PM

Performance Management
Study Manual
For Exams until June 2019

ACCA

British Library Cataloguing-in-Publication Data
A catalogue record for this book is available from the British Library

www.iaww.com/publishing

ISBN 978-1-78480-579-1

First Edition 2018

Contents

Getting Started on
Performance Management

Aim of the paper

To develop knowledge and skills in the application of management accounting techniques to quantitative and qualitative information for planning, decision-making, performance evaluation and control.

Outline of the syllabus

A. Specialist cost and management accounting techniques
B. Decision-making techniques
C. Budgeting and control
D. Performance measurement and control

Format of the exam paper

The syllabus is assessed by a three-hour examination available in both computer-based and paper-based formats. All questions are compulsory. The exam will contain both computational and discursive elements. Some questions will adopt a scenario/case study approach.

Section A of the computer-based exam comprises 15 objective test questions of 2 marks each. Section B of the computer-based exam comprises three questions each containing five objective test questions. Section C of the exam comprises two 20 mark constructed response questions.

Section A of the paper-based exam comprises 15 multiple choice questions of 2 marks each. Section B of the paper-based exam comprises three questions containing five multiple choice questions. Section C of the exam comprises two 20 mark questions.

The two 20 mark questions in both forms of the exam will come from decision making techniques, budgeting and control and/or performance measurement and control areas of the syllabus. The section A questions and the questions in section B can cover any areas of the syllabus.

Efficient and effective studying with us

1. Study when best for you in the day

Many people can double their reading speed and improve their concentration by studying early in the day. Also it has been shown that revision in the evening without major distractions afterwards (avoid late-night parties, for example!) allows your brain to work on the material once you are asleep and can significantly improve your memory.

2. Study in a good environment

There are so many potential distractions you need to avoid. Your studies require you to gain enough depth of knowledge. E-mail, mobile phones, social networking sites act as threats to you. For example, seeing that you have a new e-mail in your Inbox distracts you and it is hard not to respond to its existence, even if it is only spam e-mail. Get away from all of these and you'll have a far better retention of the knowledge you have gained. You'll stay alert if you sit at a desk so long as you don't have your PC/Mac on!

3. Get an overview of the subject early

Knowing the big picture of the subject you are about to study is a great way to study efficiently. This is hard for you to gain without knowledge of the subject, so use the knowledge of your provider of material for the exam, like the Overview given in this Study Manual.

4. Skim the chapter first for the main ideas

Read the Chapter Context and scan the structure of the main chapter sections. You'll improve your reading speed and comprehension if you understand the structure of the chapter first.

5. Form a question or questions

Boost your reading comprehension, reading speed, and concentration by formulating your own questions (write them down if it helps) and/or using the ones that we have provided. Read the chapter to obtain the answers. Your reading speed improves by doing this, and you become far more focused on your material so you will retain more. Use the following questions – **what, when, why, who, which, where, how** – and the main section titles in the chapter.

6. Take notes

Improve your overall study effectiveness by jotting brief notes immediately after reading each section of the chapter. Linking your points together, using a mind map for example, helps memory. Refer back to your notes later to test your understanding (and see point 7 below).

7. But avoid highlighting

Although some readers believe that highlighting in yellow (or any other colour, for that matter) improves their reading speed and comprehension, the reverse is actually true. Highlighting simply means they don't bother learning the material right now. The result: they end up reading the material twice, and possibly not understanding or remembering it either time! Similarly, using material that has been highlighted by the publisher is ineffective for your learning.

8. Repetition, repetition, repetition

We learn by repeating. It can be shown that if you don't repeat knowledge almost immediately then you have no chance of remembering it. We also need to repeat that knowledge again within the next 90 to 120 minutes or we will forget it. So build in time to your studies to do this, it will be very effective for you. How do we learn?

9. What's the story?

At the end of each chapter, try to generate your own story for what you have just been reading. Use the Questions at the start of the Chapter and the Key Learning Points at the end of the Chapter to help here. Making your **own** story is a very powerful way of helping you remember. It can have a start a middle and an end, just like a normal story!

Our material – how we help you

✓ Our authors are all experienced at producing targeted material for your exam. So you will gain from that wealth of knowledge, for example by understanding the Overview of the syllabus at the start of your studies and reviewing your knowledge in line with it as you progress.

✓ Our material is based on knowledge of how your brain works to help you study better.

✓ We pose you questions at the start of each chapter to assist your learning and boost your interest and retention. Look for the '3 Questions' that we have at the start of each chapter. These help you become engaged with the material and will mean you can answer the three questions better as well as the other material in the chapter. For example:

3Q	
1.	What are the problems for modern manufacturing businesses in using absorption costing methods?
2.	Can you describe the principle of activity-based costing?
3.	What is the kind of environment necessary for ABC to operate?

✓ You will be advised where you should stop and spend time learning/memorising key facts or knowledge. Look out for the 'Learn's to help your repetition of important knowledge.

 Learn

✓ Similarly if you have to be familiar with the principles behind a few paragraphs (such as a calculation) then we will prompt you with 'Principle' plus guidance on what to go back for. Take time to stop yourself and check that you are happy with these, they are key for the exam. For example:

 Principle

> Learn the steps above so you can apply them in the exam

✓ You will find when a formula or other information is given in the exam. Look out for the 'Given's.

 Given

✓ We want you to build up a 'story' based on the material to help you remember it better. When you see the 'What's the Story' at the end of each chapter, take time to link the chapter together and also link to any relevant previous chapters.

What's the story?

Stop and think through the 'story' of this chapter and how it links with other chapters (use the Overview to help).

✓ **Importantly, we don't bloat our material with extra unneeded features (for example in the margins of the page, which are inefficient for students to learn from). All the reminders to learn are in the centre of the page.**

✓ **You will leave with 'Key learning points' to go away with that will help you build up that story.**

✓ **We are interested in your feedback – please complete the Feedback Form at the end of studying this paper and have the chance to win a prize!**

Overview

This ACCA paper, Performance Management, helps you look at making good decisions in an organisation. You will learn a series of techniques that organisations use and how they are useful in helping organisations know about the costs that they are incurring, deciding what to do and, once decided, whether what they have decided has been successful.

The syllabus states that the aim of the paper is 'develop knowledge and skills in the application of management accounting techniques to quantitative and qualitative information for planning, decision-making, performance evaluation, and control'.

Let's see how this is reflected in this Study Manual and its chapters. There are chapters on the current analysis of the organisation's situation, the future plans of the business and how to decide if they are worthwhile and finally the analysis of the results that the business has obtained to decide if it has been successful.

Current analysis

Current analysis focuses on cost accounting techniques. There are a number of different techniques which can be applied. Companies must choose the most appropriate method to ensure that costs can be understood and managed carefully. The technique applied will depend on the company's current position in terms of product/service type, industry and cost types.

We cover *Activity-based Costing* (Chapter 1) which looks at how costs can be recorded in a useful way based on what an organisation is doing. We then consider *Throughput Accounting* (Chapter 2) which looks at ways to account when there are bottlenecks in production. *Target Costing and Lifecycle Costing* (Chapter 3) which relate the costs in the business to the prices that are charged to see how to control costs and then looks at how costs vary over the life of a product. Finally, *Environmental Management Accounting* (Chapter 4) looks more widely than just the financial costs an organisation incurs to wider issues of the effect the organisation has on the environment.

Future plans

In addition to understanding what the company needs at the present time, management accountants must also make decisions about what the company should do next. This section looks at a range of decisions including how scarce resources should be used, which areas of the business should be shut-down or grown in the future and how management can deal with uncertainty in decision making.

Relevant Costing and Short-term Decision-making (Chapter 5) looks at the costs to take into account when an organisation is making decisions, particularly the decisions that are relevant or not. *Limiting Factors* (Chapter 6) look at what stops an organisation doing everything it wants and deciding how to do the most it can if there are limitations on it. *Cost Volume Profit Analysis* (Chapter 7) considers the breakeven point for organisations and how to see how safe the organisation is above that point. *Pricing Decisions* (Chapter 8) are exactly that, how to price products to make a profit. *Decision-making Under Uncertainty* (Chapter 9) looks at how to cope with situations where things don't happen the same each time but there are a range of possible outcomes. Finally we move onto *Budgeting* (Chapter 10) and *Quantitative Aids to Budgeting* (Chapter 11) which tell of the systems used for budgeting, the types of budget and how to prepare them.

Results analysis

It is vital that management accountants assess the performance of the company across a wide range of areas. Are the costing systems which were implemented working for the company and ensuring product profitability? Were the decisions taken at the start of the year successful for the company? To understand this, the company performance must be analysed from both a financial and non-financial perspective.

Variance Analysis (Basic) (Chapter 12) sees where variances (differences) between our actual performance and budgeted performance have arisen. *Variance Analysis (Advanced)* (Chapter 13) looks at more complex differences we can work out, especially if we are changing the mix of products we are making and selling. *Performance Management* (Chapter 14) looks at how to judge performance without just considering numbers, this is important for the exam. Finally *Divisional Performance and Transfer Pricing* (Chapter 15) considers transfers between divisions within a business and how to account for these in a beneficial way for both the divisions and the company as a whole.

You can see the diagram covers the current analysis, future plans and results analysis that we have seen in the syllabus.

Learn this diagram so that you can see where the subjects you have learnt fits in. It will be useful to come back to so that you can see the 'big picture' for the paper.

Finally look around at businesses or other organisations that you are involved with and see if you can see the techniques being used or get involved in them yourself. Alternatively look at organisations that you are aware of, such as the supermarket you shop in and think how they might use the techniques that you have learnt. If you can see your studies coming to life in this way it will help your learning considerably and make the subject more interesting and useful.

| Current Analysis | Results Analysis | Future Plans |

Costing

· Activity-based Costing

· Throughput Accounting

· Target and Lifestyle Costing

· Environmental Management
  Accounting

· Marginal Costing

Variance Analysis

Performance Management

Divisional Performance

Decision Making

· Relevant Costing

· Limiting Factors

· CVP Analysis

· Pricing Decisions

· Decision Making
  under Uncertainty

Budgeting

· Quantitative Aids

Syllabus and Study Guide

PERFORMANCE MANAGEMENT (PM)

SEPTEMBER 2018 TO JUNE 2019

SYLLABUS AND STUDY GUIDE

GUIDE TO STRUCTURE OF THE SYLLABUS AND STUDY GUIDE

OVERALL AIM OF THE SYLLABUS

This explains briefly the overall objective of the syllabus and indicates in the broadest sense the capabilities to be developed within the exam.

RELATIONAL DIAGRAM LINKING PERFORMANCE MANAGEMENT (PM) WITH OTHER ACCA EXAMS

This diagram shows direct and indirect links between this exam and other exams preceding or following it. It indicates where you are expected to have underpinning knowledge and where it would be useful to review previous learning before undertaking study.

MAIN CAPABILITIES

The aim of the syllabus is broken down into several main capabilities which divide the syllabus and study guide into discrete sections.

RELATIONAL DIAGRAM OF THE MAIN CAPABILITIES

This diagram illustrates the flows and links between the main capabilities (sections) of the syllabus and should be used as an aid to planning teaching and learning in a structured way.

SYLLABUS RATIONALE

This is a narrative explaining how the syllabus is structured and how the main capabilities are linked. The rationale also explains in further detail what the examination intends to assess and why.

DETAILED SYLLABUS

This shows the breakdown of the main capabilities (sections) of the syllabus into subject areas. This is the blueprint for the detailed study guide.

APPROACH TO EXAMINING THE SYLLABUS

This section briefly explains the structure of the examination and how it is assessed.

STUDY GUIDE

This is the main document that students, education and content providers should use as the basis of their studies, instruction and materials. Examinations will be based on the detail of the study guide which comprehensively identifies what could be assessed in any examination session. The study guide is a precise reflection and breakdown of the syllabus. It is divided into sections based on the main capabilities identified in the syllabus. These sections are divided into subject areas which relate to the sub-capabilities included in the detailed syllabus. Subject areas are broken down into sub-headings which describe the detailed outcomes that could be assessed in examinations. These outcomes are described using verbs indicating what exams may require students to demonstrate, and the broad intellectual level at which these may need to be demonstrated (*see intellectual levels below).

INTELLECTUAL LEVELS

The syllabus is designed to progressively broaden and deepen the knowledge, skills and professional values demonstrated by the student on their way through the qualification.

The specific capabilities within the detailed syllabuses and study guides are assessed at one of three intellectual or cognitive levels:

Level 1:   Knowledge and comprehension

Level 2:   Application and analysis

Level 3:   Synthesis and evaluation

Very broadly, these intellectual levels relate to the three cognitive levels at which the Applied Knowledge, the Applied Skills and the Strategic Professional exams are assessed.

Each subject area in the detailed study guide included in this document is given a 1, 2, or 3 superscript, denoting intellectual level, marked at the end of each relevant line. This gives an indication of the intellectual depth at which an area could be assessed within the examination. However, while level 1 broadly equates with Applied Knowledge , level 2 equates to Applied Skills and level 3 to Strategic Professional, some lower level skills can continue to be assessed as the student progresses through each level. This reflects that at each stage of study there will be a requirement to broaden, as well as deepen capabilities. It is also possible that occasionally some higher level capabilities may be assessed at lower levels.

LEARNING HOURS AND EDUCATION RECOGNITION

The ACCA qualification does not prescribe or recommend any particular number of learning hours for examinations because study and learning patterns and styles vary greatly between people and organisations. This also recognises the wide diversity of personal, professional and educational circumstances in which ACCA students find themselves.

As a member of the International Federation of Accountants, ACCA seeks to enhance the education recognition of its qualification on both national and international education frameworks, and with educational authorities and partners globally. In doing so, ACCA aims to ensure that its qualifications are recognised and valued by governments, regulatory authorities and employers across all sectors. To this end, ACCA qualifications are currently recognised on the education frameworks in several countries. Please refer to your national education framework regulator for further information.

Each syllabus contains between 20 and 35 main subject area headings depending on the nature of the subject and how these areas have been broken down.

GUIDE TO ACCA EXAMINATION STRUCTURE

The structure of examinations varies within and between levels.

The Applied Knowledge examinations contain 100% compulsory questions to encourage candidates to study across the breadth of each syllabus. These are assessed by a two-hour computer based examination.

The *Corporate and Business Law* exam is a two-hour computer-based objective test examination for English and Global, and available as a paper based version for all variants.

The other Applied Skills examinations (PM, TX-UK, FR, AA, and FM) contain a mix of objective and longer type questions with a duration of three hours for 100 marks; these questions directly contribute towards the candidate result. These exams are available in computer-based and paper-based formats. Prior to the start of each exam there will be time allocated for students to be informed of the exam instructions.

Computer-based exams

For the Applied Skills (PM, TX-UK, FR, AA and FM) computer-based exams candidates will be delivered an extra 10 marks of objective test content (either five single OT questions or five OT questions based around a single scenario), for which candidates are given an extra 20 minutes. These questions are included to ensure fairness, reliability and security of exams. These questions do not directly contribute towards the candidate's score. Candidates will not be able to differentiate between the questions that contribute to the result and those that do not. All questions have been subject to ACCA's regulatory approved quality assurance process.

The total exam time is therefore 3 hours and 20 minutes. Prior to the start of the exam candidates are given an extra 10 minutes to read the exam instructions.

Paper-based exams

For paper-based exams 15 minutes are added to the three hours to reflect the manual effort required as compared to computer-based exams. All paper-based and computer-based questions have been subject to the same quality assurance process. There will be time awarded by the invigilator to read the exam instructions.

Strategic Business Leader is ACCA's case study examination at the Strategic Professional level and is examined as a closed book exam of four hours, including reading, planning and reflection time which can be used flexibly within the examination. There is no pre-seen information and all exam related material, including case information and exhibits are available within the examination. Strategic Business Leader is an exam based on one main business scenario which involves candidates completing several tasks within which additional material may be introduced. All questions are compulsory and each examination will contain a total of 80 technical marks and 20 Professional Skills marks. The detail of the structure of this exam is described in the Strategic Business Leader syllabus and study guide document.

The other Strategic Professional exams are all of three hours and 15 minutes duration. All contain two Sections and all questions are compulsory. These exams all contain four professional marks. The detail of the structure of each of these exams is described in the individual syllabus and study guide documents.

ACCA encourages students to take time to read questions carefully and to plan answers but once the exam time has started, there are no additional restrictions as to when candidates may start writing in their answer books.

Time should be taken to ensure that all the information and exam requirements are properly read and understood.

The pass mark for all ACCA Qualification examinations is 50%.

GUIDE TO ACCA EXAMINATION ASSESSMENT

ACCA reserves the right to examine anything contained within the study guide at any examination session. This includes knowledge, techniques, principles, theories, and concepts as specified. For the financial accounting, audit and assurance, law and tax exams except where indicated otherwise, ACCA will publish *examinable documents* once a year to indicate exactly what regulations and legislation could potentially be assessed within identified examination sessions.

For examinations, regulation **issued** or legislation **passed** on or before 31 August annually, will be examinable from 1 September of the following year to 31 August of the year after that. Please refer to the examinable documents for the exam (where relevant) for further information.

Regulation issued or legislation passed in accordance with the above dates may be examinable even if the **effective** date is in the future.

The term issued or passed relates to when regulation or legislation has been formally approved.

The term effective relates to when regulation or legislation must be applied to an entity transactions and business practices.

The study guide offers more detailed guidance on the depth and level at which the examinable documents will be examined. The study guide should therefore be read in conjunction with the examinable documents list.

PERFORMANCE MANAGEMENT (PM) SYLLABUS AND STUDY GUIDE

This syllabus and study guide is designed to help with planning study and to provide detailed information on what could be assessed in any examination session.

AIM

To develop knowledge and skills in the application of management accounting techniques to quantitative and qualitative information for planning, decision-making, performance evaluation, and control

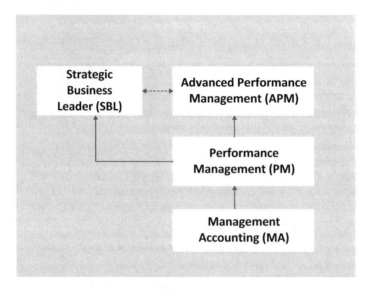

RELATIONAL DIAGRAM LINKING PERFORMANCE MANAGEMENT (PM) WITH OTHER ACCA EXAMS

This diagram shows direct and indirect links between this exam and other exams preceding or following it. Some exams are directly underpinned by other exams such as Advanced Performance Management by Performance Management. These links are shown as solid line arrows. Other exams only have indirect relationships with each other such as links existing between the accounting and auditing exams. The links between these are shown as dotted line arrows. This diagram indicates where you are expected to have underpinning knowledge and where it would be useful to review previous learning before undertaking study.

MAIN CAPABILITIES

On successful completion of this exam, candidates should be able to:

A. Explain and apply cost accounting techniques
B. Select and appropriately apply decision-making techniques to facilitate business decisions and promote efficient and effective use of scarce business resources, appreciating the risks and uncertainty inherent in business and controlling those risks
C. Identify and apply appropriate budgeting techniques and methods for planning and control and use standard costing systems to measure and control business performance and to identify remedial action
D. Identify and discuss performance management information and measurement systems and assess the performance of an organisation from both a financial and non- financial viewpoint, appreciating the problems of controlling divisionalised businesses and the importance of allowing for external aspects

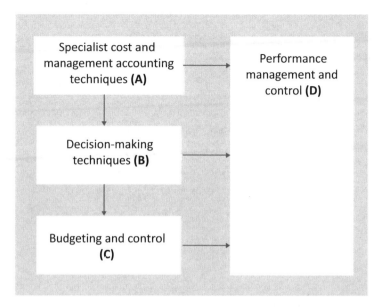

This diagram illustrates the flows and links between the main capabilities (sections) of the syllabus and should be used as an aid to planning teaching and learning in a structured way.

RATIONALE

The syllabus for Performance Management (PM), builds on the knowledge gained in Management Accounting (MA) and seeks to examine candidates' understanding of how to manage the performance of a business. It also prepares candidates for more specialist capabilities which are covered in Advanced Performance Management (APM).

The syllabus begins by introducing more specialised management accounting topics. There is some knowledge assumed from Management Accounting (MA) - primarily overhead treatments. The objective here is to ensure candidates have a broader background in management accounting techniques.

The syllabus then considers decision-making. Candidates need to appreciate the problems surrounding scarce resource, pricing and make-or-buy decisions, and how this relates to the assessment of performance. Risk and uncertainty are a factor of real-life decisions and candidates need to understand risk and be able to apply some basic methods to help resolve the risks inherent in decision-making.

Budgeting is an important aspect of many accountants' lives. The syllabus explores different budgeting techniques and the problems inherent in them. The behavioural aspects of budgeting are important for accountants to understand, and the syllabus includes consideration of the way individuals react to a budget. The preparation of fixed, flexible and incremental budgets is assumed knowledge from Management Accounting (MA).

Standard costing and variances are then built on. All the variances examined in Management Accounting (MA) are assumed knowledge in Performance Management (PM). Mix and yield variances, and planning and operational variances are explored

21

here and the link is made to performance management. It is important for accountants to be able to interpret the numbers that they calculate and ask what they mean in the context of performance.

The syllabus concludes with performance management systems, measurement and control. This is a major area of the syllabus. Accountants need to understand how a business should be managed and controlled and how information systems can be used to facilitate this. They should appreciate the importance of both financial and non-financial performance measures in management. Accountants should also appreciate the difficulties in assessing performance in divisionalised businesses and the problems caused by failing to consider external influences on performance. This section leads directly to Advanced Performance Management (APM).

All of the subject areas covered in this syllabus could be examined in either a public sector or private sector context.

DETAILED SYLLABUS

A. Specialist cost and management accounting techniques
1. Activity-based costing
2. Target costing
3. Life-cycle costing
4. Throughput accounting
5. Environmental accounting

B. Decision-making techniques
1. Relevant cost analysis
2. Cost volume analysis
3. Limiting factors
4. Pricing decisions
5. Make-or-buy and other short-term decisions
6. Dealing with risk and uncertainty in decision-making

C. Budgeting and control
1. Budgetary systems and types of budget
2. Quantitative analysis in budgeting
3. Standard costing
4. Material mix and yield variances
5. Sales mix and quantity variances
6. Planning and operational variances
7. Performance analysis

D. Performance measurement and control
1. Performance management information systems
2. Sources of management information
3. Management reports
4. Performance analysis in private sector organisations
5. Divisional performance and transfer pricing
6. Performance analysis in not-for-profit organisations and the public sector

7. External considerations and behavioural aspects

APPROACH TO EXAMINING THE SYLLABUS

The syllabus is assessed by a three-hour examination available in both computer-based and paper-based formats. *

All questions are compulsory. The exam will contain both computational and discursive elements.

Some questions will adopt a scenario/case study approach.

Candidates are provided with a formulae sheet.

Computer-based exams

*For computer-based exams an extra 20 minutes is provided to candidates to reflect the additional content as per below. The total exam time is therefore 3 hours and 20 minutes. Prior to the start of the exam candidates are given an extra 10 minutes to read the exam instructions.

Section A of the computer-based exam comprises 15 objective test questions of 2 marks each plus additional content as per below.

Section B of the computer-based exam comprises three questions each containing five objective test questions plus additional content as per below.

For the computer-based exam candidates will be delivered an extra 10 marks of objective test content (either five single OT questions **OR** five OT questions based around a single scenario), for which candidates are given an extra 20 minutes. These questions are included to ensure fairness, reliability and security of exams. These questions do not directly contribute towards the candidate's score. Candidates will not be able to differentiate between the questions that contribute to the result and those that do not.

Section C of the exam comprises two 20 mark constructed response questions. The two 20 mark questions will come from decision making techniques, budgeting and control and/or performance measurement and control areas of the syllabus. The section A questions and the questions in section B can cover any areas of the syllabus.

Paper-based exams

*For paper-based exams an extra 15 minutes is provided to candidates to reflect the manual effort required as compared to the time needed for the computer-based exams. The total exam time is therefore three hours and 15 minutes. Prior to the start of the exam candidates are given an extra 10 minutes to read the exam instructions.

Section A of the paper-based exam comprises 15 multiple choice questions of 2 marks each

Section B of the paper-based exam comprises three questions containing five multiple choice questions.

Section C of the exam comprises two 20 mark questions.

The two 20 mark questions will come from decision making techniques, budgeting and control and/or performance measurement and control areas of the syllabus. The section A questions and the questions in section B can cover any areas of the syllabus.

STUDY GUIDE

A. Specialist cost and management accounting techniques

1. Activity based costing

(a) Identify appropriate cost drivers under ABC. [1]

(b) Calculate costs per driver and per unit using ABC.[2]

(c) Compare ABC and traditional methods of overhead absorption based on production units, labour hours or machine hours.[2]

2. Target costing

(a) Derive a target cost in manufacturing and service industries.[2]

(b) Explain the difficulties of using target costing in service industries.[2]

(c) Suggest how a target cost gap might be closed.[2]

3. Life-cycle costing

(a) Identify the costs involved at different stages of the life-cycle.[2]

(b) Derive a life cycle cost or profit in manufacturing and service industries.[2]

(c) Identify the benefits of life cycle costing.[2]

4. Throughput accounting

(a) Discuss and apply the theory of constraints.[2]

(b) Calculate and interpret a throughput accounting ratio (TPAR).[2]

(c) Suggest how a TPAR could be improved.[2]

(d) Apply throughput accounting to a multi-product decision-making problem.[2]

5. Environmental accounting

(a) Discuss the issues business face in the management of environmental costs.[1]

(b) Describe the different methods a business may use to account for its environmental costs.[1]

B. Decision-making techniques

1. Relevant cost analysis

(a) Explain the concept of relevant costing.[2]

(b) Identify and calculate relevant costs for a specific decision situations from given data.[2]

(c) Explain and apply the concept of opportunity costs.[2]

2. Cost volume profit analysis

(a) Explain the nature of CVP analysis.[2]

(b) Calculate and interpret the breakeven point and margin of safety.[2]

(c) Calculate the contribution to sales ratio, in single and multi-product situations, and demonstrate an understanding of its use.[2]

(d) Calculate target profit or revenue in single and multi-product situations, and demonstrate an understanding of its use.[2]

(e) Prepare break even charts and profit volume charts and interpret the information contained within each, including multi-product situations.[2]

(f) Discuss the limitations of CVP analysis for planning and decision making.[2]

3. Limiting factors

(a) Identify limiting factors in a scarce resource situation and select an appropriate technique.[2]

(b) Determine the optimal production plan where an organisation is restricted by a single limiting factor, including within the context of "make" or "buy" decisions.[2].

(c) Formulate and solve multiple scarce resource problem both graphically and using simultaneous equations as appropriate.[2]

(d) Explain and calculate shadow prices (dual prices) and discuss their implications on decision-making and performance management. [2]

(e) Calculate slack and explain the implications of the existence of slack for decision-making and performance management.[2] (Excluding simplex and sensitivity to changes in objective functions)

4. Pricing decisions

(a) Explain the factors that influence the pricing of a product or service.[2]

(b) Explain the price elasticity of demand.[1]

(c) Derive and manipulate a straight line demand equation. Derive an equation for the total cost function(including volume-based discounts).[2]

(d) Calculate the optimum selling price and quantity for an organisation, equating marginal cost and marginal revenue[2]

(e) Evaluate a decision to increase production and sales levels, considering incremental costs, incremental revenues and other factors.[2]

(f) Determine prices and output levels for profit maximisation using the demand based approach to pricing (both tabular and algebraic methods). [1]

(g) Explain different price strategies, including:[2]

(i) All forms of cost-plus

(ii) Skimming

(iii) Penetration

(iv) Complementary product

(v) Product-line

(vi) Volume discounting

(vii) Discrimination

(viii) Relevant cost

(h) Calculate a price from a given strategy using cost-plus and relevant cost.[2]

5. Make-or-buy and other short-term decisions

(a) Explain the issues surrounding make vs. buy and outsourcing decisions.[2]

(b) Calculate and compare "make" costs with "buy-in" costs.[2]

(c) Compare in-house costs and outsource costs of completing tasks and consider other issues surrounding this decision.[2]

(d) Apply relevant costing principles in situations involving shut down, one-off contracts and the further processing of joint products.[2]

6. Dealing with risk and uncertainty in decision-making

(a) Suggest research techniques to reduce uncertainty e.g. Focus groups, market research.[2]

(b) Explain the use of simulation, expected values and sensitivity.[1]

(c) Apply expected values and sensitivity to decision-making problems.[2]

(d) Apply the techniques of maximax, maximin, and minimax regret to decision-making problems including the production of profit tables.[2]

(e) Draw a decision tree and use it to solve a multi-stage decision problem

(f) Calculate the value of perfect and imperfect information.

C. Budgeting and control

1. Budgetary systems and types of budget

(a) Explain how budgetary systems fit within the performance hierarchy.[2]

(b) Select and explain appropriate budgetary systems for an organisation, including top-down, bottom-up, rolling, zero-base, activity- base, incremental and feed-forward control.[2]

(c) Describe the information used in budget systems and the sources of the information needed.[2]

(d) Indicate the usefulness and problems with different budget types (including fixed, flexible, zero-based, activity- based, incremental, rolling, top-down, bottom up, master, functional).[2]

(e) Prepare flexed budgets, rolling budgets and activity based budgets.[2]

(f) Explain the beyond budgeting model, including the benefits and problems that may be faced if it is adopted in an organisation. [2]

(g) Discuss the issues surrounding setting the difficulty level for a budget.[2]

(h) Explain the benefits and difficulties of the participation of employees in the negotiation of targets.[2]

(i) Explain the difficulties of changing a budgetary system or type of budget used.[2]

(j) Explain how budget systems can deal with uncertainty in the environment.[2]

2. Quantitative analysis in budgeting

(a) Analyse fixed and variable cost elements from total cost data using high/low method.

(b) Estimate the learning rate and learning effect[2]

(c) Apply the learning curve to a budgetary problem, including calculations on steady states [2]

(d) Discuss the reservations with the learning curve.[2]

(e) Apply expected values and explain the problems and benefits.[2]

(f) Explain the benefits and dangers inherent in using spreadsheets in budgeting. [2]

3. Standard costing

(a) Explain the use of standard costs.[2]

(b) Outline the methods used to derive standard costs and discuss the different types of cost possible.[2]

(c) Explain and illustrate the importance of flexing budgets in performance management.[2]

(d) Explain and apply the principle of controllability in the performance management system.[2]

4. Material mix and yield variances
(a) Calculate, identify the cause of, and explain material mix and yield variances.[2]
(b) Explain the wider issues involved in changing material mix e.g. cost, quality and performance measurement issues.[2]
(c) Identify and explain the relationship of the material usage variance with the material mix and yield variances.[2]
(d) Suggest and justify alternative methods of controlling production processes.[2]

5. Sales mix and quantity variances
(a) Calculate, identify the cause of, and explain sales mix and quantity variances.[2]
(b) Identify and explain the relationship of the sales volume variances with the sales mix and quantity variances.[2]

6. Planning and operational variances
(a) Calculate a revised budget.[2]
(b) Identify and explain those factors that could and could not be allowed to revise an original budget.[2]
(c) Calculate, identify the cause of and explain planning and operational variances for:

(i) sales, including market size and market share;

(ii) materials;

(iii) labour, including the effect of the learning curve.[2]

(d) Explain and discuss the manipulation issues involved in revising budgets.[2]

7. Performance analysis
(a) Analyse and evaluate past performance using the results of variance analysis.[2]
(b) Use variance analysis to assess how future performance of an organisation or business can be improved.[2]
(c) Identify the factors which influence behaviour.[2]
(d) Discuss the effect that variances have on staff motivation and action.[2]
(e) Describe the dysfunctional nature of some variances in the modern environment of JIT and TQM.[2]
(f) Discuss the behavioural problems resulting from using standard costs in rapidly changing environments.[2]

D. Performance measurement and control

1. Performance management information systems
(a) Identify the accounting information requirements and describe the different types of information systems used for strategic planning, management control and operational control and decision-making.[2]
(b) Define and identify the main characteristics of transaction processing systems; management information systems; executive information systems; and enterprise resource planning systems.[2]
(c) Define and discuss the merits of, and potential problems with, open and closed systems with regard to the needs of performance management.[2]

2. Sources of management information

(a) Identify the principal internal and external sources of management accounting information.[2]

(b) Demonstrate how these principal sources of management information might be used for control purposes.[2]

(c) Identify and discuss the direct data capture and process costs of management accounting information.[2]

(d) Identify and discuss the indirect costs of producing information.[2]

(e) Discuss the limitations of using externally generated information.[2]

3. Management reports

(a) Discuss the principal controls required in generating and distributing internal information.[2]

(b) Discuss the procedures that may be necessary to ensure security of highly confidential information that is not for external consumption.[2]

4. Performance analysis in private sector organisations

(a) Describe, calculate and interpret financial performance indicators (FPIs) for profitability, liquidity and risk in both manufacturing and service businesses. Suggest methods to improve these measures.[2]

(b) Describe, calculate and interpret non-financial performance indicators (NFPIs) and suggest methods to improve the performance indicated.[2]

(c) Analyse past performance and suggest ways for improving financial and non-financial performance.[2]

(d) Explain the causes and problems created by short-termism and financial manipulation of results and suggest methods to encourage a long term view.[2]

(e) Explain and interpret the Balanced Scorecard, and the Building Block model proposed by Fitzgerald and Moon.[2]

(f) Discuss the difficulties of target setting in qualitative areas.[2]

5. Divisional performance and transfer pricing

(a) Explain and illustrate the basis for setting a transfer price using variable cost, full cost and the principles behind allowing for intermediate markets.[2]

(b) Explain how transfer prices can distort the performance assessment of divisions and decisions made.[2]

(c) Explain the meaning of, and calculate, Return on Investment (ROI) and Residual Income (RI), and discuss their shortcomings.[2]

(d) Compare divisional performance and recognise the problems of doing so.[2]

6. **Performance analysis in not for profit organisations and the public sector**
(a) Comment on the problems of having non-quantifiable objectives in performance management.[2]
(b) Comment on the problems of having multiple objectives in this sector.[2]
(c) Explain how performance could be measured in this sector.[2]
(d) Outline Value for Money (VFM) as a public sector objective.[1]
(e) Describe, calculate and interpret non-financial performance indicators (NFPIs) and suggest methods to improve the performance indicated.[2]
(f) Discuss the difficulties of target setting in qualitative areas.[2]
(g) Analyse past performance and suggest ways for improving financial and non-financial performance.[2]
(h) Explain the causes and problems created by short-termism and financial manipulation of results and suggest methods to encourage a long term view.[2]

7. **External considerations and behavioural aspects**
(a) Explain the need to allow for external considerations in performance management, including stakeholders, market conditions and allowance for competitors.[2]
(b) Suggest ways in which external considerations could be allowed for in performance management.[2]
(c) Interpret performance in the light of external considerations.[2]
(d) Identify and explain the behaviour aspects of performance management.[2]

SUMMARY OF CHANGES TO PERFORMANCE MANAGEMENT (PM)

ACCA periodically reviews its qualification syllabuses so that they fully meet the needs of stakeholders such as employers, students, regulatory and advisory bodies and education providers.

The main areas of change to the syllabus are summarised in the table below.

Section and subject area	Syllabus content
A3b)	This has been amended to include the calculation of a life cycle profit.

1

Activity-based Costing

Context

You have developed an understanding of the traditional techniques of absorption costing and marginal costing in your Management Accounting studies. We will now develop these costing techniques to consider the various industries and situations to which different costing techniques can be applied. This chapter will address the concept of activity-based costing (ABC).

ABC is a refined version of absorption costing, and attempts to find a more accurate method whereby overhead cost can be charged into cost units.

Traditional absorption costing techniques allocate and apportion overheads to large 'cost centres' (usually a department or machine) and then absorb these overheads into cost units, usually at a predetermined hourly rate.

ABC focuses on how overheads can be more reasonably charged to cost units in a manner which reflects the cost units' 'usage' of the specific overhead. This may lead to a business having multiple absorption rates using ABC. However, these rates are likely to lead to a more accurate product costing.

It is important to be able to calculate how to absorb overheads using both traditional absorption techniques and ABC. However, the examiner expects you to be able to understand and interpret your results and also know the drawbacks of the techniques. This written understanding will inevitably have to be applied to the scenario in the question.

3Q

1. What are the problems for modern manufacturing businesses in using absorption costing methods?

2. Can you describe the principle of activity-based costing?

3. What is the kind of environment necessary for ABC to operate?

1.1 Absorption costing – revisited

In order to fully understand activity-based costing (ABC), we need to remind ourselves about the principles of traditional absorption costing.

1.1.1 Absorption costing

We aim, when using absorption costing, to calculate a full cost per unit of production.

$$\frac{\text{Production cost}}{\text{Unit}} = \frac{\text{Direct cost}}{\text{Unit}} + \frac{\text{Indirect cost}}{\text{Unit}}$$

Direct costs, such as materials or productive labour, can be clearly 'attached' to each unit of production. Indirect costs are overhead costs which cannot clearly be charged to individual units of production (for example, factory rent and rates). For overheads we have to adopt a process to estimate the amount of overhead that we can charge to each cost unit.

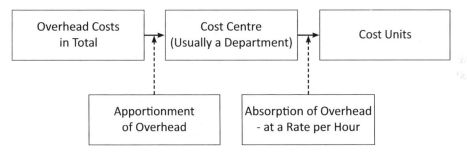

Overheads are identified in total and then usually apportioned or shared between cost centres (departments such as assembly or finishing). For example, factory rent and rates could be shared between cost centres on the basis of floor area (square metres).

Once accumulated in a cost centre the overheads can then be absorbed into cost units on an hourly basis – often either labour hours (if the cost centre is labour intensive) or machine hours (if the cost centre is capital or machine intensive).

$$\text{Overhead absorption rate (OAR)} = \frac{\text{Total cost centre overhead}}{\text{Cost centre direct labour hours}}$$

 Learn

The absorption costing per unit can then be used to:

- Assess the costs incurred per unit for performance assessment (e.g. variance analysis);
- Value inventory stock for financial accounting purposes;
- Calculate sales prices based on a cost-plus basis.

1.1.2 Problems associated with absorption costing

There are problems for modern manufacturing businesses in using absorption costing methods.

- **Increased product complexity**

  Modern manufacturers tend to produce a wide range of products at different volumes. Because all overhead costs are absorbed using one OAR, there is a high risk that some products may be charged too much overhead and others too little. This in turn could lead to inappropriate pricing of products.

- **Increased capital intensity of modern manufacturing techniques**

  Many modern manufacturers are highly machine intensive. This means that direct labour hours used in production have reduced significantly. Using labour hours to absorb overheads can lead to extremely high absorption rates that bear little resemblance to the underlying overhead and how it is incurred.

- **Greater proportion of overhead costs**

  Overhead costs are likely to be a greater percentage of total cost now than they were in the past. Therefore, the overhead cost per unit of product is also higher. This means that it is important that companies are able to estimate the overhead cost per unit accurately as it can significantly affect product profitability.

 Principle

The limitations of absorption costing

EG **Learning example 1.1**

Armstrong manufactures small handheld hammers and 12-metre containers used in the transportation of goods by road, rail and sea. It operates a highly mechanised production system. Overheads are absorbed on a direct labour hour basis.

The following information is available for the manufacture of these products over a period:

	Handheld hammers	Containers
Budgeted production units	20,000	1,000
Labour hours/unit	0.5	2
Labour cost/unit @ $20/hour	$10	$40
Direct material cost/unit	$5	$300
Prime cost/unit	$15	$340

Factory overhead costs for the period are expected to be $960,000.

> **Required:**
>
> Calculate the amount of overhead to be absorbed into each product.
>
> The business calculates sales price on a full cost plus 40% basis. Calculate the selling price of each product.

1.2 Activity-based costing (ABC)

ABC tackles the problems of absorption costing by adopting a much more accurate way of charging overhead to cost units.

In essence the business carefully considers what the primary **activities** are of the business. In making units of production what does the business actually do to be able to make those units?

IE Illustrative example 1.1

A business that bakes pizzas to then package them, freezes them and subsequently distributes them to supermarkets may undertake the following activities:

- Setting up ovens in order to bake the pizzas;
- Chopping the ingredients to put on to the pizzas;
- Preparing/mixing the pizza dough etc.

Traditional absorption costing may collect all of the activities together in say the 'cooking' cost centre. Any factory overheads are then apportioned to that cost centre.

Under ABC, overheads are (wherever possible) specifically allocated to a 'cost pool' relating to a particular activity. For example the power consumed by the dough mixer can be allocated to the dough mixing activity.

Rather than then absorbing all overheads from a cost pool under one uniform basis (e.g. labour hours), ABC absorbs overhead into cost units by identifying the relevant **cost driver.** This is likely to mean that there will be multiple absorption rates within a business.

IE Illustrative example 1.2

In our pizza business, the oven set-up overheads are driven by the number of batches of pizza cooked. For example if 50 batches are cooked, then the ovens need to be set up 50 times incurring 50 'lots' of overhead. If only 20 batches need to be cooked in a period then only 20 'lots' of overhead are incurred.

One of the most important attributes of ABC is that to control costs, the business needs to focus on reducing the amount of cost drivers. In our example, to cook pizzas in larger batches, causes less frequent oven set-up and hence lowers oven set-up overhead cost.

1.2.1   Overall summary of ABC

- A **cost pool** is an activity for which costs can be ascertained. All factory overhead costs must be allocated to the appropriate cost pool.
- A **cost driver** is the factor which causes the overhead costs to increase. A cost driver must be identified for each cost pool.
- A cost driver rate is calculated for each cost pool. Individual cost driver rates are used to charge activity overheads to individual cost units on the basis of specific usage.
- ABC analysis provides a more accurate estimate of overhead cost/unit.

Learn

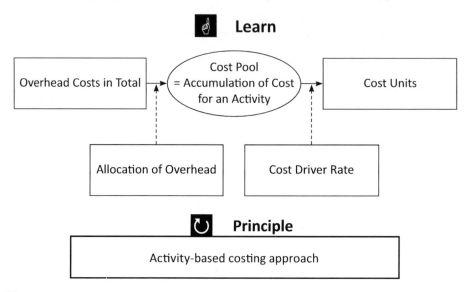

Principle

Activity-based costing approach

IE   Illustrative example 1.3

Hensau Ltd has a single production process for which the following costs have been estimated for the period ending 31 December 20X1:

	$
Material receipt and inspection costs	15,600
Power costs	19,500
Material handling costs	13,650

Three products X, Y, and Z are produced by workers who perform a number of operations on material blanks using hand held electrically powered drills. The workers are paid $4 per hour.

The following budgeted information has been obtained for the period ending 31 December 20X1:

	Product X	Product Y	Product Z
Production quantity (units)	2,000	1,500	800
Batches of material	10	5	16
Data per product unit:			
Direct material (square metres)	4	6	3
Direct material cost ($)	5	3	6
Direct labour (minutes)	24	40	60
No. of power drill operations	6	3	2

Overhead costs for material receipt and inspection, process power and material handling are presently each absorbed by product units using rates per direct labour hour.

An activity-based costing investigation has revealed that the cost drivers for the overhead costs are as follows:

Material receipt and inspection	Number of batches of material
Process power	Number of power drill operations
Material handling	Quantity of material (square metres) handled

Required:

Prepare a summary which shows the budgeted product cost per unit for each product of X, Y, and Z for the period ending 31 December 20X1 detailing the unit costs for each cost element using:

(i)   the existing method for the absorption of overhead costs and

(ii) an approach which recognises the cost drivers revealed in the activity-based costing investigation.

1.3 Budgeted cost per unit using absorption costing

Firstly we can calculate the direct costs for the three products. This will NOT differ between absorption costing and ABC.

	Product X $	Product Y $	Product Z $
Direct material cost/unit	5	3	6
Direct labour: X: 24/60 × $4 Y: 40/60 × $4 Z: 60/60 × $4	1.6	2.67	4

Next we need to calculate the production overhead attributable to each product. We will calculate an OAR using:

$$\frac{\text{Budgeted overhead cost}}{\text{Total direct labour hours}}$$

$$\text{OAR} = \frac{\$15,600 + \$19,500 + \$13,650}{\left(\frac{24}{60} \times 2,000 \text{ units}\right) + \left(\frac{40}{60} \times 1,500 \text{ units}\right) + \left(\frac{60}{60} \times 800 \text{ units}\right)}$$

$$= \frac{\$48,750}{2,600 \text{ Direct labour hours}} = \frac{\$18.75}{\text{Direct labour hour}}$$

These overheads can now be absorbed into each product on the basis of labour hour usage:

	Product X $	Product Y $	Product Z $
Direct material	5.00	3.00	6.00
Direct labour:			
$\frac{24}{60}, \frac{40}{60}, \frac{60}{60} \times \$4/\text{hour}$	1.60	2.67	4.00
Prime cost	6.60	5.67	10.00
Overhead absorbed:			
$\frac{24}{60}, \frac{40}{60}, \frac{60}{60} \times \$18.75/\text{hour}$	7.50	12.50	18.75
Total absorption cost/unit	14.10	18.17	28.75

The absorption costs per unit that we have calculated do not truly reflect an accurate valuation of these products. We need to calculate a much fairer valuation using ABC methodology.

1.4 Budgeted cost per unit using ABC

To calculate the cost per unit with ABC, the following steps must be applied:

1. For each cost pool, calculate the cost driver rate.

   $$\text{Cost driver rate} = \frac{\text{Budgeted overhead cost}}{\text{Total cost drivers}}$$

2. Apportion the cost pool out across the products based on usage of the cost drivers. For each product the overhead cost apportioned will be equal to:
   Cost driver rate × Total cost drivers for the product

3. Repeat Steps 1 and 2 for all cost pools and then calculate the total overhead cost for each product.

   $$\frac{\text{Overhead cost}}{\text{Unit}} = \frac{\text{Total overhead cost for the product}}{\text{Total units for the product}}$$

 Principle

Steps to calculate cost per unit with ABC

The steps that are needed to calculate cost per unit with ABC are as follows:
Cost driver rates

- Material receipt and inspection costs
  Total number of batches = 10 + 5 + 16 = 31

  $$\text{Cost driver rate} = \frac{\$15,600}{31} = \$503.23 \text{ per batch}$$

- Process power
  Total number of power drill operations = 2,000 × 6 + 1,500 × 3 + 800 × 2 = 18,100

  $$\text{Cost driver rate} = \frac{\$19,500}{18,100} = \$1.0773 \text{ per power drill operation}$$

- Material handling
  Total quantity of material handled = 2,000 × 4 + 1,500 × 6 + 800 × 3 = 19,400

  $$\text{Cost driver rate} = \frac{\$13.650}{19,400} = \$0.7036 \text{ per metre squared of material}$$

Please note that it is important to calculate these rates per cost driver with a reasonable degree of accuracy.

1.5 Calculating the overhead cost for each product

1.5.1 Activity-based costing approach

IE Illustrative example 1.4

Hensau Ltd has a single production process for which the following costs have been estimated for the period ending 31 December 20X1:

	$
Material receipt and inspection costs	15,600
Power costs	19,500
Material handling costs	13,650

Three products X, Y, and Z are produced by workers who perform a number of operations on material blanks using hand held electrically powered drills. The workers are paid $4 per hour.

The following budgeted information has been obtained for the period ending 31 December 20X1:

	Product X	Product Y	Product Z
Production quantity (units)	2,000	1,500	800
Batches of material	10	5	16
Data per product unit:			
Direct material (square metres)	4	6	3
Direct material cost ($)	5	3	6
Direct labour (minutes)	24	40	60
No. of power drill operations	6	3	2

Overhead costs for material receipt and inspection, process power and material handling are presently each absorbed by product units using rates per direct labour hour.

An activity-based costing investigation has revealed that the cost drivers for the overhead costs are as follows:

Material receipt and inspection	Number of batches of material
Process power	Number of power drill operations
Material handling	Quantity of material (square metres) handled

Required:

Prepare a summary which shows the budgeted product cost per unit for each product of X, Y, and Z for the period ending 31 December 20X1 detailing the unit costs for each cost element using:

(i)   the existing method for the absorption of overhead costs and

(ii) an approach which recognises the cost drivers revealed in the activity-based costing investigation.

We use this example to illustrate absorption costing and activity-based costing procedures.

1.5.2   Material receipt and inspection costs

	Product X $	Product Y $	Product Z $
Cost driver (batches)	10	5	16
Cost per batch	503.23	503.23	503.23
Total cost for product	5,032.3	2,516.15	8,051.68

Note that the total material receipt and inspection cost is unchanged. At this point, all we have done is divide out that cost across the products on the basis of cost drivers used.

The material receipt and inspection cost/unit for each product can now be calculated.

	Product X ($)	Product Y ($)	Product Z ($)
Total cost for product	5,032.3	2,516.15	8,051.68
Production quantity (units)	2000	1500	800
Material receipt and inspection cost/unit	2.52	1.68	10.06

We can see from the above that since the batch sizes of Product X are much larger than Z, far less overhead is absorbed into each cost unit of X in comparison to Z. Product Z being made in small batches causes or drivers the overhead to a much greater degree

 **Principle**

Be able to link cost driver rates to products

1.5.3   Process power

	Product X ($)	Product Y ($)	Product Z ($)
Cost driver (drill operations)	12,000	4,500	1,600
Cost per operation	1.0773	1.0773	1.0773
Total cost for product	12,927.60	4,847.85	1,723.68
Production quantity (units)	2000	1500	800
Power cost/unit	6.46	3.23	2.15

Note that if the number of cost drivers per unit is already known, then the cost/unit can be more directly calculated as cost drivers/unit × cost driver rate.

So for Product X above, the power cost/unit = 6 × $1.0773 = $6.46

1.5.4   Material handling

	Product X ($)	Product Y ($)	Product Z ($)
Cost driver (quantity of material)	8,000	9,000	2,400
Cost per metre squared	0.7036	0.7036	0.7036
Total cost for product	5,628.8	6,332.4	1,688.64
Production quantity (units)	2000	1500	800
Power cost/unit	2.81	4.22	2.11

1.5.5 The overall standard cost card

The full production cost/unit for each product can now be calculated using the results from the ABC analysis. Note that the prime cost will be the same as under an absorption costing approach.

	Product X ($)	Product Y ($)	Product Z ($)
Direct material	5	3	6
Direct labour	1.6	2.67	4
Prime cost	6.60	5.67	10.00
Overhead:			
Material receipt and inspection	2.52	1.68	10.06
Process power	6.46	3.23	2.15
Material handling	2.81	4.22	2.11
Total unit cost	18.39	14.80	24.32

Overall we have now constructed a much more accurate cost per unit, given the complexity of the overheads of Hensau.

1.6 Comparison between absorption costing and ABC

	Product X	Product Y	Product Z
Absorption cost per unit	$14.10	$18.70	$28.75
ABC cost per unit	$18.40	$14.80	$24.32
Difference in cost per unit	($4.30)	$3.90	$4.43

We can see from the above data that the differences between the costs per unit under the two techniques are quite significant.

Product X appears to have been **undercosted** using absorption costs whereas products Y and Z appear to have been **overcosted.** This may have led to inappropriate inventory valuations in Hensau's financial and management accounting records.

Product **profitability** may have been inappropriately assessed under absorption costing. Product X for example is actually less profitable than we previously thought. Products Y and Z are in fact more profitable than previously recognised. This may cause the business to alter its selling and marketing strategies.

Linked to this point is whether the products have been appropriately priced. If Hensau uses cost-plus **pricing** techniques then there is scope to decrease the price of Product X and increase the prices of both products Y and Z.

 **Principle**

Impact of changing from absorption costing to ABC

1.7 Impact of changing from absorption costing to ABC

For example if Hensau had operated a 40% cost-plus pricing strategy then the following prices would have been attained under both absorption and ABC techniques:

	Product X	Product Y	Product Z
Absorption cost plus 40%	$14.10 + 40% = $19.74	$18.70 + 40% = $26.18	$28.75 + 40% = $40.25
ABC plus 40%	$18.40+ 40% = $25.76	$14.80 + 40% = $20.72	$24.32 + 40% = $34.05
Difference in sales price per unit	**($6.02)**	**$5.46**	**$6.20**

1.8 Assumptions behind ABC

A key assumption behind ABC is that (certainly in the long run) all costs are variable. Costs may vary (or importantly be driven) on the following bases:

- **Unit level.** For example, for a wooden furniture manufacturer, the more units that are made, the more glue, varnish and power is likely to be used in their manufacture.
- **Batch related.** The wooden furniture manufacturer may have to pack the finished furniture onto a pallet for transportation. Batches of furniture will be packaged onto a pallet. The larger the pieces of furniture, the fewer that can be packaged and hence the higher the packaging overhead cost per unit.
- **Product sustaining.** The wooden furniture manufacturer may have to pay a patent registration fee which varies with the number of types of product that the business manufactures.

1.9 Environment necessary for ABC to operate

ABC tends to operate most commonly in a manufacturing or production environment where:

- The repetitive nature of production. Unless products are made repetitiously, it is difficult to establish a clear cause and effect link between activities and the units produced.

- Production processes are complex. If for example a business made one or two products in a simple environment, it is unlikely to benefit greatly from ABC. Traditional absorption costing is likely to a reasonable estimate of overheads per unit.
- Overhead expenditure needs to be high. Businesses that find a considerable proportion of their input costs to be direct costs are unlikely to benefit from ABC.

It is important as well for management to clearly understand the relationship between overheads, activities and cost drivers. Only through a clear understanding of this relationship and a robust management accounting system are management likely to be able to use ABC to plan effectively (through setting accurate standards and budgets) and control operations effectively (e.g. through accurate variance analysis).

 Principle

Environments where ABC is appropriate

1.10   Problems in using ABC

Many businesses have decided not to use ABC. The main reasons for this are:

- The cost of implementing an ABC system does not generate a large enough benefit to justify the expense.
- Too much focus is placed on cost allocation between cost pools. Instead of worrying about accurate allocation, a business would be better placed focusing on reducing overhead costs at source rather than worrying about allocating the costs it has incurred more accurately. By driving the source overhead down, the business becomes more profitable as a whole.
- In reality, it is difficult to identify each individual activity and equally (if not more) difficult to clearly identify the cost driver for that activity.

EG **Learning example 1.2**

If a company makes only ball point pens and nothing else, would it get more accurate product cost data by using ABC?

Key Learning Points

- Absorption costing and ABC both provide methods for calculating the overhead (indirect) cost per unit. (A1c)
- Traditional absorption costing calculates a 'blanket' absorption rate for each cost centre, commonly:
  - Total cost centre overhead.
  - Cost centre direct labour hours. (A1c)

- ABC allocates costs more accurately between cost pools reflecting different activities. (A1a)
- For each cost pool, ABC calculates a rate per cost driver for each cost pool of:
  - Budgeted overhead cost for the cost pool.
  - Total number of cost drivers for the cost pool. (A1b)

- Using ABC, the cost/unit for each cost pool can then be calculated as:
  - Number of cost drivers/unit × rate per cost driver (A1b)

 What's the story?

Stop and think through the 'story' of this chapter and how it links with other chapters (use the Overview to help).

Learning example solutions

EG Solution 1.1

$$OAR = \frac{\$960{,}000}{(20{,}000 \times 0.5 \text{ hours}) + (1{,}00 \times 2 \text{ hours})} = \$80/\text{hour}$$

The standard cost card for each product becomes:

	Handheld hammers	Containers
Direct material/unit	$5	$300
Direct labour/unit		
0.5 hours @ $20/hour	$10	
2 hours @ $20/hour		$40
Prime cost/unit	$15	$340
Overhead per unit		
0.5 hours × $80/hour	$40	
2 hours × $80/hour		$160
Total absorption cost/unit	$55	$500

The sales price of each product becomes:

	Handheld hammers	Containers
Absorption cost/unit	$55	$500
+ 40% profit margin	$22	$200
Sales price	$77	$700

It would appear very unreasonable indeed to expect to get such a high sales price for hand-held hammers. The overhead of $40 charged to the product is some 73% of the overall product cost ($55).

Similarly it is likely that if the containers are sold for $700, this will be significantly below the market price. It also appears strange that for such a large and bulky product, only 32% of the product's cost is made up of overhead. Each container appears relatively 'cheap' to make in overhead terms because of the relatively small amount of direct labour required to make it. The bulk of the productive input to make the container is machine overhead, yet the labour rate absorption rate does not recognise this.

EG Solution 1.2

Since the company manufactures just one product in a simple production system, it is unlikely to get more accurate product cost data by using ABC. ABC would be a waste of time and expense. To bring in an ABC system would have significant implementation risk.

Throughput Accounting

Context

In this chapter, we first need to understand the theory of constraints to see what could be holding a business back. Then we move on, to consider how costing techniques can operate when a business is focusing on just-in-time (JIT) manufacturing techniques ie where a company holds little stock and makes everything as required by its customers.

Throughput accounting helps us look at where there are constraints in a JIT environment. Throughput accounting is similar in its objectives to marginal costing and contribution analysis. It focuses on the most efficient and profitable production to be undertaken when there is a restriction on productive capacity.

3Q

1. Do you know the five focusing steps in the Theory of Constraints?

2. Can you list some measures to relieve bottlenecks in the just-in-time process?

3. What do different values of the throughput accounting ratio indicate?

2.1 Constraints

Although you will come across constraints in the mathematical model of linear programming, it has a slightly different application when dealing with management and management accounting.

Basically, a constraint is anything that will stop a system, organisation or process from producing as much as it could, and prevents an organisation from achieving its goal. There might be many constraints but some will be more important and critical than others: this is termed a 'bottleneck'.

An internal constraint exists when the environment demands more of an organisation than it can deliver. Examples of these internal constraints include equipment, people with the right skills, policies and regulations.

IE Illustrative example 2.1

A hospital might have a target of treating all patients for hip replacements within 18 weeks. Factors enabling it to achieve this goal include availability of hospital beds, availability of consultants and surgeons, availability of other medical staff.

An **external constraint** is where the environment does not require or want the output of the organisation, so making it difficult to achieve its goal. For example, a university may have space for lots of students on certain courses, but it may be that these courses are not popular. This affects the funding the university receives.

The theory of constraints holds that organisations or processes can be analysed by variations on three measures:

- Throughput: this is the rate the system achieves its goals. In a business this is the rate at which it hits sales. In the hospital example above, this is the number of hip operations carried out, and funded.
- Inventory is the investment the business has made in creating items to sell. In a business selling goods, inventory is physical stocks. In a hotel, you could say that inventory is the 'stock of time slots' available, that is, the number of nights available for customers to spend in the hotel's rooms.
- Operational expenses are the money the system spends in order to turn inventory into throughput, for example selling stocks or paying consultants and nurses to carry out operations.

In most cases there is at least one key constraint.

IE Illustrative example 2.2

In the example of the hospital, this might well be the fixed availability of beds, compared to the demand for hip replacements. The limited number of beds limits the number of operations that can be performed in any period. Only by increasing throughput can the goal be achieved. Somehow, the hospital has to provide more ways to do this.

So what to do about constraints that prevent an organisation from achieving its goal? The Theory of Constraints offers **five focusing steps**.

Step 1: Identify the system's constraint that stops the goal being achieved	The hospital may determine that it simply does not have enough beds to meet the demand for surgery in 18 weeks.
Step 2: Decide how to get best use from the constraint.	An example might be to reschedule operations at different times of day, perhaps to squeeze in some extra usage from the beds. It may be beds are out of usage if all patients are admitted in the morning.
Step 3: Subordinate everything else to the above decision.	A policy could be to discharge some patients earlier if this is possible without breaching clinical guidelines, for example by discharging after three, as opposed to four, days. New surgical techniques can be used.
Step 4: Elevate the constraint. In other words make other major changes needed to increase the constraint's capacity. If a constraint's throughput capacity is elevated to the point where it is no longer the system's limiting factor, this is said to "break" the constraint. The limiting factor is now some other part of the system, or may be external to the system (an external constraint).	This is a more fundamental change. Step 2 and 3 involved tinkering with the usage patterns of the constraining resource. In Step 4 the hospital determines it will increase the number of beds by buying more.
Step 5: If in steps 2, 3 and 4, a constraint has been 'broken' – in other words it is no longer a constraint - go back to step 1	There will come a time when bed availability is not an issue, in which case it is no longer a constraint – and something else! The hospital may have enough beds, but if it is still not meeting its 18 month target, there may be other constraints to look at.

2.2 Throughput accounting

Throughput accounting is an extension of costing techniques seen so far. It is a technique which is closely related to the culture of just-in-time (JIT) manufacturing techniques.

2.2.1 JIT (just-in-time) manufacturing

JIT is used extensively in highly mechanised businesses, particularly the car industry. The ultimate **aim** is to **carry zero stock** lines, since holding large inventories ties up cash reserves, is expensive to store, and may become damaged or indeed obsolete. In other words, carrying inventory is expensive for the business.

The philosophy is that finished goods are only to be made when an order has been placed for them by a customer. This in turn means that since no work-in-progress is held, then the workforce needs to be reallocated and machinery needs to be set up in order to manufacture that product. If this is to happen then since no raw material stocks are held, an order needs to be placed and met by the supplier instantaneously. At each point in the production process, the business manufactures enough 'units' just in time for the next processes' requirements.

The factory needs to be considered as a **whole process** in its own right. We view the factory as a whole process rather than considering each individual process in its own right. This **holistic** approach aims to ensure that the factory can make the required units of production in the least possible time and using the least possible resources.

IE Illustrative example 2.3

A typical car manufacturer has highly automated production lines, capable (often through robotic flexible manufacturing systems) of manufacturing different types and models of motor cars. The workforce is highly trained to quickly switch production techniques from one type of car to another as and when required (eg by a new customer order). When the production run is due to start, the suppliers will already have delivery lorries on site to offload the right amount of components (guaranteed quality is a necessity!) onto the production line. Once the cars are finished, they are delivered straight to the customer.

2.2.2   Throughput accounting – bottlenecks

If we are considering the output/efficiency of a factory as a whole, we need to consider *internally* where there may be sticking points which could hamper the overall efficiency and effectiveness of the factory operations.

IE Illustrative example 2.4

A factory has three processes which run concurrently. Process P1 feeds into process P2 and P2 in turn feeds into process P3. The maximum possible output of units (capacity) in a given period is:

	P1	P2	P3
Capacity	200	250	150
			bottleneck

If we operate a JIT philosophy, there is no point in P1 making 200 or P2 making 250 units, since production of the factory is constrained overall to the 150 P3 is capable of making. For P1 and P2 to manufacture to their own capacity, they would end up 'stockpiling'; P1 some (200–150) 50 units and P2 some (250–150) 100 units each time period.

Process P3 limits the capacity of the factory and is known as the **bottleneck.** It is in essence the limiting factor on factory production. If a JIT system is operated, the production in P1 and P2 would need to be scaled back to 150 units.

2.2.3 Relieving the bottleneck

Bottlenecks (here in P3) can be relieved by practical measures to increase capacity:

- **Increasing** the length of **time** that **machines run** for – for example moving form a 12 hour per day production process to 24 hour operations (common in many mass production processes);
- **Divert** more **productive labour** to the bottleneck process. This may be easier to perform if staff are multi-skilled and can operate different processes.
- **Invest** in new and **more efficient machinery.** Businesses have historically moved more toward capital than manual or labour intensive production processes
- **Outsource** part or all of the production of the bottleneck if this is more efficient and cost-effective.

However, relieving a bottleneck in one process will create another elsewhere.

IE Illustrative example 2.5

Continuing from Illustrative example 2, if P3's capacity increases to 300, the bottleneck shifts now to P1:

	P1	P2	P3
Capacity	200	250	300
	Bottleneck		

Process P1 can now be investigated further to improve potential output, although processes P2 and P3 scale production now to 200 units.

 Principle

The throughput accounting approach

2.2.4 Throughput accounting – a summary so far:

- **Identify the bottleneck** – this is the process within the factory which prevents all the other processes from reaching their maximum capacity.
- **Scale back production in the factory to the bottleneck throughput** – all other processes need to be making the same number of units as the bottleneck process can make at its existing maximum capacity. It is rather like a group of mountain walkers travelling at the pace of the slowest walker.

- **Ease the bottleneck** – procedures will need to be undertaken to increase the capacity of the bottleneck.

 Learn

2.2.5 Throughput accounting – measurement

It is easiest to understand the concept of throughput accounting performance measurement by comparing it with marginal costing from your Management Accounting studies. The differences are largely in terms of definitions.

Marginal costing (MC)	Throughput accounting (TA)
Variable costs are identified as those costs which vary directly with activity. This is likely to include, direct materials, **direct labour, direct expenses and variable overhead.**	The only **variable cost** recognised by TA is **direct material cost**. If more units are made, then more material is needed. Other costs are assumed to be fixed. For example, in reality direct labour is likely to be salaried and work a set number of hours as specified in an employment contract. Direct Labour is in essence a fixed cost.
The more units that are made, the more of these costs that are incurred.	
Fixed costs are assumed to be other costs which do not vary with activity levels.	Fixed costs are now classified as **total factory cost**. It is important to note that his will **include direct labour costs** and all overheads.
Contribution is calculated as **sales revenue** *less* **variable costs**. The resultant contribution is then compared to the fixed costs of a business to identify if a profit has been made.	**Throughput** is calculated as **sales revenue** less **direct material cost**. The throughput will hopefully exceed the Total Factory Costs of the business

2.2.6 Key throughput measures

Throughput per unit = Selling price - Direct material cost

$$\text{Return per factory hour} = \frac{\text{Throughput per unit}}{\text{Hours per unit in the bottleneck}}$$

 Learn

This can be measured for each process in question and is the 'equivalent' of contribution per hour that would occur in marginal costing. It is extremely useful to calculate the return per factory hour for the bottleneck resource, since it enables the business to make appropriate decisions with reference to its product mix. For example the business can decide which products are getting the 'best' return per hour of scarce bottleneck resource.

$$\text{Cost per factory hour} = \frac{\text{Total factory cost}}{\text{Total factory hours}}$$

 Learn

This identifies across the factory, the total (unvarying!) fixed costs that need to be recovered and we can assess this on an hourly basis using the Throughput Accounting Ratio (TPAR):

$$\text{Throughput accounting ratio (TPAR)} = \frac{\text{Return per factory hour}}{\text{Cost per factory hour}}$$

 Learn

In essence we are comparing a 'contribution' per hour against a 'fixed cost' per hour.

TPAR	Interpretation
TPAR = 1.00	The return being generated by the product per hour exactly recovers the fixed cost per hour. This is like a 'breakeven' position where no profit and no loss is made.
TPAR > 1.00	The product is generating a return in excess of the fixed costs per hour. It is 'profitable'.
TPAR < 1.00	The product is generating a return per hour less than the fixed costs that business incurs per hour. It is 'loss making'.

 Learn

EG Learning example 2.1

Shopland has two production departments: assembly and finishing. It manufactures two products, Product alpha and Product beta. It operates a JIT manufacturing system.

Processing capabilities are shown here:

	Processing time in minutes	
	Assembly	Finishing
Product alpha	30	45
Product beta	30	60

Total time available in the period for both departments is 12,000 hours. Factory overhead for the period is $180,000

Cost data is as follows:

	Product alpha	Product beta
Units sales price	$20	$15
Direct materials cost per unit	$11	$9

- Identify the bottleneck process.
- Calculate:

  - Return per factory hour for the bottleneck process

  - Cost per factory hour

  - TPAR for each product.

2.3 Interpreting and improving the TPAR

In Learning example 2.1, Product alpha appears worthwhile to produce since it is getting a return per factory hour (in finishing) in excess of the factory fixed cost per hour. Product beta however appears to not be so worthwhile to produce, since it is 'loss making'.

In order to improve beta's TPAR, consider the constituent parts of the ratio. For example its TPAR would improve if:

- The selling price could be increased. This may be possible if the market is not overly competitive.

- Its material cost and/or usage could be decreased. Possibly the business could drive a harder bargain with suppliers or redesign the product to use less material. Maybe lower quality and hence cheaper material could be used, although this may impair the product quality.

- Cost savings programmes on factory cost, for example labour saving schemes, cutting fixed overhead by operating from cheaper premises etc may help, although this is likely to be a more long-term decision.

- Improving the efficiency of the process in the bottleneck could help. For example if each alpha and beta could be made in 30 minutes by the finishing department (as in assembly), a marked improvement would be noted in TPAR.

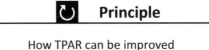 **Principle**

How TPAR can be improved

EG Learning example 2.2

Gemma Ltd manufactures two products Alpha and Beta which are used in the chemical industry. Due to limited plant capacity demand it cannot meet the demand at present. The managing director aims to make use of its plant in the most efficient way by producing products in order of profitability.

The following are details extracted from the management accounts for the current period:

	Alpha	Beta
Demand (units) per day	250	300
Selling price per unit ($)	10	7
Direct material cost per unit ($)	6	4
Machine time per unit (minutes)	1.5	1

Conversion costs including labour and overheads: $1,200 per day

The plant operates 8 hours per day.

Required:

1. Calculate throughput return per hour for each product.
2. Calculate factory cost per hour
3. Calculate throughput accounting ratio for each product
4. Determine the optimum production schedule

➡ Key Learning Points

- Key throughput accounting techniques:
  - Identify the bottleneck.
  - Scale back production in the factory to the bottleneck capacity.
  - Increase capacity in the bottleneck.

- Key throughput accounting formulae:
  - Return per factory hour

$$\frac{\text{Sales price per unit - Direct material cost per unit}}{\text{Hours per unit in the bottleneck}}$$

  - Cost per factory hour

$$\frac{\text{Total factory cost}}{\text{Total factory hours}}$$

- Throughput accounting ratio (TPAR)

$$\frac{\text{Return per factory hour}}{\text{Cost per factory hour}} \quad (A4b)$$

What's the story?

Stop and think through the 'story' of this chapter and how it links with other chapters (use the Overview to help).

Learning example solutions

EG **Solution 2.1**

Bottleneck process

The bottleneck process is finishing, since both products will take the longest production time in that process. Numerically we can calculate the maximum units of alpha and beta that can be manufactured by each process:

	Processing capacity	
	Assembly	**Finishing**
Product alpha	$12,000 \div \left(\dfrac{30 \text{ minutes}}{60 \text{ minutes}} \right) = 24,000$ units	$12,000 \div \left(\dfrac{45 \text{ minutes}}{60 \text{ minutes}} \right) = 16,000$ units
Product beta	$12,000 \div \left(\dfrac{30 \text{ minutes}}{60 \text{ minutes}} \right) = 24,000$ units	$12,000 \div \left(\dfrac{60 \text{ minutes}}{60 \text{ minutes}} \right) = 12,000$ units

We can see that Assembly is capable of making 24,000 product alpha and 24,000 product beta. Finishing however is only capable of making 16,000 product alpha and 12,000 product beta. Assembly will need to scale back its production of alpha and beta to 16,000 and 12,000 units respectively if the business is to maintain its zero inventory policy.

Return per factory hour for the bottleneck process

The bottleneck process is finishing. Therefore the return per factory hour in assembly is calculated:

$$\text{Return per factory hour} = \frac{\text{Sales price per unit - Direct material cost per unit}}{\text{Factory hours per unit in finishing department}}$$

Product alpha: $\dfrac{\$20 - \$11}{0.75} = \$12.00$

Product beta: $\dfrac{\$15 - \$9}{1.00} = \$6.00$

Cost per factory hour

$$\text{Cost per factory hour} = \frac{\text{Total factory cost}}{\text{Total hours on bottleneck resource}}$$

$$= \frac{\$180,000}{12,000 \text{ hours}} = \$15 \text{ per hour}$$

TPAR

$$\text{Throughput Accounting Ratio (TPAR)} = \frac{\text{Return per factory hour}}{\text{Cost per factory hour}}$$

For each product:

Product alpha: $\dfrac{\$12.00}{\$15} = 0.8$

Product beta: $\dfrac{\$6.00}{\$15} = 0.4$

EG Solution 2.2

1. Return per factory hour for each product

	Alpha ($)	Beta ($)
Selling price	10	7
Less: direct materials	6	4
Throughput per unit	4	3
÷ Time per unit	1.5	1
Throughput return per minute	$2.67	$3

To get throughput return per factory hour we need to multiply above by 60:

Alpha	Beta
$160	$180

2. Cost per factory hour

   Conversion costs per day: $1,200

   ÷ bottleneck time per day: 8 hours

   = $150 per hour

   Or $150/60 minutes = $2.50 per minute

   $$\text{Throughput accounting ratio} = \frac{\text{Throughput return per hour}}{\text{Factory (conversion) costs per hour}}$$

   Alpha = $\dfrac{\$160}{\$150} = 1.07$

   Beta = $\dfrac{\$180}{\$150} = 1.2$

3. Optimum production plan

   The issue here is that Gemma Ltd are unable to meet daily demand for both products. There are only 8 plant hours available per day which equates to 8 ×

60 = 480 minutes. To meet demand for both products more processing hours would be required:

Alpha: 250 × 1.5 minutes = 375 minutes

Beta: 300 × 1 minute = 300 minutes

So 675 minutes are required in total. Since the company cannot meet demand for both products, they instead want to ensure they maximise profits given the limited hours available. To determine this, first we must rank the products:

	Alpha	Beta
TPAR	1.07	1.2
Ranking	2	1

Beta is a more profitable product as the returns per hour for this product are greater than the returns per hour for product Alpha.

Therefore, to maximise profits, Gemma will first produce as many units of Beta as possible, up to the maximum demand. If there are any machine minutes left after this, they can be used to produce Alpha.

The optimum production plan will therefore be:

Machine minutes available	Alpha (units)	Beta (units)
480 minutes		
(300) Beta production 180 minutes remaining		300
(180) Alpha production 1.5 × 120 0 minutes remaining	120	

From this table, once the Beta units have been produced, there are 180 minutes remaining. These are used to produce as many units of Alpha as possible = 180/1.5 minutes per unit = 120 units.

3

Target Costing and Lifecycle Costing

Context

In this chapter, we will consider two new costing techniques: target costing and lifecycle costing.

Target costing is an important concept for many businesses. Here the business responds to what customers are willing to pay, and tries to manage its own internal costs accordingly.

Lifecycle costing tries to identify all the costs associated with a product over its whole life, and spread these over the number of units that the business is aiming to make and sell over the product's life.

These techniques are largely discursive areas where you will not only need to know the attributes of the pricing techniques, but also how to apply them to exam scenarios and assess whether the costing method chosen is appropriate.

3Q

1. Can you explain the concept of target costing?

2. What steps can companies take to close the gap between the actual cost base and target cost base?

3. What is the formula for life cost/unit and given the product selling price, how would you determine if the product is profitable over its lifecycle?

3.1 Target costing

3.1.1 Introduction

Target costing is a technique widely used by many companies. Lots of businesses operate in a highly competitive market where it is virtually impossible for the producer to determine the price that the goods will sell at in the market.

Factors such as strong and innovative competition and knowledgeable customers who can easily shop around and demand specific attributes that a product should possess, contribute to how the market determines the price of the goods sold rather than the company itself.

Therefore a business, through proper marketing research, will try to find out how much customers are willing to pay. Once this is established, the business will deduct its required profit margin in order to identify the cost ceiling that it will need to work to if a profit is to be made.

3.1.2 Target costing steps

1. Identify the sales price at which the product may be sold.
2. Identify the required margin that the business wishes to secure. This may be a profit or indeed a contribution margin.
3. Target cost = Sales price - Required margin
4. 'Close the gap' – ie the difference between the actual cost base and the target cost base.

 Learn

IE Illustrative example 3.1

Stanisavljevic has designed a new machine which should sell in the market for $7,800. Stanisavljevic wishes to make a profit margin of 18% and currently estimates from design work undertaken that the machine will cost (using current specifications) $6,550 to manufacture.

What is the target cost and the target cost gap?

Target cost

Sales price = $7,800

Required margin = $7,800 × 18% = $1,404

Target cost = $7,800 – $1,404 = $6,396

Target cost gap = $6,550 – $6,396 = $154

Target costing versus cost-plus pricing

It could be argued that target costing is the exact opposite of cost-plus pricing techniques. Cost-plus is an 'inside-out' technique, where the business calculates the cost per unit and adds on a desired margin in order to establish the sales price that it will set. The problem with this approach can be if the price is actually quite different to that which the customer is willing to pay. If the sales price is too high, the product will not sell. If the sales price is set too low, the product will sell, but the business could easily have sold it for a higher price and made more profit.

Target costing is an 'outside-in' approach to pricing, where the start point is what the customers are actually willing to pay, in order to purchase a product of given quality and specification.

 Principle

How target costing differs in its principle from cost-plus pricing

3.1.3   'Closing the gap'

The problem most businesses find is that:

Actual cost base > target cost base

Therefore they need to focus on reducing the 'gap' between the two to zero so that they can charge the sales price that the customers are willing to pay in order to receive the desired margin.

This closure of the gap is most likely to happen at the design stage, where the product can be adapted to incorporate different methods of achieving acceptable output, but at a different cost. If a product has already reached commercial production and sale, it is unlikely to be successfully adapted.

3.1.4   Methods of reducing the gap

To illustrate we could consider a business that makes frozen pizzas to be sold via supermarkets:

Reduce the number of components used in manufacture.

IE **Illustrative example 3.2**

For example the pizza may be wrapped just in shrink-wrap cellophane, rather than wrapped in both cellophane and then an external cardboard box. The first method would clearly be cheaper. If other simple reductions in components could be achieved then the product cost would fall further still. For example the pizza may not contain artificial additives and colourants which would not only be cheaper, but may improve the eating quality of the pizza as well.

Reduce production complexity.

IE Illustrative example 3.3

The pizza could be made by using fewer processes. For example, the pizza topping could be pre-mixed and then put on each pizza in one step rather than each topping being put on the pizza in individual steps. If the business puts five different toppings on to the pizzas in five separate stages, then by mixing the toppings in one process and putting them on the pizza in a second process, dramatic cost savings can be achieved.

Revise the specification of the product.

IE Illustrative example 3.4

Some toppings could be excluded from the pizza completely, or cheaper ingredients could be used. This would reduce the cost of producing the pizzas. Clearly the danger here is decreasing the quality of the pizza to such an extent that customers would no longer wish to buy it.

↻ Principle

How the cost gap could be closed

3.1.5 Target costing and service businesses

Service businesses differ from manufacturers in the characteristics of the 'product' that they make. Examples of services are:

- Dentistry
- Hairdressing
- Pensions advice
- Banking
- Air travel

The characteristics of service businesses make it difficult to accurately cost their 'products'.

IE Illustrative example 3.5

If a person is paying a visit to a hairdresser, the hairdresser will not know exactly how much time is needed or hair products are required to perform the haircut. The bulk of costs involved in a haircut are also not directly associated with the haircut itself. For example the hairdresser may be salaried, the premises may be rented, etc.

IE | **Illustrative example 3.6**

At a hairdresser's, suppose the target price to charge for each haircut is $40. The required profit margin per haircut is 15%. Therefore the target cost is:

$40 – 15% × $40 = $34

But each haircut provided will be unique in some way. So for two different customers, the data may be as follows:

	Customer 1	Customer 2
Time taken (hours)	0.5	1
Material cost (hair products)	$10	$15

If overhead costs are allocated on the basis of time taken, then the overhead cost of each haircut will also be different. Therefore, some service units provided will achieve the target cost but others will not.

Furthermore, in service industries there are fewer product innovations. As target costing is most successful when applied to a new product, there is less opportunity to use this in service organisations. For example, if an airline starts selling flights on a new route, this is not a brand new product being provided, it is just a different version of the existing products.

 Principle

Product costing in services organisations

3.2 Life cycle costing

Life Cycle Costing addresses two important issues that have arisen in recent years:

- Products tend to have shorter product lifecycles. There is less time between products being introduced to the market and subsequently withdrawn.
- Increased initial costs to design, develop and launch a new product.

The difficulty from a costing perspective is how to link the costs of development to the products they relate to. It is important here to distinguish between the financial reporting issues of how to deal with development expenditure and how management accountants need to cost the product range.

3.2.1   Product lifecycle

Many products pass through a typical product lifecycle as shown below. The phases of the cycle are:

- **Development** – Research and product development costs can be huge for many businesses. For example a pharmaceutical manufacturer will spend vast sums of money researching new drugs, testing and trialling those drugs and so on. A major issue with life cycle costing is how to effectively account for these costs.
- **Introduction** – The product needs to be effectively marketed and advertised in the launch stage. Significant promotional costs and possibly product redesign costs can be incurred here (if product needs adapting due to customer feedback).
- **Growth** - If successful, the product will be attractive to customers, sales revenues and volumes climb rapidly and profits increase. The business may incur further promotional and product adaptation costs to maintain growth rates
- **Maturity** – The product will reach a stage where sales demand starts to stabilise. It is possible at this phase that there is intense competition and the business may need to update its product to 'extend' its life.
- **Decline** – Demand will start to fall when the market tires of the product. The product may cease to be produced as demand falls away.

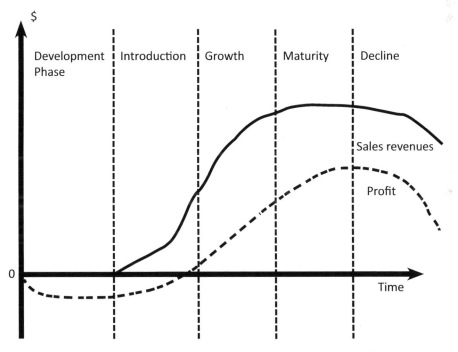

For many modern businesses, this lifecycle may be as short as 12–18 months (eg the lifecycle of a computer game!).

3.2.2 The benefits of lifecycle costing

(a) The most suitable performance measures can be applied at different stages in the product's life.
(b) It will be easier to predict cash flows and investment requirements for a product
(c) When a business has a portfolio of several different products at different stages in the lifecycle, it will be easier to predict costs.
(d) Learning curve effects can be incorporated
(e) Standard costs do not have to be regularly changed

3.2.3 Issues arising with lifecycle costing

- **Ensuring costs are recouped during the product life** – The business must be able to identify all costs associated with the product. Prices may be inappropriately set if all costs are not identified effectively. Businesses may also seek where possible to extend the lifecycle of a product. This may involve launching new updated versions of the product or seeking new (for example foreign) markets in which the product can be sold.
- **Understand the cost from year to year** – if the business spreads the costs over each year, but does not reflect the number of expected units to be made in each year it may again price incorrectly. If for example a high cost is recognised in the launch year, yet few units are due to be sold, the resultant unit cost may be excessively high causing an unrealistically high sales price to be set. The business must have a robust budgeting system and accurate performance measures to assess whether the product is giving a sufficient return over its life.

  Principle

> Product lifecycle and the principle, issues and benefits of lifecycle costing

3.2.4 Calculation of life cost per unit

We aim to take all of the costs associated with its product over its entire life and spread these over all of the units that are expected to be sold over the entire life of the product.

$$\frac{\text{Life cost}}{\text{Unit}} = \frac{\text{Estimated total lifecycle costs}}{\text{Estimated lifecycle units produced}}$$

3.2.5 Life cycle profit

Life cycle profit is the total profit that a product will make over its lifecycle. In simple terms this takes the total revenue less total costs in the life cycle to calculate the profit. Businesses are likely to want to manage the costs and revenues as much as they can, via control of production and marketing, to make a product as profitable as possible.

  Learn

EG Learning example 3.1

Ponting is to design a new style of cricket bat. Ponting operates a JIT manufacturing system. The new cricket bat is expected to have a life of 4 years and the following costs:

	Year 1 ($)	Year 2 ($)	Year 3 ($)	Year 4 ($)
Development costs	320,000			
Marketing and advertising costs	30,000	15,000	10,000	5,000
Manufacturing costs per bat	30	25	20	15
Selling and distribution costs	25,000	40,000	30,000	15,000
Bats (units made and sold)	5,000	12,500	20,000	3,000

Ponting is aiming to sell the bat for $40. Is the bat likely to be profitable over its life cycle?

EG Learning example 3.2

A company is considering the development of a new product. The following costs and sales have been estimated over the life of the product:

	2008 ($)	2009 ($)	2010 ($)	2011 ($)
Selling price/unit		3	3.25	2.50
Production costs				
Variable		1	1	1
Fixed		100,000	110,000	120,000
Development costs	100,000			
Marketing	100,000	50,000	50,000	50,000
Volumes (units)		100,000	150,000	125,000

Required:

    (a) Calculate total contribution over lifecycle and per unit.
    (b) Calculate total life cycle profit and per unit.

EG Learning example 3.3

Megna Ltd is trying to develop a new washing powder introducing a stain removal formula. The following are the details extracted from working papers of the project.

Research costs	$5,000
Development costs	$20,000
Branding & legal costs	$3,000
Initial marketing	$10,000
Further marketing	$4,000 per annum
Variable production costs	$1 per kg
Fixed production costs	$100,000 per annum
Terminal costs	$15,000

The life of the washing powder is expected to be two years after which a new formula will be launched into the market. Expected volume is 500,000 kg per annum which is normal capacity of the plant. Following extensive market research, the company has established a target selling price of $1.5 per kg. The required profit margin is 20%.

Required:

(a) Calculate total life cycle cost per kg.
(b) Calculate the cost gap per kg if a life cycle costing approach is adopted.

➡ Key Learning Points

- Target costing ensures that the selling price charged will be competitive. (A2a)
- The key steps in target costing are:
  - Identify the sales price at which the product may be sold.
  - Identify the required margin that the business wishes to secure.
  - Target cost = sales price *minus* required margin.
  - 'Close the gap' – ie the difference between the actual cost base and the target cost base. (A2a, A2b)

- Lifecycle costing ensures that all the costs incurred in the life of the product are recovered in the selling price. (A3a)
- Life cost/unit

$$\frac{\text{Estimated total lifecycle costs}}{\text{Estimated lifecycle units produced}} \quad \text{(A3b)}$$

What's the story?

Stop and think through the 'story' of this chapter and how it links with other chapters (use the Overview to help).

Learning example solutions

EG Solution 3.1

	$
Total development costs	320,000
Total marketing and advertising costs	60,000
Total manufacturing cost	
5,000 x 30 = 150,000	
12,500 x 25 = 312,500	
20,000 x 20 = 400,000	
3,000 x 15 = 45,000	907,500
Selling and distribution costs	110,000
Total lifecycle costs	1,397,500
Total lifecycle units	40,500
Cost per unit	**$34.51**

Since the bat has an expected cost of $34.51, it should be profitable if sold at a sales price of $40. There is however only a relatively small margin that is likely to be earned on average ($5.49 – a mark-up on lifecycle cost of 15.9%).

Ponting may wish to investigate whether costs can be saved or whether it may be able to charge a higher price, for example at launch to reflect the desirability and novelty of the bat.

EG Solution 3.2

(a) Total contribution and contribution per unit

	$
Sales revenue:	
2009: 100,000 × $3	300,000
2010: 150,000 × $3.25	487,500
2011: 125,000 × $2.5	312,500
Total revenue	1,100,000
Variable costs: 375,000 × $1	(375,000)
Total contribution	725,000
Contribution/unit: 725,000/375,000	$1.93

(b) Total profit and profit per unit

	$
Total contribution	725,000
Less:	
Fixed production costs	(330,000)
Research and development	(100,000)
Marketing costs	(250,000)
Total lifecycle profit	45,000
Profit/unit: $45,000/375,000	$0.12

EG Solution 3.3

(a) Life cycle cost per kg

Cost type	$
Research	5,000
Development	20,000
Branding and legal	3,000
Initial marketing	10,000
Further marketing $4,000 × 2	8,000
Variable production costs $1 × 1,000,000kg	1,000,000
Fixed production costs	200,000
Terminal costs	15,000
Total lifecycle costs	1,261,000
Lifecycle cost/kg: 1,261,000/1,000,000	$1.261

(b) Cost gap

	$
Target price	$1.5
Required margin: 20% x $1.5	$0.3
Target cost/kg	$1.2
Life cost/kg	$1.261
Cost gap: $1.261 – $1.2	$0.061

Environmental
Management Accounting

Context

An issue that is becoming increasingly important in the business world is that of protecting the environment. As organisations are now accountable for the impact of their operations on the environment they have to become much more aware of the problems that they can cause to the environment, such as carbon emissions.

In order to become more environmentally aware, and to minimise the impact to the environment, an organisation will incur costs and, therefore, there is a need to focus on managing and accounting for these environmental costs.

There will be no calculations within this area of the syllabus. However, the examiner expects you to be able to discuss and describe the issues in the management of environmental costs and the different methods to account for such costs.

1. Why is it important from a non-financial perspective for companies to be environmentally aware?

2. In relation to the environment, what are image and relationship costs?

3. Can you describe the input outflow analysis method of calculating environmental costs?

4.1 Environmental management accounting

Environmental management accounting (EMA) is part of management accounting and it focuses on the costs to the environment caused by decisions made by the company.

 Learn

IE Illustrative example 4.1

Examples of costs to the environment made by company decisions can include:

- **Energy** – there may be many inefficiencies within energy use that could be damaging to the environment and causing unnecessary costs to the organisation.
- **Waste disposal** – costs associated with waste disposal could be fines for polluting or costs associated with having the correct wastage systems in place.
- **Transport** – carbon emissions given off by transport could be reduced by using more fuel efficient vehicles or alternative fuel vehicles.
- **Raw materials** – recycling of materials could bring both cost savings to the company and help reduce the waste that would impact the environment.

 Learn

However there is not only a focus on the financial costs but also the non-financial impact of being environmentally aware, such as the effect on the public perception of not abiding by environmental legislation or using a supplier that is not environmentally friendly.

Businesses have to externally report on these issues however for the purpose of this paper we are focusing on the generation of internal information for decision-making purposes. Its aim is to make managers aware of the environmental costs associated with their decision so that they can try and strike a balance between providing a benefit to the company and reducing the harmful impact to the environment.

4.1.1 Importance of environmental management accounting

1. Organisations have increasing regulations and legal requirements to meet relating to environmental management which can lead to fines for non-compliance.
2. Organisations need to manage the risk and potential impact of environmental disasters.
3. Cost savings can be made through the reduction of waste and efficient use of resources such as water and energy.
4. Society is now becoming more and more environmentally aware and so environmental management accounting could be used to an organisation's advantage to try and attract customers.
5. Environmental costs are becoming a major part of an organisations cost and therefore need to be managed well.

IE **Illustrative example 4.2**

A relevant example which demonstrates the importance of EMA in particular managing the risks and potential impact of environmental disasters is that of the Deepwater Horizon oil spill. In April 2010 a BP drilling rig exploded releasing approximately 4.9 million barrels of crude oil into the Gulf of Mexico. This resulted in BP reporting its first annual loss since 1992 most likely due to the serious damage to their reputation and the cash needed for compensation and the clean-up operation, which was estimated at $32 billion.

 Principle

Understand the importance of environmental management accounting

4.1.2   Defining environmental costs

In order for management to be aware of the environmental costs and identify areas for improvement and cost saving it is important to try and make these costs visible and give them a clear definition of environmental costs.

There are many definitions of environmental costs which can vary significantly:

- **Conventional costs**
  These are costs such as raw materials and energy costs that will have an impact on the environment. This category could also include waste through inefficiency and regulatory fines.

- **Potentially hidden costs**
  These costs usually lose their identity due to being hidden within general overheads but are captured by accounting systems. It is important that they are separated from general overheads otherwise they will not be a high priority for management as they cannot be seen.

- **Contingent costs**
  These are costs that are incurred at a future date such as clean-up costs. They can be large costs that because they are in the future may not be given high priority by managers who may be concerned with short-term financial measures.

- **Image and relationship costs**
  These costs are intangible in nature and are concerned with maintaining the reputation of the organisation and may include costs associated with producing information for public reporting. These reports will show the public the importance that the organisation attaches to being environmentally aware.

 Learn

4.1.3 Methods to account for environmental costs

There are four methods which were identified by United Nations Divisions for Sustainable Development (UNDSD) and are examinable in this paper. These methods are input/outflow analysis, flow cost accounting, activity-based costing and lifecycle costing.

Input/outflow analysis

This method works on the theory that 'what goes in must come out' and the inflow regarded as 100% must be balanced with the outflows as shown by the diagram below. This will enable waste or any costs that remain unaccounted for to be identified.

By examining the outflows of a process it enables relevant information needed for environmental cost analysis to be identified in both physical units and monetary units.

Flow cost accounting

This method used both material flows and organisational structures to make material flows more transparent. It will focus on quantities, costs and values of the material flows and also identify material losses throughout the production process. It will divide the material flows into three categories:

- **Material** – these are costs and values of the materials involved in the production processes.
- **System** – these are costs and values of the internal handling of the materials eg personnel costs
- **Delivery and disposal** – these are costs of the material flows leaving the company eg. transport costs or waste disposal.

The aim of flow cost accounting is to reduce the quantities of material which should be beneficial to the environment as well as saving costs for the organisation.

Activity-based costing

Activity-based costing (ABC) is a detailed cost allocation system which allocates costs to cost centres based on the activities that are deemed to cause the costs.

Within environmental management accounting ABC distinguishes between environment-related costs and environmentally-driven costs. Environment-related costs are costs that can be attributed specifically to an environmental cost centre, for example sewerage plants or incinerators.

Environment-driven costs are usually hidden within general overheads and do not relate to a specific cost centre but however relate to environmental drivers such as higher costs of staff or increased depreciation.

In order to allocate the environment-driven costs to cost centres it is important to find adequate cost drivers. In order to do this the production processes must be analysed to establish the volumes of waste and emissions, the toxicity of emissions and the costs associated with treating emissions.

Life cycle costing

This method considers costs and revenues throughout the life of a product from the initial design stage right through the end of the life where it will be removed from the market.

As mentioned previously there are future environmental costs associated with products such as clean-up of industrial sites and also disposal costs. By using the lifecycle costing method these environmental costs will have an early focus which can aid decision making such as pricing and the design of the product.

 Principle

> How environmental costs can be managed in existing costing systems

EG **Learning example 4.1**

It was alleged that BluePaint Ltd, a company manufacturing dyes for clothing, was letting liquid waste from its manufacturing unit into a nearby river without treating it sufficiently. The company vehemently denied this allegation and launched a publicity campaign to prove its environmental awareness. How would you classify the cost associated with this publicity campaign?

A. Marketing cost
B. Conventional cost
C. Contingent cost
D. Image and relationship cost

EG **Learning example 4.2**

Can you differentiate between environment-related costs and environment-driven costs?

Key Learning Points

- Environmental costs are important to a business to ensure they comply with legislation, to ensure accurate pricing and to minimise costs. (A5a)
- Environments costs can be categorised as conventional, hidden, contingent and relationship costs. (A5a)
- The UNDSD identified four methods to account for environmental costs as input/outflow analysis, flow cost accounting, activity-based costing and lifecycle costing. (A5b)

 What's the story?

Stop and think through the 'story' of this chapter and how it links with other chapters (use the Overview to help).

Learning example solutions

EG **Solution 4.1**

D. Image and relationship cost

EG **Solution 4.2**

Environment-related costs are costs that can be attributed specifically to an environmental cost centre, for example sewerage plants or incinerators.

Environment-driven costs are usually hidden within general overheads and do not relate to a specific cost centre but however relate to environmental drivers such as higher costs of staff or increased depreciation.

5

Relevant Costing and Short-term Decision-making

Context

We have developed an understanding of various techniques of costing. We now need to extend this and focus on decisions that need to be made by a business, largely in the short-term.

We will develop a number of techniques largely built around the important concepts of marginal costing (contribution analysis) and relevant costing.

Contribution analysis focuses on the costs and revenues in a decision that vary in respect of volume of activity. Fixed costs are largely ignored since they are costs that are common to all decisions and are unlikely to vary in the short term as a result of a decision being undertaken.

Relevant costing focuses on situations where often a one-off decision is being made (for example whether or not to accept a contract from a customer). The key is to focus on whether a cashflow will occur in the future as a direct consequence of the decision in hand.

It is key to be able to deal quickly and effectively in terms of contribution when looking at volume-related decisions. Fixed overheads are rarely relevant, but examiners may try to confuse you by giving a fixed overhead absorption rate in a standard cost card. This can be used to calculate total fixed costs but is rarely important to the decision in hand.

Relevant cost questions can be very confusing. Remember that it is very important to be able to explain your treatment of costs and revenues. This is important as well for costs and revenues that you think are not relevant to the decision. You need to be able to explain why they are irrelevant.

3Q	1. What are the conditions for a cost to be relevant to a decision?
	2. What is the criterion for a make-or-buy decision?
	3. What is the decision criterion for further processing?

5.1 Marginal costing

Decision-making is key to this paper. A business may have to evaluate different courses of action (for example which of two products to make or what price to charge for a product). Two topics of particular importance covered in this session are:

- Marginal costing; and
- Relevant costing.

Marginal costing focuses on the different cost behaviours and the concept of contribution analysis, where:

Total contribution = Sales revenue – Total variable costs

And on a per unit basis:

Contribution per unit (CPU) = Sales price/unit – Variable cost/unit

Contribution is the contribution earned towards covering fixed costs and earning a profit.

IE Illustrative example 5.1

Suppose a company provides a delivery service in country A and management are considering opening a regional office in country B. As part of their decision-making they would need to consider:

- What fixed costs would be incurred from opening up a regional office in country B?
- What contribution would be earned from providing the delivery service in country B?

5.1.1 Variable Costs

By their very nature, variable costs in total increase with the activity of a business (for example direct material or direct labour). Graphically below, as output increases from 20 to 50 units, total variable cost increases from $60 to $150:

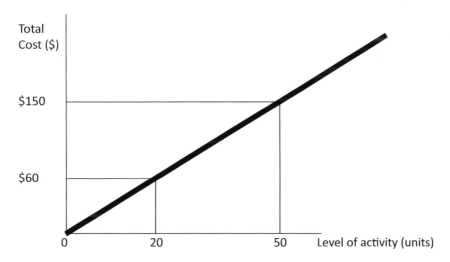

On a variable cost per unit basis, each extra unit manufactured causes a variable cost per unit of $3 to be incurred.

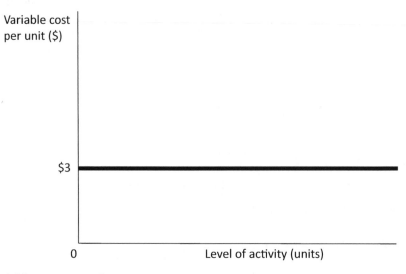

Variable cost per unit ($)

$3

0   Level of activity (units)

Variable costs **per unit** are a **constant**.

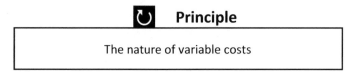

Principle

The nature of variable costs

5.1.2 Fixed costs

Fixed costs by contrast do not increase in line with the activity levels of a business (for example rent, rates, factory depreciation etc.).

Graphically below, fixed costs remain at $50,000 irrespective of the output levels of the business.

Fixed costs in **total** are a **constant.**

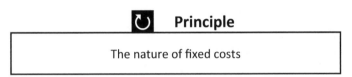

Principle

The nature of fixed costs

5.2 Relevant cost analysis

Relevant costing focuses on identifying and considering only the costs or cashflows that are going to be affected by the decision being made. If the costs or cashflows are not altered by the decision being made, then those cashflows are irrelevant to the decision and can be ignored.

IE Illustrative example 5.2

Suppose a company is considering discontinuing one of their products. The relevant costs of making this decision would typically include:

- The variable cost of production (as the company will no longer spend cash producing units of this product)
- The revenue lost (as the company will no longer earn the cash inflow from sale of the product)

These are the cashflows which will change as a result of the decision to discontinue the product.

For any short-term decision we must consider relevant costing principles. These principles build upon everything that we have seen so far!

For a cost to be relevant to a decision it must have three properties:

- It must arise in the **future.** Anything that occurs in the past cannot be relevant to decisions being made now. For example, if you bought a machine three years ago for $4,500, that amount has no relevance now for a decision whether or not the machine should be replaced. It is a sunk cost.
- It must be a **cash flow.** Cash flows have a direct link to the wealth of the owners of a business. They are an objective way of measuring the success or otherwise of any decision.
- It arises as a direct result of the decision being taken **(incremental).** As we have already seen, it is important to identify how cash flows in the future will *differ* as a result of the decision being made.

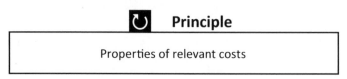

Principle

> Properties of relevant costs

In summary for a cost (or revenue!) to be relevant to a decision it must be a future cash flow which arises as a result of the decision being taken.

It is important to consider the **cash flows for the business as a whole** and not just the decision being made in isolation, when considering relevant costs.

We need to explore this principle in more detail.

Non-relevant costs:

- **Sunk costs:** Any cost arising as a result of a past decision cannot influence a current decision. For example, if the business has incurred a cost for purchasing materials, it is not going to be able to get that money back, it has been spent.
- **Committed costs:** Some businesses may have agreed to pay cash sums in the future. For example the business may have agreed to pay its insurance premium in 12 monthly installments. These cash outflows will have to occur whatever decisions the business takes today.
- **Non-cash flows:** The most common non-cash flow is depreciation (also amortisation). Depreciation only ever affects the reported profit of a business and never affects the cashflows of a business or a decision being made. Indeed the only relevant capital cashflows are the initial outlay to acquire the asset and the proceeds when the asset is sold.
- **Fixed overhead absorbed:** Fixed overhead absorbed relates to an underlying fixed cost that will not vary as a result of the decision being made. Overhead absorbed relates to the arbitrary re-allocation of a cost and not a true cash flow. Fixed costs are **not** incurred on a per unit or 'variable' basis! Therefore fixed cost per unit cannot be relevant.

Learn

Relevant costs:

- **Opportunity costs:** A business must recognise that there is often an alternative option to the decision being made by the entity. Opportunity costs attempt to quantify the *next best alternative for the business as a whole* to the decision being made.

IE Illustrative example 5.3

A business may have some inventory in its storeroom. It is thinking of selling this material for $10 since it has no use for it. A new project being considered could use that material. If the decision is to go ahead with the project, the business as a whole loses the opportunity to sell that material. Hence the opportunity cost of using the material in the project is $10 – reflecting the lost sales opportunity.

- **Variable costs:** Most variable costs will be incurred if the business decides to undertake a new project, but would not be incurred if the business did not go ahead with the project. For example by deciding to make more units of a project, more direct costs (and hence cash outflow) will be incurred as a result.
- **Incremental costs:** A decision may cause other incremental costs to be incurred. For example a retailer may be considering opening a new shop. By going ahead with this project, it will acquire new premises. If the new shop is not opened, then the new premises will not be acquired. **Fixed costs** may **in total** change as a result of a decision. For our retailer, they may incur a higher insurance premium if the new shop is opened.
- **Avoidable costs:** Costs may be avoided as a result of a decision. For example by opening a new shop in a town, our retailer may no longer need to rent its existing premises.

 Learn

5.2.1   Relevant cost of materials

Exam questions can be quite involved when using relevant cost principles. The following diagram will help to identify the appropriate relevant cost to use in different circumstances.

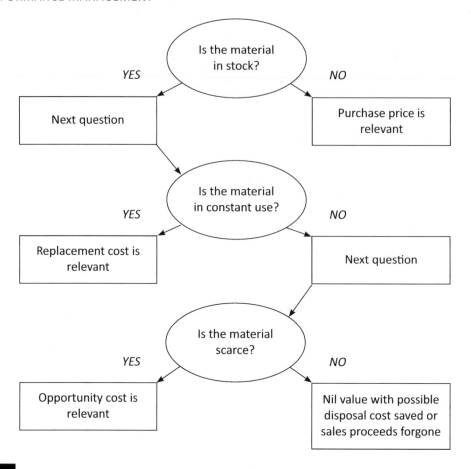

Illustrative example 5.4

Salako needs 10 kg of material X to undertake a new project. What is the relevant cost of material X in the following independent situations?

- Material X is not in stock and is currently available at a market price of $ 15/kg.

  The relevant cash flow is the purchase cost of the material. If Salako goes ahead with the project it must pay 10 kg x $ 15/kg = **$150** to purchase the material. If the project was not undertaken, no material would be purchased.

- Material X is regularly used by Salako. It has 4 kg in stock which cost $13/kg three months ago. Material X is currently available at a market price of $15/kg.

  By undertaking the project and using the 4 kg in stock, Salako will need to replace this 4 kg in order to undertake other projects in the future. The relevant cost is again the purchase price or replacement cost of material:

  10 kg x $15/kg = **$150**

- 15 kg of material X is in stock but is no longer available from suppliers. It is used by Salako in the manufacture of the Pemberton. The Pemberton has the following standard cost card:

	$	$
Sales price		40
Direct material: 1 kg of material X @ $15/kg	15	
Direct labour: 2 hours @ $8/hour	16	
		(31)
Contribution per unit		9

It is important to understand the concept of opportunity cost. If Salako uses 10 kg of material X on the new project, it loses the *opportunity* to use material X on the Pemberton. This means that for each kg of material used on making the new product, Salako will lose the chance of getting $40 revenue from a Pemberton although the direct labour cost of $16 will be saved (the historic cost of the material in Pemberton's standard cost card is irrelevant). Therefore the opportunity cost becomes:

10 kg × ($40 – 16) per kg = **$240.**

The 5 kg of material X remaining could be used in the manufacture of the Pemberton.

- 15 kg of material X is in stock but is no longer available from suppliers. It is not used by Salako in the manufacture of any other products and is about to be scrapped at a cost of $2.50/kg.

By undertaking the new project, Salako will no longer need to scrap 10 kg of material X. (5 kg of material X will be disposed of whether or not the new project is undertaken). The relevant cash flow is now a **saving** of 10 kg × $2.50/kg = **$25** (this is effectively a cash inflow of $25).

 Principle

Establishing the relevant cost of materials

5.2.2   Relevant cost of labour

The following diagram will help to identify the appropriate relevant cost to use in different circumstances for labour costs.

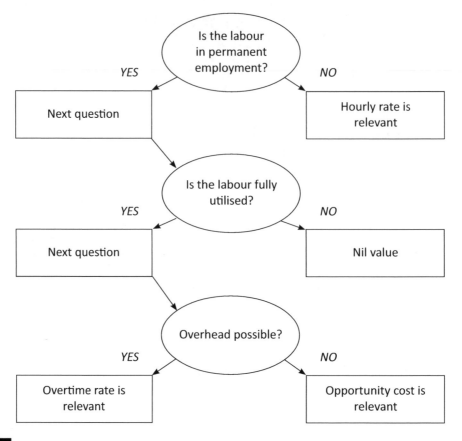

Is the labour in permanent employment?

YES → Next question

NO → Hourly rate is relevant

Is the labour fully utilised?

YES → Next question

NO → Nil value

Overhead possible?

YES → Overtime rate is relevant

NO → Opportunity cost is relevant

IĖ Illustrative example 5.5

Martyn needs 6 hours of Grade A labour to undertake a new project. What is the relevant cost of Grade A labour in the following independent situations?

- Grade A labour is hired on a freelance basis at the rate of $12.50 per hour.

  Grade A labour is not employed on a permanent contract basis, therefore the relevant cost is the rate paid per hour: 6 hours × $12.50/hour = $75.

- Grade A labour is contracted to a 35 hour working week at a pay scale of $10.50/ hour. Currently the workforce is only working at 80% capacity. 20% of their time is currently unutilised.

  Each member of the workforce could work an additional 20% × 35 hours = 7 hours without any effect on current output and activity. Therefore since the workforce is paid for 35 hours and is currently only productive for 28 of those hours, there is no relevant cost in taking up the 'slack' hours working on the new project. Relevant cost of labour is therefore $nil.

- Grade A labour is contracted to a 35 hour working week at a pay scale of $10.50/hour. Currently the workforce is working at 100% capacity. They are willing to work overtime at a rate of normal time + a 50% premium ('time and a half').

  Whether the output of the new project is done in normal or overtime hours, the business as a whole would have to pay 6 hours at a rate of ($10.50 + 50%) $15.75. The relevant cost of labour is therefore 6 hours × $15.75 = $94.50.

- Grade A labour is contracted to a 35 hour working week at a pay scale of $10.50/hour. Currently the workforce is working at 100% capacity. No overtime work is possible due to all machinery working to full capacity in the manufacture of the Pemberton Plus which has a standard cost card of:

	$	$
Sales price		40
Direct material: 1 Kg of material X @ $15/kg	15	
Direct labour: 2 hours @ $10.50/hour	21	
		(36)
Contribution per unit		4

If Salako undertakes the project, then it will not be able to make 6 hours.

$$\frac{6 \text{ hours}}{2 \text{ hours per Pemberton Plus}} = 3 \text{ Pemberton Plus}$$

The relevant cost of undertaking the project is the $40 sales price foregone less the $15 material saved per Pemberton Plus – ie $25 per Pemberton Plus. The labour cost is incurred whatever project is undertaken.

The relevant cost of labour is therefore 3 × $25 = $75.

 **Principle**

Establishing the relevant cost of labour

EG Learning example 5.1

You are the management accountant of Tricks an organisation which has been asked to quote for the production of a pamphlet for an event. The work could be carried out in addition to the normal work of the company. Due to existing commitments, some overtime working would be required to complete the printing of the pamphlet. A trainee has produced the following cost estimate based upon the resources required as specified by the operations manager:

			$
Direct materials	paper (book value)		4,000
	inks (purchase price)		2,400
Direct labour	highly-skilled	250 hours @ $4.00	1,000
	semi-skilled	100 hours @ $3.50	350
Variable overhead		350 hours @ $4.00	1,400
Printing press depreciation		350 hours @ $4.00	500
Fixed production costs		350 hours @ $6.00	2,100
Estimating department costs			400
			12,150

You are aware that considerable publicity could be obtained for the company if you are able to win this order and the price quoted must be very competitive.

The following notes are relevant to the cost estimate above:

1. The paper to be used is currently in stock at a value of $5,000. It is of an unusual specification (texture and weight) and has not been used for some time. The replacement price of the paper is $9,000, whilst the scrap value of that in stock is $2,500. The stores manager does not foresee any alternative use for the paper if it is not used on the pamphlet.
2. The inks required are presently not held in stock. They would have to be purchased in bulk at a cost of $3,000. 80% of the ink purchased would be used in producing the pamphlet. There is no foreseeable alternative use for the remaining unused ink.
3. Highly skilled direct labour is in short supply, and to accommodate the production of the pamphlet, 50% of the time required would be worked at weekends for which a premium of 25% above the normal hourly rate is paid. The normal hourly rate is $4.00 per hour.

4. Semi-skilled labour is presently under-utilised, and 200 hours per week are currently recorded as idle time. If the printing work is carried out, 25 unskilled hours would have to occur during the weekend, but the employees concerned would be given two hours' time off during the week in lieu of each hour worked at the weekend.
5. Variable overhead represents the cost of operating the printing press and binding machines.
6. When not being used by the company, the printing press is hired to outside companies for $6.00 per hour. This earns a contribution of $3.00 per hour. There is unlimited demand for this facility.
7. Fixed production costs are those incurred by and absorbed into production, using an hourly rate based on budgeted activity.
8. The cost of the estimating department represents time spent in discussions with the organisation concerning the printing of its pamphlet.

Required:

Prepare a revised cost estimate using the opportunity cost approach, showing clearly the minimum price that the company should accept for the order. Give reasons for each resource valuation in your cost estimate.

EG Learning example 5.2

A company is considering whether or not to undertake an order from a customer, and to establish the minimum price using relevant costing principles.

The order would require 3,000 kilos of material S. There are over 3,000 kilos already held in inventory. Material S is no longer in regular use by the company and could be sold as scrap for $1.50 per kilo. It could also be used as a substitute for material L, which is in regular use. Conversion costs of $1.60 per kilo would have to be spent on the material S. One kilo of material S after conversion would be a substitute for one kilo of material L. The purchase price of material L is $4/kg.

Skilled labour needed to fulfil the order would be specifically recruited for $50,000.

Unskilled labour needed to fulfil the order would be transferred from another department. The cost of the labour time (3000 hours) would be $30,000 in wages. However, 1,500 of these hours would be idle time if the order is not undertaken. The other 1,500 hours would be spent on a work that would provide a contribution of $5,000.

Required:

Calculate the relevant costs of material and labour for this customer order.

EG Learning example 5.3

Pearl Ltd manufactures material A which is sold to overseas factories. It is approached by a customer for a one-off job to produce 15,000 units of a product Limo which requires the use of material A.

It is expected to use 1 kilo of A in one unit of Limo. Variable costs of producing material A are $200 per kg which is produced in batches of 20,000 kg. A set-up cost of $80,000 is incurred per batch.

The external selling price of material A is $225 per kg. Pearl Ltd has a total capacity to produce 80,000 kg per annum but current demand is only 70,000 kg per annum.

Required:

Calculate the relevant cost of one kg of Limo.

5.3 Make or buy decision

The make or buy decision is a practical situation where marginal and relevant costs can be considered. In this decision, the business is deciding whether to make a product in-house, or whether to outsource its production.

The underlying assumption of this decision is that all the **fixed costs** of manufacture are general to the organisation as a whole and **do not alter** with the decision to make or buy externally. Hence only the **marginal cost** of making the component is **relevant.** Therefore we focus only on the variable element of the costs.

Decision criterion: Compare the marginal cost of making to the purchase price (the marginal cost of buying).

 Learn

IE Illustrative example 5.6

Clemence Ltd produces a number of components, two of which the production manager is considering buying in, components X and Y:

Cost of making ($)	X	Y
Variable	14	28
Fixed	4	4
Total	18	32
Purchase price	17	25
(from outside supplier)		

Should Clemence Ltd make or buy in?

	X	Y
	$	$
Variable cost (marginal cost) of making in-house:	14	28
Variable cost of buying in:	17	25
Amount saved by making in-house	3	
Amount saved by buying in		3
Decision?	Make in house	Buy in

From this we can establish that it is cheaper by $3 to make X in-house, there is no point in paying a supplier $17 in order to save yourself $14 by making the product internally.

Similarly, it makes sense to buy in Y from the outside supplier, who can manufacture the product $3 cheaper than Clemence.

Clemence would need to be confident that:

- The supplier can continue in the long term to supply at a competitive price;
- The supplier can meet Clemence's needs in terms of flexibility of supply and quality;
- No extra costs will arise from the decision to stop making X in-house. For example staff may have to be made redundant or machinery may need to be scrapped.

5.4 Shut down decision

As an extension of this analysis, we can consider situations where the business may consider shutting down part of its operations. It is important here to recognise the importance of relevant costing principles.

By closing part of the business, revenues from the products made and sold from that part of the business will be lost (foregone).

However costs will also be saved (avoidable costs). Avoidable costs will include the variable costs of the part of the factory being closed. It is important however to note that some fixed costs may be avoided as well. The fixed costs that can be avoided are known as **specific fixed costs** (for example plant, machinery and salaried staff that are specifically employed in making the products in the part of the division to be closed). Fixed costs of a more general nature will not be avoided if the section of the business is closed.

Decision criteria: Shut down if avoidable costs > Revenues foregone

 Learn

IE Illustrative example 5.7

Jones Ltd operates three divisions within a larger company. The CEO has been shown the latest profit statements and is concerned that division C is losing money.

You are required to advise her whether or not to close down division C.

Division	A	B	C
($000s)			
Sales	100	80	40
Variable costs	60	50	30
Fixed costs	20	20	20
Profit/(loss)	20	10	(10)

You are also informed that 40% of the fixed cost is product specific, the remainder being allocated arbitrarily to the divisions from head office.

Should division C be shut down?

Division C	$'000	$'000
Revenue foregone		(40)
Avoidable costs		
Variable costs	30	
Specific fixed costs		
($20,000 x 40%)	8	
		38
Net cost of closure		(2)

The decision should be to **retain** Division C. If closed, the business would lose $2,000 in overall profit. In essence the contribution foregone of $10,000 ($40,000 revenue − $30,000 variable costs) exceeds the specific fixed costs saved.

5.5 Further processing decisions

As an extension to our previous studies on process costing we can consider the relevant costing decision issue of whether or not it is worthwhile processing a product further through a production system.

For example in a petroleum refining process, crude oil is refined in a **'joint process'**. Once refined, separate products can be clearly identified such as; petrol, kerosene, lubricating oils etc. These are known as **'joint products'** and are usually identified at the **split-off point.**

The business needs to decide whether it is worthwhile selling unrefined products at this 'split off' point. Alternatively the business can process/refine the product further and then sell the more refined product at a higher sales price.

The choice becomes:

Sell at split-off point or sell after further processing.

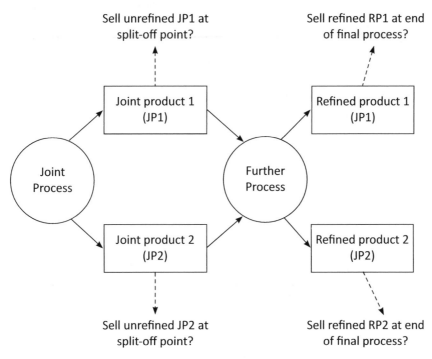

The joint process costs cannot be part of any decision that we make. These costs are common to all products whether refined further or not. For example, the cost of buying the crude oil is common to all refined petroleum-based products that can be derived by processing that crude oil further.

Decision criteria: Process further (beyond the split off point) if incremental revenues generated by further processing > incremental costs of further processing.

 Learn

IE Illustrative example 5.8

Unrefined Product A can be sold at the separation point for $5 per unit. If it is further processed, at a cost of $8 per unit, it can then be sold in its more refined state for $16 per unit. Should it be processed further?

The word 'incremental' is important for relevant cost decisions because it identifies the extra cost, revenue or cash flow that will occur as a result of a decision. Here, if Product A is processed further, incremental revenue and costs will be earned/incurred:

	$	$
Sales price if processed further (refined Product A)	16	
Sales price if sold at split off point (unrefined Product A)	5	
Incremental revenue		11
Incremental costs of processing further		(8)
Extra profit by further processing		3

We can see that further processing is worthwhile because the incremental revenue of $11 outweighs the incremental costs of $8.

If we altered the example so that only $12 is earned after further processing, then the decision would change and it would no longer be worthwhile processing further and Product A should be sold at the split-off point:

	$	$
Sales price if processed further (refined Product A)	12	
Sales price if sold at split off point (unrefined Product A)	5	
Incremental revenue		7
Incremental costs of processing further		(8)
Extra loss by further processing		(1)

EG Learning example 5.4

Heighway Ltd operates a joint process from which four products arise. The products may be sold at the separation point of the process or can be refined further and be sold at a premium. Information regarding the products and the refining process can be found below:

Product	E	F	G	H
Selling price – at the split-off point	12	16	15	18
Selling price – after further processing	20	23	25	22
Costs				
Joint process cost per unit	8	8	8	8
Refining cost per unit	5	5	5	5
Specific fixed cost (total)	1,000	2,000	3,000	4,000
Budgeted units	2,000	500	5,000	6,000

General fixed costs for the period are $20,000 if further processing is undertaken.

Required:

Which products should be further processed?

Key Learning Points

- Relevant cost decisions are made by looking at the future cash flows which arise as a result of the decision being taken. (B1a)
- Shutdown decisions: a division could be shut down if the avoidable costs > revenue forgone. (B5d)
- Further processing decisions: Process further (beyond the split-off point) if incremental revenues > incremental costs of further processing. (B5d)
- Make or buy decisions: Compare marginal cost of making to the purchase price (the marginal cost of buying). (B5b)

What's the story?

Stop and think through the 'story' of this chapter and how it links with other chapters (use the Overview to help).

Learning example solutions

EG Solution 5.1

To address relevant cost questions of this size, it is important not to get bogged down in any one area. It is also extremely important to ensure that you can explain and justify your workings. For example, there are usually marks awarded in the exam for ignoring non-relevant cash flows but importantly explaining **why** you have ignored the cash flow.

In this situation we are trying to calculate the relevant costs, using an opportunity cost approach, that Tricks needs to ensure are 'covered' by the sales price that is charged to the client. Obviously Tricks would like to charge a price higher than this minimum value. However a typical exam requirement is to identify the minimum price that can be charged to a customer using a relevant/opportunity cost approach.

Taking each cost in turn:

- **Paper:** The paper required is in stock but has not alternative use. It is not scarce and will be sold if not used on this contract. The book value of $4,000 and the current valuation of the paper ($5,000) are non-relevant costs. They are historic valuations and of no relevance to our decision and are therefore ignored. Since there is no alternative use for this paper, then the next best alternative (the opportunity cost) would be to sell it for $2,500. This amount is foregone by using the paper in our contract. There is no point in replacing the material at a cost of $9,000 if it is not to be used within the business.

The relevant cost of the paper is **$2,500**.

- **Inks:** The ink has to be bought in bulk for $3,000. Unfortunately for Tricks, 20% of the ink will not be used and has to be thrown away. There is no alternative use for this material.

The relevant cost of the ink is **$3,000**.

- **Highly skilled labour**: This labour is scarce. To accommodate full production of the pamphlets (50% × 250 hours) 125 hours will have to be worked in overtime at a cost of ($4.00 + 25%) $5.00 per hour. The other 50% of time (125 hours) will be worked in normal working hours. If we assume that the highly skilled labour is in permanent employment then there is no extra cost for these workers operating in normal hours.

The relevant cost is therefore: overtime hours: 125 hours × $5.00/hour = **$625**

- **Semi-skilled labour**: This labour is currently under-utilised and has 200 hours of spare capacity. We can assume that the workforce is permanently employed. However, 25 hours must be undertaken at the weekend and 75 hours during the week. If the workers are to work at the weekend then they will take off (2 x 25 hours) 50 hours during the week in lieu of payment. This means that only 200-50 hours = 150 hours are available in the week to use up the unutilised hours. However, we only need 75 of those 150 unutilised hours for this project, so no incremental cost is incurred.

The relevant cost of unskilled labour is **$nil**.

- **Variable overhead**: This cost appears to be directly variable in line with the activity levels of the business. Therefore by printing these pamphlets, an incremental production cost will be incurred for the 350 hours worked by both the skilled and semi-skilled workers – i.e. 350 hours x $4.00/hour = $1,400

The relevant cost of variable overhead is **$1,400**.

- **Printing press depreciation:** Depreciation is of course a non-cash flow and is not relevant to the decision.

The relevant cost of depreciation is **$nil**.

- **Printing press rental income foregone:** However, the lost contribution of renting the machine out is an opportunity cost for the business. By using 200 hours of printing time to make the pamphlets, the opportunity to rent out the machine is lost. Although Tricks can generate $6/hour rental per hour, it also appears to incur a $3 per hour variable cost for each hour of rental. Therefore the relevant cashflow is the $3/hour contribution foregone, some 200 hours × $3/hour = $600.

The relevant cost of printing press rental is **$600.**

- **Fixed production costs:** The fixed production costs are absorbed into each unit using an hourly absorption rate. The underlying fixed costs will not change as a result of accepting this contract. They are fixed in total and therefore not relevant to the decision.

The relevant cost of the fixed production costs is **$nil.**

- **Estimating department costs:** These costs are either sunk or committed costs. They have either already been incurred (sunk) or will be incurred whether or not the contract is accepted.

The relevant cost of the estimating department costs is **$nil.**

Overall summary

The overall relevant costs that need to be considered in establishing a minimum contract price are:

Cost	$
Materials: paper	2,500
Materials: inks	3,000
Labour: highly-skilled	625
Labour: semi-skilled	Nil
Variable overhead	1,400
Printing press depreciation	Nil
Printing press rental income foregone	600
Fixed production costs	Nil
Estimating department costs	Nil
Total	**8,125**

The minimum price that is acceptable on an opportunity cost basis is $8,125.

In reality Tricks would obviously wish to charge a higher price than this. Indeed in the long-term all costs of the business (including fixed costs) need to be covered through sales revenues.

EG Solution 5.2

Relevant cost

	£
Material S (3000 kilos × 2.4)	**7,200**
Skilled labour	50,000
Unskilled labour:	
Use of idle time	0
Use of other time (50% × 30,000) + 5000 lost contribution	20,000
Total relevant cost	77,200

Notes:

- The relevant cost of material S is the benefit that would be obtained from the most profitable alternative use. The alternatives from using material S are

  - to sell for scrap and earn $1.5 per kilo

  - to use as a substitute for material L, and save $2.4 per kilo (4 − 1.60)

  - therefore the relevant cost of material S is $2.4 per kilo (greater opportunity cost)

- The full $50,000 will be the relevant cost of the skilled labour as all represent incremental cost.
- The relevant cost of the unskilled labour, which will be paid wages of $30,000 anyway, is the loss of cash flow from having to move the labour from other work. Contribution is calculated after deducting labour cost as a variable cost, therefore 50% of the labour cost - $15,000 must be included in the relevant cost along with the $5,000 contribution lost.

EG Solution 5.3

Set up costs	nil
Variable costs per kilo	$200 (for 10,000 kg)
Opportunity cost per kg	$225 (for 5,000 kg)

Notes:

1. As the company is producing A in batches and setup cost would be incurred anyway whether this offer is accepted or not.
2. The company has a spare capacity of 10,000 kg against which variable cost can be charged on this contract.
3. For the remaining 5,000 kg above the capacity, the company would have to forgo 5,000 kg external sales at a price of $225 per kg, which can be treated as opportunity cost.

EG Solution 5.4

Product	E	F	G	H
Selling price – after further processing ($)	20	23	25	22
Selling price – at the split-off point ($)	12	16	15	18
Incremental revenue/unit ($)	8	7	10	4
Less: incremental variable cost/unit of processing further (refining cost) ($)	(5)	(5)	(5)	(5)
Incremental contribution per unit (CPU) ($)	3	2	5	(1)
× budgeted production/sales units	2,000	500	5,000	Sell at split off point

Incremental total contribution	$6,000	$1,000	$25,000	-
Specific fixed cost (total)	($1,000)	($2,000)	($3,000)	-
Net 'contribution'	**$5,000**	**($1,000)**	**$22,000**	
		Sell at split off point		

From the table above we can see firstly that it is not worthwhile processing Product H beyond the split off point. To do so would earn incremental revenue of $4, but at an incremental variable cost per unit of $5.

Similarly Product F creates an incremental contribution per unit of $2 and an incremental contribution overall of $1,000. This is however insufficient to cover the extra fixed overhead *specifically* incurred if Product F is processed beyond the split off point.

Finally we can compare the extra amounts earned by products E and G against the extra general fixed costs of further processing:

	$	$
E – net 'contribution'	5,000	
G – net 'contribution'	22,000	27,000
General fixed costs		(20,000)
Incremental profit of further processing		**7,000**

We can see that it is worthwhile processing Products E and G beyond the split off point since they not only are profitable when compared to their own specific fixed costs, they also create a profit of $7,000 after the general fixed costs have been paid off.

6

Limiting Factors

Context

Limiting factor decisions apply contribution analysis techniques to situations where the activity of the company is limited due to reduced availability of resources.

For example, if a company has two pieces of machinery within the factory and one of them breaks down, then machine hours will be a scarce resource until the first machine can either be fixed or replaced.

Management must decide how the limited resource available should be used in order to maximise company profits.

There are two techniques which can be applied in limiting factor decisions:

- Rank products according to contribution per unit of limiting factor (if there is only one limiting factor)
- Linear programming (if there are two or more limiting factors)

A rigorous exam technique must be followed in order to maximize the marks available. There are a lot of easy marks to obtain provided that you follow a methodical and complete approach. For example, too many candidates lose marks by failing to label graphs or identify all of the constraints.

Take care as well to clearly show all workings and draw graphs carefully.

3Q

1. What are the steps involved in limiting factor decision questions?

2. Do you know the key steps involved in linear programming problems?

3. Can you define shadow price?

6.1 Single limiting factor decisions

This section looks at situations where there is only one factor limiting the company's activities. This would typically be a short term restriction on one of the following:

- Limited availability of materials
- Key staff shortages
- Productive capacity etc.

In the **long-term,** the business could rectify this by (for example) sourcing from different suppliers, recruiting new workers (or re-training existing workers), purchasing new machinery etc.

In the **short-term,** we aim to maximise contribution by choosing production combinations of products which make the 'best use' of the scarce resource. Again we assume that fixed costs in total will not change as a result of our decision.

Decision criteria: Select and produce products which maximise the contribution per unit of the limiting factor

 Learn

The steps involved in limiting factor decision questions are:

- Step 1: Calculate the contribution per unit of sale (contribution of each product);
- Step 2: Calculate the contribution per unit of scarce resource (contribution per unit of sale ÷ limiting factor per unit of sale);
- Step 3: Rank production schedule in order of step 2 – starting with the highest first;
- Step 4: Use up the resource in order of the ranking.

 Principle

Decision-making steps when there is a single limiting factor

IE Illustrative example 6.1

Neal Ltd produces two products using the same machinery. The hours available on this machine are limited to 5,000. Information regarding the two products is detailed below:

Products (per unit data)	M	N
Selling price ($)	40	30
Variable cost ($)	16	15
Fixed cost ($)	10	8
Profit ($)	14	7
Machine hours	8	3
Budgeted sales (units)	600	500

Calculate the maximum profit that may be earned.

The limiting factor in this scenario is given in this question, namely machine hours. In reality the business in the long-term could look to acquire a new machine, but is constrained in the short-term by the machine capacity available.

	Product M	Product N
Step 1:		
Contribution/unit		
Sales price $	40	30
Variable costs $	(16)	(15)
Contribution per unit (CPU)	24	15

Step 2: Contribution per machine hour

CPU ÷ machine hours/unit	$24 ÷8 hours	$15 ÷3 hours
	=3/machine hour	= $5/machine hour
Step 3:	2nd	1st
Rank production		

Step 4: Production schedule

	Machine hours	Production schedule	Contribution	
Hours available:	5,000			
(500 units x 3 machine hours)	(1,500)	Product N 500 units	$7,500	(500 units x $15)
	3,500			
3,500 hours ÷ 8 hours/unit = 437.5 units	(3,500)	Product M 437.5 units	$10,500	
	nil	Total Contribution	$18,000	

In order to calculate fixed cost we MUST remember that the OAR for each product is based on budgeted levels of activity.

$$OAR = \frac{\text{Budgeted overhead cost}}{\text{Budgeted level of activity}}$$

Therefore in order to calculate the fixed costs in **total** we work 'backwards':

Budgeted overhead cost = Budgeted level of activity × OAR

Product	Budgeted activity × OAR	Fixed cost $
M	600 units × $10/unit	6,000
N	500 units × $8/unit	4,000
Total fixed cost		**$10,000**

Therefore the overall profit for Neal Ltd becomes:

	$
Total contribution	18,000
Less: Fixed costs	(10,000)
Overall profit	**$8,000**

6.2   Linear programming

In the limiting factor analysis we have performed so far, we have considered just **one limitation.**

We now extend this analysis to consider situations where **multiple** restrictions or limiting factors exist. We only consider two products in this situation.

We solve this problem by using **linear programming.** 'Linear' implies the use of straight line relationships and 'programming' involves formulating and solving the problem using mathematical techniques.

6.2.1   Key features of linear programming:

- Multiple output variables
- Multiple constraints on our output (input variables)
- Overall aim is (usually) to maximize contribution. Fixed costs are assumed to be irrelevant to the decision.

 **Principle**

When linear programming is used

6.2.2 Key steps involved in linear programming problems:

The key steps to tackling linear programming questions are fairly 'standard' to all questions set:

1. Identify the variables – these are usually two output variables (on the 'x' and 'y' axes of a graph) and relate to the output quantities of two products that the business can make
2. Identify the objective function. This is our aim and is usually to maximize contribution (although occasionally may be to minimise costs).
3. Identify the constraints. These will be the limitations on activity and could be a maximum number of labour or machine hours available.
4. Graph the information. We need to be able to deal with a graphical solution to our problem. This is why we can only ever consider two products, one on the 'x' axis and one on the 'y' axis of the graph.
5. Compute the optimal solution. We may need to use a number of techniques to find the optimal solution. This will allow is to identify the maximum possible contribution that a business can make, and how many units the business should make of each product.
6. We may then extend the above analysis and calculate shadow prices. This identifies what the effect would be of a small amount more of a key resource that is scarce. For example if a material is scarce and another kg of that material became available, what would the effect on contribution be of having that extra material?

 Principle

> Steps involved in linear programming

IE Illustrative example 6.2

A company makes two products (R and S) within three departments (A, B and C). Production times per unit, contribution per unit and the hours available in each department are shown below:

	Product R	Product S	Capacity (hours)
Contribution/unit	$4	$8	
	Hours/unit	Hours/unit	
Department A	8	10	11000
Department B	4	10	9000
Department C	12	6	12000

Determine the optimum production plan and calculate the maximum contribution which can be earned.

We need to take a methodical approach to this problem.

Define the problem – identify the key variables

This sets out the key variables, namely the quantity of the two products that we can look to manufacture and the overall objective. We need to make sure that Products R and S relate to one of each axes on a graph (x-axis and y-axis). Therefore we define the variables as:

- Let x = number of units of R produced;
- Let y = number of units of S produced;
- Objective: maximize total contribution = z.

Identify the objective function

This sets out the overall aim of what we are trying to achieve.

- Maximize contribution = z where:
- $z = 4x + 8y$

This reflects that every x we make and sell secures $4 contribution and each y we sell secures $8 contribution. So if for example we sold 10x and 20y, we are in fact selling 10 R and 20 S and making (10 × $4) + (20 × $8) = $200 contribution. We wish to maximize the overall contribution that we can make.

Identify the constraints

Our activity (output of R and S) is restricted by the lack of production time available in each of the three departments A, B and C. This needs to be reflected in our problem and is done so using inequalities (to reflect that hours in each department will be less than or equal to a maximum output in hours.

So for Department A, hours are limited to 11,000. For each product, the total hours required in Department A will be the time taken per unit in Department A multiplied by the number of units.

Department A production hours	Product R	Product S
Hours per unit	8	10
Number of units (unknown)	X	Y
Total production hours	8x	10y

Therefore the total hours used in Department A = 8x + 10y. The inequality for Department A is:

$8x + 10y \leq 11,000$

Similarly, we can construct the inequalities for Departments B and C, which will be:

- Department B hours: $4x + 10y \leq 9,000$
- Department C hours: $12x + 6y \leq 12,000$

Additionally, we need to recognise that it is not possible to make a negative number of units of products R and/or S. Therefore we have a non-negativity constraint:

- Non negativity: x, y ≥ 0

Plotting the graph

If we know the constraints we are able to plot the limitations on a graph as straight lines. The linearity of the problem means that we need only identify two points on each constraint boundary or line. The easiest to identify will be the intersections with the x and y-axes.

We can also identify the **feasible** (and non-feasible) region. The feasible region shows a production combination of x and y (product R and product S) which is possible given all of the constraints.

Constraint	Inequality	y = 0, x = ?	x = 0, y = ?
Department A	8x + 10y ≤ 11000	1,375	1,100
Department B	4x + 10y ≤ 9000	2,250	900
Department C	12x + 6y ≤ 12000	1,000	2,000
Non-negativity	x, y ≥ 0	any value	any value

Scanning the above table we can see that the maximum value our constraints reach on the x-axis is 2,250 and the maximum on the y-axis is 2,000. In drawing our graph we need to ensure that it is large enough to be usable and to easily accommodate these values.

The graph **must show** (to score marks):

- a title;
- labelled axes and;
- labelled constraints.

If we plot the Department A constraint on to the graph (using the previous table which gave us two co-ordinates for the line) we get:

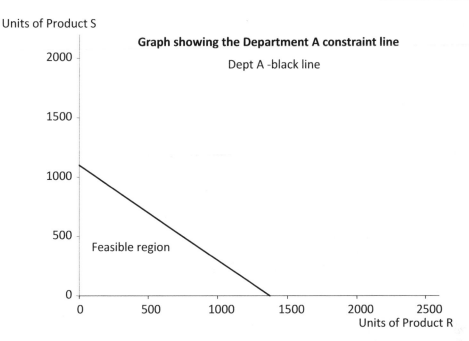

Graph showing the Department A constraint line

It is possible to produce R and S in any combination in the area below and to the left of the constraint line. This is known as a 'feasible region'. For example at an output of 800 units of R and 400 units of S, this would use:

Product R: 800 × 8 hours	6,400
Product S: 400 × 10 hours	4,000
Total hours required	10,400
Total hours available	11,000
Is this feasible?	Yes

If we subsequently plot the other constraints onto the graph we get:

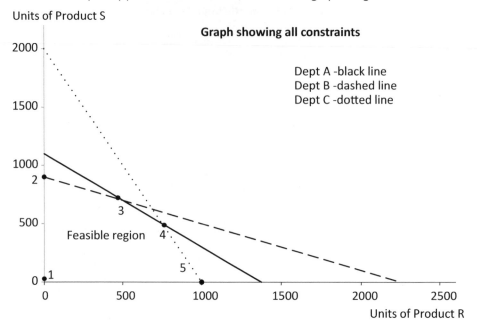

Units of Product S

Graph showing all constraints

Dept A -black line
Dept B -dashed line
Dept C -dotted line

Units of Product R

The non-negativity constraints permit only positive quantities of R and S to be made. The constraints from Departments A, B and C allow production combinations below and to the left of their constraint lines.

The feasible region is any production combination in the area 12345.

Point 1 is at the origin, i.e. where no R and no S is made. Clearly at this point contribution will be zero.

One of points 2, 3, 4 or 5 will give the maximum contribution. We need techniques to help us identify which one is the optimum point.

Note: Contribution will always be maximised at one of the corners of the feasible region. The final question to answer is – which corner?

Identifying the optimal solution

Iso-contribution (IC line):

The iso-contribution line is a key tool in helping identify the optimal solution (i.e. the production combination of R and S which maximises contribution). This line indicates production combinations of (here) products R and S that would give the **same** contribution.

The iso-contribution line therefore represents the objective function for a given value of z (contribution):

$$4x + 8y = 100$$

The first step is to draw the iso-contribution line on our graph.

To plot an iso-contribution line, we can select a reasonable value for contribution and use this value of contribution (z) to compute value of x and y.

We know z = 4x + 8y.

If we select z = 4,000 (divisible by both 4 and 8) – we have:

4,000 = 4x + 8y

If x = 0 then 8y = 4,000.

Therefore $y = \dfrac{4,000}{8} = 500$

We have the co-ordinate x = 0; y = 500 or (0, 500)

If y = 0 then 4x = 4,000.

Therefore $x = \dfrac{4,000}{4} = 1,000$

We have the co-ordinate y = 0; x = 1,000 or (1,000, 0)

Units of Product S

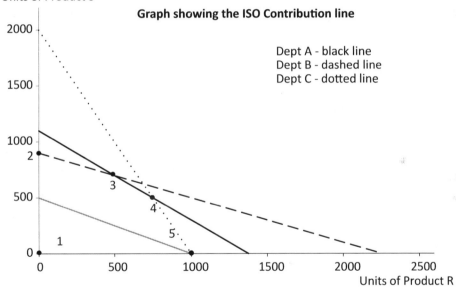

Graph showing the ISO Contribution line

Dept A - black line
Dept B - dashed line
Dept C - dotted line

Units of Product R

Plotting these on our graph, we get an iso-contribution line:

In the previous graph, we plotted the iso-contribution line based on a value of 4,000 for z. We could have selected many other arbitrary values for z.

Let's see what happens to the iso-contribution line if the value for z is increased.

For example if we choose 6,000 = 4x + 8y:
If x = 0 ==> y = 750 and if y = 0 ==> x = 1,500

This line could be plotted on the graph:

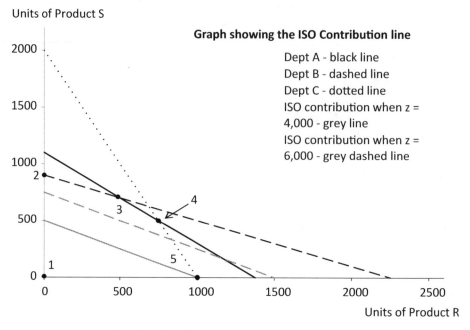

Units of Product S

Graph showing the ISO Contribution line

Dept A - black line
Dept B - dashed line
Dept C - dotted line
ISO contribution when z = 4,000 - grey line
ISO contribution when z = 6,000 - grey dashed line

Units of Product R

As we can see, when the value for z is increased, the iso-contribution line is 'pushed' upwards on the graph. The gradient of the line does not change (i.e. the new ISO-contribution line is parallel to the old one).

Note that the iso-contribution line is still partially within the feasible region. This means it is possible for the company to earn contribution of $6,000 and still be within all constraints.

If a very high value was selected for z (for example, z = 1,000,000) this would 'push' the iso-contribution line far above the feasible region.

So the question is what is the maximum value of z which can be selected before the iso-contribution line goes above the feasible region in full?

In the exam, you need to use a ruler to 'push out' the iso-contribution line as far as possible from the origin whilst it remains parallel to the original iso-contribution line we have drawn. This will find the optimum point where contribution is maximised.

Note: Contribution will be maximised at the last corner of the feasible region the iso-contribution line touches before it leaves the feasible region.

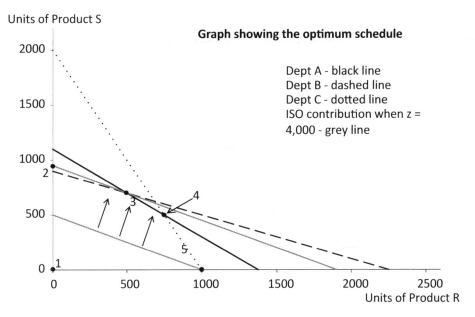

By pushing our iso-contribution line upwards, we find that the optimal solution must be at point 3. If we push the iso-contribution line up any further, it will have left the feasible region entirely.

Compute the optimal solution

The optimal solution is at point 3. This is the interception of the Department A and Department B constraints.

We solve by using simultaneous equations, what values of x and y satisfy both the Department A and Department B constraints at point 3 where they intercept.

Equation 1	8x + 10y = 11,000	Department A
Equation 2	4x + 10y = 9,000	Department B

Equation 1	8x + 10y = 11,000
Less: Equation 2	4x + 10y = 9,000
	4x = 2,000

Therefore $x = \dfrac{2,000}{4} = 500$ units or **500 units of product R**

We can substitute this value of x into equation 2:

4x + 10y = 9,000 giving: 4(500) + 10y = 9,000

Therefore $y = \dfrac{9,000 - 2,000}{10} = 700$ units or **700 units of product S**

Therefore the maximum contribution that can be made, **given the constraints** is obtained by substituting values of x = 500 and y = 700 into the objective function z = 4x + 8y:

Product R	500 units x $4 =		$2,000
Product S	700 units x $8 =		$5,600
Maximum contribution			$7,600

Therefore the maximum contribution is **$7,600.**

6.3 Slack and binding constraints

It is important that management understand which constraints are currently limiting the company's activities.

Definition

Slack constraints are constraints which currently have some spare capacity (slack).

Definition

Binding constraints are constraints which are currently fully utilised. Production of products cannot be increased unless further capacity is added to the binding constraints.

IE Illustrative example 6.3

In the example we have been working through, there are 3 constraints namely the hours available in each of the departments A, B and C. We need to determine which of these are slack constraints and which are binding.

As the optimum solution was calculated as 500 units of R and 700 units of S, we can calculate how many hours are currently being used in each department. This is done by multiplying the time taken in each department by the number of units for each product.

Department		Current usage (hours)	Capacity (hours)	Slack hours
A	8 × 500 + 10 × 700	11,000	11,000	0
B	4 × 500 + 10 × 700	9,000	9,000	0
C	12 × 500 + 6 × 700	10,200	12,000	1,800

Based on this, we can see that departments A and C are binding constraints. All of the hours available in these departments are being used.

Department C is a slack constraint. There are currently 1,800 hours of spare capacity in department C.

 Principle

Slack and binding constraints

EG Learning example 6.1

In which type of constraint can the production of products not be increased unless further capacity is added?

Definition

A **shadow price** or dual price is the amount by which total contribution would increase if an additional unit of limiting factor was made available.

 Learn

Shadow prices can only be calculated for the binding constraints. Adding an additional unit to a slack constraint would have no impact as there is spare capacity in the slack constraints anyway.

Therefore in this example, we can calculate shadow prices for departments A and B.

6.3.1 Shadow price of department A

Here we are looking at how much contribution would increase if there were one more hour available in department A. Graphically, we can show the impact of this on our linear programming graph. Note that we only need to consider the binding constraints.

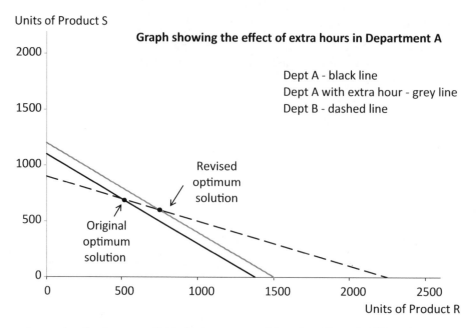

Units of Product S

Graph showing the effect of extra hours in Department A

Dept A - black line
Dept A with extra hour - grey line
Dept B - dashed line

Units of Product R

Increasing the hours available in department A has the effect of shifting the constraint line further away from the original and parallel to the existing constraint. The department A line has moved from its original position (black line) up to the grey line position.

The effect of this is to move the optimal solution to the right such that more units of R would be made and less of S. This should also in turn lead to a higher contribution being made.

To calculate the shadow price the following steps must be followed:

1. Add 1 unit (hour) to the binding constraint and calculate the new optimum production schedule
2. Calculate the new maximum contribution
3. Shadow price = New maximum contribution – Maximum contribution under the existing production schedule

Step 1 – new optimum production schedule
The revised constraint lines will now be:

Department A: $8x + 10y = 11,001$

Department B: $4x + 10y = 9,000$

Solving these equations, we are left with:

$4x = 2,001$

$x = 500.25$ units of product R

Therefore $4(500.25) + 10y = 9,000$

$10y = 6,999$

y = 699.9 units of product S

Step 2 – new maximum contribution
Using our objective function, we know that contribution, z = 4x + 8y

Under the new optimum production schedule:

Z = 4 x 500.25 + 8 x 699.9 = 7,600.2

Step 3 – shadow price
The shadow price of department A = $7,600.2 = $7,600 = $0.2

So each additional hour added to department A will increase total contribution by $0.2.

Therefore, the extra amount per hour (over and above existing hourly variable costs) that the business would be willing to pay for an additional hour in department A is $0.2/hour.

 **Principle**

Calculating the shadow price for binding constraints

6.3.2   Overall summary

Units of x (product R)	500.25 units – 500 units =	↑ by 0.25 units
Units of y (product S)	699.9 units – 700 units =	↓ by 0.1 units
Contribution	(0.25 x $4) – (0.1 x $8) =	↑ by $0.20
Department C hours	(0.25 x 12 hours) – (0.1 x 6 hours) =	↓ by 2.4 hours

6.3.3   Ranges where shadow prices apply

It is important to note that, for example, Department C it still has slack hours available. However this is not the case indefinitely.

From our previous analysis, Department C had 1,800 slack hours at the original optimum position of 500 units of x and 700 units of y. If we obtain one extra hour of time in Department A, this has the effect of 'using up' 2.4 hours of slack in Department C.

Department C will only have slack for $\dfrac{1{,}800 \text{ hours}}{2.4 \text{ hours per extra hour in Department A}}$

= 750 extra hours in department A.

If Department A were to obtain more hours than this, then Department C would become a binding constraint.

From the graph above we can see that if more hours become available in Department A, Department A will have a shadow price of $0.20/hour up to and including all production combinations to point 6 on the diagram where the constraint for Department A and Departments B and C intercept. Beyond this point, Departments B and C become the binding constraints. There would be no point in paying for an additional hour of Department A time when it is now departments B and C that are the binding constraints. Therefore there are a finite number of extra hours in Department A where the business will be willing to pay the shadow price of $0.20/hour for an extra hour of Department A time.

As computed above, the shadow price of $0.20 only holds for an **extra** 750 hours of time on Department A (i.e. to a maximum of 11,000 + 750 = 11,750 hours).

Similarly, if the number of hours available in Department A falls, once the constraint falls below and to the left of point 2 (the interception with the constraint x = 0), the business will only ever consider making y (albeit in decreasing numbers, given the slope of the iso-contribution line). Therefore the shadow price will alter from its current level of $0.20/hour to:

$$\frac{\text{Contribution of product Y} = \$8}{\text{Department A hours required to make one unit of Y} = 10 \text{ hours}} = \$0.80/\text{hour}.$$

Since the interception the y-axis at point 2 is 900 units of Y, this would require 900 units x 10 hours/unit = 9,000 hours of Department A time.

Therefore the shadow price of $0.20/hour of Department A time only applies over the range:

9,000 ≤ Department A hours ≤ 11,750

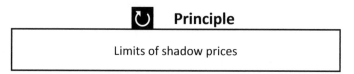

Principle

Limits of shadow prices

6.3.4   Shadow price of department B

The shadow price for department B can be calculated using the same approach, except this time the extra hour is being added to department B and we use the original constraint line for department A.

Looking at this graphically, we can see the following:

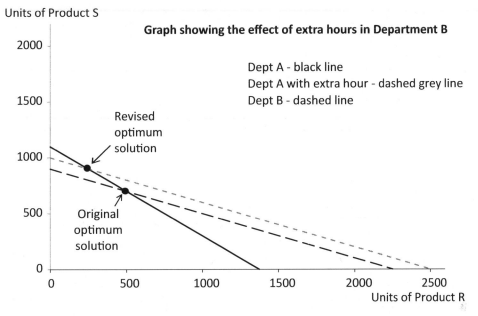

Units of Product S

Graph showing the effect of extra hours in Department B

Dept A - black line
Dept A with extra hour - dashed grey line
Dept B - dashed line

Revised optimum solution

Original optimum solution

Units of Product R

Increasing the hours available in department B has the effect of shifting the constraint line further away from the original and parallel to the existing constraint. The dept. B line has moved from its original position (black dashed) up to the grey dashed line position.

The effect of this is to move the optimal solution to the left such that more units of S would be made and less of R. This should also in turn lead to a higher contribution being made.

To calculate the shadow price the same steps as above should be followed.

Step 1 – new optimum production schedule

The revised constraint lines will now be:

Department A: $8x + 10y = 11{,}000$

Department B: $4x + 10y = 9{,}001$

Solving these equations, we are left with:

$4x = 1{,}999$

$x = 499.75$ units of product R

Therefore $4(499.75) + 10y = 9{,}001$

$10y = 7{,}000.2$

$y = 700.2$ units of product S

Step 2 – new maximum contribution

Using our objective function, we know that contribution, $z = 4x + 8y$

Under the new optimum production schedule:
$Z = 4 \times 499.75 + 8 \times 700.2 = 7,600.6$

Step 3 – shadow price

The shadow price of department B = $7,600.6 = $7,600 = $0.6

So each additional hour added to department B will increase total contribution by $0.6.

Therefore, the **extra** amount per hour (over and above existing hourly variable costs) that the business would be willing to pay for an additional hour in department A is $0.6/hour.

EG Learning example 6.2

Bravo International manufactures two products A and B. There will be limited availability of a number of key resources in the next quarter. The following details are available for the two products.

Product	A	B	Maximum available
Raw materials/unit	16kg	4kg	400kg
Labour hours/unit	6hrs	6hrs	240hrs
Machine hours/unit	3hrs	10hrs	330hrs
Contribution/unit	$50	$70	

Demand for both products is unlimited and the company can sell as many units as it can produce for the next period. The company has signed an agreement with a customer to supply a minimum of 12 units of product B.

Required:

Using a linear programming model, calculate the maximum number of each product which should be produced over the next quarter if Bravo International wishes to maximise its contribution and calculate the maximum contribution.

Key Learning Points

- Limiting factor decisions arise where a company cannot meet the full demand for all products due to limitations in production e.g. limited availability of machine hours, materials or labour hours. (B3a)
- Single limiting factor: select and product the products which maximise the contribution per unit of limiting factor. (B3b)
- In multi limiting factor situations, linear programming must be used to determine the optimal production plan:
  - Identify the key variables – usually the x and y axes and the aim of maximising contribution
  - Identify the key constraints and express an inequalities: eg, for departmental restrictions 5x + 6y ≤ 8,500
  - For non-negativity constraints x ≥ 0, y ≥ 0.
  - Graph the information – plot one product on the x axis and the other product on the y axis.
  - Identify the optimal solution using an ism-contribution line and simultaneous equations.
  - Consider sensitivity analysis – including the calculation of shadow prices. (B3c, B3d)

 What's the story?

Stop and think through the 'story' of this chapter and how it links with other chapters (use the Overview to help).

Learning example solutions

EG Solution 6.1

Binding constraints, as these are constraints which are currently fully utilised.

EG Solution 6.2

Define the unknowns:

- X = units of product A
- Y = units of product B

Constraints

- Machine hours 3x + 10y ≤ 330
- Materials 16x + 4y ≤ 400
- Labour 6x + 6y ≤ 240
- Units of Product B Y ≥ 12

Note that because there is an agreement in place with a customer, Bravo Ltd must produce at least 12 units of Product B.

Objective function

- Maximise Contribution
- Z = Total contribution

Z = 50x + 70y

Graph the constraints

First, 2 points on each of the constraint lines can be calculated.

Constraint	x = 0, y =	y = 0, x =	Points
Machine hours	33	110	(0,33) (110,0)
Materials	100	25	(0,100) (25,0)
Labour	40	40	(0,40) (40,0)

On the line y = 12, we can plot any two points where y = 12, e.g. y = 12, x = 0 and y = 12, x = 100.

Finally, the ISO – contribution line will also need to be plotted on the graph. Remember this line represents the objective function: Z = 50x + 70y

To plot this, we select any arbitrary value for Z. Suppose Z = 1,000, then:

50x + 70y = 1,000

On this line, when x = 0, y = 14 and when y = 0, x = 20. Therefore the two points on the line are: (0, 14) and (20, 0).

Plotting the above on a graph gives us:

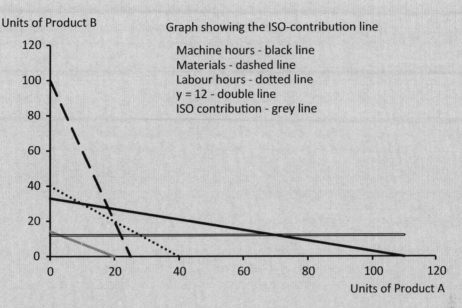

Units of Product B

Graph showing the ISO-contribution line

Machine hours - black line
Materials - dashed line
Labour hours - dotted line
y = 12 - double line
ISO contribution - grey line

Units of Product A

Determining the optimum production schedule

If we move the ISO contribution line upwards, we can see that the optimum production plan is the point where the labour constraint line meets the machine hours constraint line

Machine hours: $3x + 10y = 330$

Labour $6x + 6y = 240$

If we multiply the machine hours equation by two that will give us:

Machine hours: $6x + 20y = 660$

Labour $6x + 6y = 240$

Subtracting the labour constraint from the machine constraint, we are left with:

$14y = 420$

$y = 30$

Solving for x;

$6x + 6(30) = 240$

$x = 10$

Maximum contribution: $50 \times 10 + 70 \times 30 = 2,600$

7

Cost Volume Profit Analysis

Context

Cost volume profit (CVP) analysis examines the effect that changes in activity have on the financial results of an organisation. It uses marginal costing principles and involves preparing calculations to aid short-term decision-making such as:

- How many units do we need to sell to break even?
- How many units do we need to sell to make a profit of $50,000?

In this exam you may be asked to perform a CVP analysis in **either** a multi-product or a single product environment.

In CVP analysis, there are a number of formulae which must be learnt so that you are able to perform the computational elements of a CVP question.

3Q

1. Do you know the formula to calculate sales volume to achieve a target profit?

2. Can you draw and describe the contribution breakeven chart?

3. What are the limitations of cost volume profit analysis?

7.1 Cost volume profit (CVP) analysis – Single product

7.1.1 Nature and purpose of CVP analysis

When we are looking at CVP Analysis we are focussing on how short-term operating decision can affect profit. As we know from previous studies on this paper, in short-term decision making fixed costs are assumed to remain constant and therefore the focus needs to be on sales activity and contribution.

There is more of a focus on sales activity primarily, as to a certain degree sales price and variable costs and therefore contribution per unit are known with certainty in the short term. So in the short term profit usually hinges upon how many units are sold as this is fairly unpredictable. For example we may know that material, labour and variable overheads cost us $60 per unit and that we wish to set a selling price of $80 giving us a contribution of $20 per unit. However we do not know what our profit will be until we know how many units we are going to sell.

Therefore we can use different levels of activity to estimate what the profit will be but most importantly CVP Analysis will answer questions such as how many units we need to sell in order to cover all of our costs and breakeven or how many units do we need to sell to reach our target profit.

 Principle

Uses of cost volume profit analysis

7.1.2 Calculating the breakeven point

The breakeven point is when total revenue equals total costs or as mentioned previously we can use marginal costing principles to examine the breakeven point.

Contribution is calculated as sales revenue less variable costs and this contributes towards paying the fixed costs of the organisation. Once the fixed costs have been paid any remaining contribution is profit.

Therefore when contribution is equal to fixed costs this is when the company is at its breakeven point as there is no profit or loss made.

IE **Illustrative example 7.1**

Contribution per unit = $15 per unit

Fixed costs = $30,000

If the company sold 3,000 units total contribution = $15 × 3,000 = $45,000.

After paying fixed costs of $30,000 there is $15,000 contribution remaining, which is profit.

If the company sold 2,000 units, total contribution = $15 × 2,000 = $30,000.

After paying fixed costs of $30,000 there is no profit made because contribution is equal to the fixed costs.

So we know that

Profit = Contribution – Fixed costs

Rearranging this formula we can say that

Contribution = Fixed costs + Profit.

 Learn

Remember that contribution equals the number of sales units multiplied by contribution per unit. At the breakeven point there is no profit and so the formula to calculate the breakeven point in units is as follows:

$$\text{Breakeven (units)} = \frac{\text{Fixed costs}}{\text{Contribution per unit}}$$

 Learn

Using Illustrative example 7.1, Breakeven units = $30,000/$15 = 2,000 units

7.1.3 Calculating sales volume to achieve a target profit

We can use the formula **Contribution = Fixed Costs + Profit** to also calculate how many units we would need to sell in order to achieve a desired profit. It is very similar to the breakeven units calculation, however this time we have to bring profit into the calculation.

$$\text{Units to achieve target profit} = \frac{\text{Fixed costs} + \text{Target profit}}{\text{Contribution per unit}}$$

 Learn

EG **Learning example 7.1**

Contribution per unit	$30
Fixed costs	$45,000
Required profit	$15,000

(a) Calculate the breakeven point in units.
(b) Calculate the number of sales units needed to reach the required profit.

7.1.4 Margin of safety

This is a measure of sensitivity or riskiness of the budget. It measures how much that budgeted sales can decrease before the business will fall into a loss making position, and therefore the excess of budgeted sales over the breakeven sales.

It can be measured in terms of revenue, units or as a percentage:

Margin of safety (units) = Budgeted sales units – Breakeven sales units

 Learn

Margin of safety (%) = $\dfrac{\text{Budgeted sales units} - \text{Breakeven sales units}}{\text{Budgeted sales units}}$

 Learn

Margin of safety (Revenue) = (Budgeted sales units – Breakeven sales units) × Sales price

 Learn

EG Learning example 7.2

Sales price/unit	= $50
Marginal cost/unit	= $30
Contribution/unit	= $20
Total fixed costs	= $100,000
Budgeted sales	= 16,000 units

Calculate the margin of safety in units, revenue and as a percentage.

7.1.5   Contribution to sales ratio

This ratio calculates just how much each $ sold contributes towards paying the fixed costs and will become very important when we look at multi-product breakeven analysis. It is calculated as:

C/S ratio = $\dfrac{\text{Contribution per unit}}{\text{Sales price}}$

 Learn

It can also be calculated using total contribution and total sales revenue, it does not have to be calculated per unit.

IE **Illustrative example 7.2**

Units sales price	= $20
Unit variable costs	= $8
Contribution per unit	= $12
C/S ratio	= $12/$20
	= 0.6 or 60%

This shows that for every $1 of sales revenue, $0.60 of contribution is generated and contributes towards the fixed costs.

The C/S ratio can be used to calculate breakeven sales revenue and also the revenue required to achieve the target profits. These formulae are as follows:

$$\text{Breakeven sales revenue} = \frac{\text{Fixed costs}}{\text{C/S ratio}}$$

 Learn

$$\text{Revenue to achieve target profit} = \frac{\text{Fixed costs} + \text{Profit}}{\text{C/S ratio}}$$

 Learn

EG **Learning example 7.3**

Unit sales price	= $40
Unit variable costs	= $24
Contribution per unit	= $16
Fixed costs	= $160,000

Calculate the C/S ratio, breakeven sales revenue and required revenue to achieve a profit of $56,000.

7.1.6 Breakeven, contribution and profit/volume charts

We can calculate breakeven points and visually examine the effect that a change in activity will have on financial results of an organisation by using a graphical method.

Traditional breakeven chart

This chart plots total sales revenue, total cost and fixed cost and the breakeven point is where the total sales revenue and total cost line intersect.

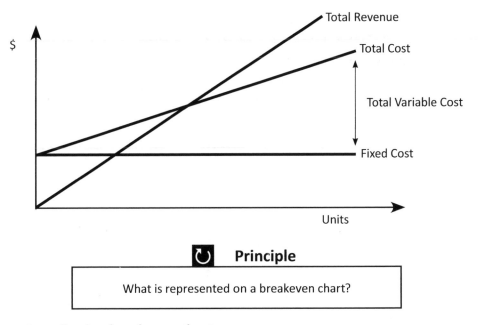

Principle

What is represented on a breakeven chart?

Contribution breakeven chart

The contribution breakeven chart is very similar to the traditional one however instead of having a fixed cost line there is now a total variable cost line. The fixed costs is represented as the distance between the total cost and the total variable cost line. Therefore on this chart it is clear to see contribution at different levels of activity as it is the distance between total revenue and total variable cost.

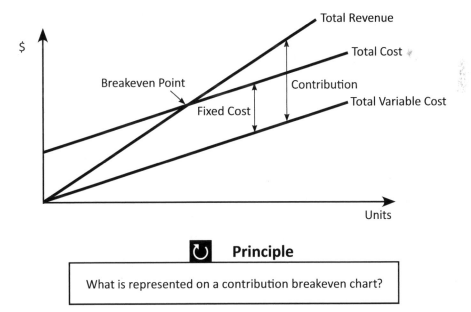

Principle

What is represented on a contribution breakeven chart?

The breakeven point is where the total revenue and the total cost line intersect, however on this chart this also represents when contribution is equal to the fixed costs.

Profit/volume chart

This chart emphasises how different activity levels impacts on the level of profit and is an important chart for this paper.

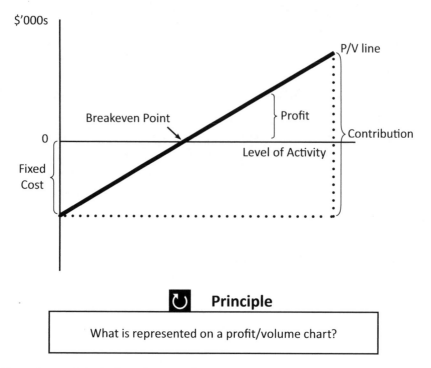

Principle

What is represented on a profit/volume chart?

Drawing a simple breakeven chart

To draw a breakeven chart you need to be able to draw the three lines required and following some simple steps should make this straightforward.

IE Illustrative example 7.3

Campbell Ltd has the following sales and cost information:

Sales price per unit	$50
Variable cost per unit	$35
Fixed cost per annum	$500,000
Budgeted sales per annum	50,000 units

Step 1

First of all you will need to draw and label your axis and therefore you will need to know the maximum values for your axis. This will be the number of sales units and the maximum sales revenue.

Maximum value for x axis (units)	50,000
Maximum value for y axis	50,000 × $50 = $2,500,000

Draw your chart as big as possible as this will enable the examiner to clearly see what you have done and award marks. Make sure you label your axis and give your chart a title.

Step 2

Next you can draw and label the fixed costs line as this will be a horizontal straight line parallel to the x axis. The starting point will be 0 on the x-axis and the amount of fixed costs on the y axis which in this example is $500,000.

Step 3

Now draw the total cost line and label it. You will need two points for your straight line and therefore work out the total cost when activity is 0 units and when activity is the maximum sales units which is 50,000 in this example. Remember total cost is total fixed cost + total variable cost.

When activity is 0 units total cost $= \$500,000 + (0 \times \$35)$

$= \$500,000$

When activity is 50,000 units total cost $= \$500,000 + (50,000 \times \$35)$

$= \$500,000 + \$1,750,000$

$= \$2,250,000$

Step 4

Draw the total revenue line and label it. This line will start in the origin (0,0) as if there are no units sold there is no revenue. The other point for drawing this line will be the maximum sales revenue which will be budgeted units multiplied by selling price, which was calculated earlier as $2,500,000.

Your chart should look like the one below. Make sure you highlight relevant information on the chart such as breakeven point and the margin of safety.

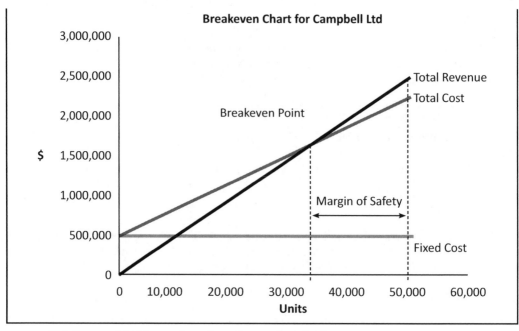

Breakeven Chart for Campbell Ltd

7.1.7 Multi-product breakeven analysis

When carrying out breakeven analysis for organisations that sell more than one product we have to make an assumption that those products are always sold in a constant sales mix. For example if an organisation makes products P and Q then we assume that they are always sold together in a constant ratio such as 3:1. So that whenever 3 units of P are sold 1 unit of Q is sold.

By assuming this ratio it enables us to calculate a weighted average contribution for each sales mix on the basis of the proportion of each product in the mix. However this assumption will only allow an estimated analysis as it will assume the products are always sold in a particular mix which may not always be the case. It could be that the organisation will sell more units of one product or that it may choose to sell its most profitable product first. We will examine the effects of selling the products in a different order when we look at multi-product breakeven charts.

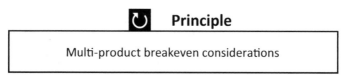

Principle

Multi-product breakeven considerations

Breakeven point

In multi-product situation we can calculate a breakeven point as a number of product mixes by calculating the contribution per sales mix.

$$\text{Breakeven point (mixes)} = \frac{\text{Fixed costs}}{\text{Contribution per mix}}$$

 Learn

IE Illustrative example 7.4

Bat Plc produces two products, the ball and the racket. Below is the sales and cost information for the two products:

	Ball	Racket
Sales price	$3	$5
Variable cost	$1.75	$2.30
Contribution per unit	$1.25	$2.70

Bat plc have estimated that these products will always be sold in the ratio of 4:1. So for every 4 balls that are sold 1 racket is also sold. Fixed costs are estimated to be $27,000.

Contribution per mix	= ($1.25 × 4) + ($2.70 × 1)
	= $7.70
Breakeven point (mixes)	= $27,000/$7.70
	= 3,507 mixes

To determine how many units of each product need to be sold to reach this breakeven we need to multiply the number of mixes by the proportion of units in the mix.

Breakeven (no. of units of each product)	= (3,507 × 4) = 14,028 units of balls
	= (3,507 × 1) = 3,507 units of rackets

Please note that these two figures should never be added together to give a breakeven point in units as the assumption is that they are sold in this constant sales mix.

Weighted average contribution/sales ratio

Again assuming that the products are always sold in the same constant sales mix we can calculate a weighted average contribution to sales ratio, which will enable us to calculate a breakeven sales revenue:

Breakeven sales revenue = Fixed costs/Weighted average CS ratio

 Learn

IE **Illustrative example 7.5**

Using the example of Campbell Ltd:

Sales revenue per mix	= ($3 × 4) + ($5 × 1)
	= $17

Contribution per mix (calculated previously) = $7.70

Weighted average C/S ratio	= $7.70/$17
	= 0.453 or 45.3%
Breakeven sales revenue	= $27,000/0.453
	= $59,603

In order to calculate the breakeven sales revenue for the individual products we need to calculate the ratio of revenue.

Revenue Ratio	= ($3 × 4) : ($5 × 1)
	= 12 : 5
Therefore breakeven sales are:	Ball $59,603 × 12/17 = $42,073
	Bat $59,603 × 5/17 = $17,530

Margin of safety

Margin of safety in multi-product breakeven analysis is exactly the same as in single product breakeven analysis, however we use the breakeven sales in the standard mix.

IE **Illustrative example 7.6**

Again using the example of Campbell Ltd, we now have further information that the budgeted sales revenue for the year is $85,000.

Margin of safety (Revenue) = $85,000 – $59,603 (calculated previously) = $25,397

Remember that this is in total and therefore relates to the standard mix.

Margin of safety (%) = $25,397 / $85,000 = 0.299 or 29.9%

Target profit calculations

This formula is very similar to that of single product breakeven analysis, however this time we will be calculating the number of mixes of products in order to achieve the target profit.

It is calculated as:

No. of mixes to achieve target profit = (Fixed costs + Target profit)/Contribution per mix

 Learn

IE Illustrative example 7.7

Again we will use the previous example of Campbell Ltd:

Fixed costs	= $27,000
Contribution per mix	= $7.70
Target profit	= $50,000

No. of mixes to achieve target profit = ($27000 + $50,000) / $7.70

=10,000 mixes

We can then calculate this in terms of the number of units of each product that need to be sold and the required sales revenue of each product.

Ball 10,000 × 4	= 40,000 units × $3	= $120,000 sales revenue
Racket 10,000 × 1	= 10,000 units × $5	= $50,000 sales revenue

Therefore, in total, $170,000 sales revenue will generate the profit of $50,000 if the products are sold in the ratio of 4:1.

7.1.8   Breakeven charts in multi-product organisations

You could be asked to draw a breakeven chart for a multi-product situation and there are different approaches to how we do this based on the assumptions we make.

A contribution chart is not specifically covered, however you could be asked to draw a traditional breakeven chart or a profit volume chart. Due to the amount of lines drawn on a breakeven chart then a new one will need to be drawn for each approach we use. However on a profit volume chart we can draw both approaches on the same chart.

The different approaches that we will use to draw these charts are as follows:

1. A constant product mix
2. Products sold in sequence – most profitable first.

IE Illustrative example 7.8

Walters PLC sells three products D, A and Z and they sell for $16, $12 and $12 respectively. Their variable costs are $6, $8 and $10 respectively. Fixed cost for Walters Plc are $20,000 per annum.

Walters Plc predicts that sales for next year will be 4,000 units for D, 8,000 units for A and 6,000 units for Z. The three products are always sold in the ratio of 2:4:3.

Breakeven chart – assuming constant product mix

As we did when drawing a simple breakeven chart we need to establish the points for the three lines on the graph and also for drawing the axis.

Fixed cost line - this will be a horizontal line parallel to the x axis at $20,000.

Total revenue line	- the first point will be in the origin and the second point is maximum sales revenue calculated below.
D = 4,000 x $16	= $64,000
A = 8,000 x $12	= $96,000
Z = 6,000 x $12	= $72,000
Total	**= $232,000**

Total cost line	- the first point for this line will be when the x axis is equal to 0 and y axis is equal to fixed costs of $20,000.
	- The second point for this line will be the total cost of the three products calculated below.

Variable Cost

D = 4,000 × $6	= $24,000
A = 8,000 × $8	= $64,000
Z = 6,000 × $10	= $60,000
Total variable cost	= $148,000
Total fixed cost	= $20,000
Total cost	= $168,000

Now that we have the points for the lines and have establish the values for our axis we can now draw the breakeven chart.

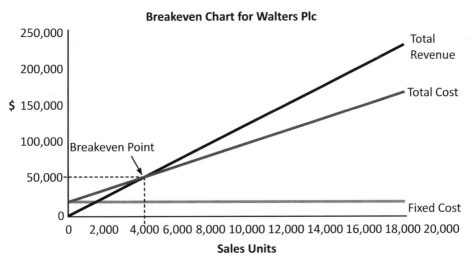

The breakeven point is approximately $55,000 of sales revenue. This can be shown by solving this mathematically.

Contribution per mix	= ($10 × 2) + ($4 × 4) + ($2 × 3)
	= $42 per mix
Breakeven (mixes)	= $20,000/$42
	= 477 mixes (rounded)
Breakeven sales revenue	
D (477 × 2) × $16	= $15,264
A (477 × 4) × $12	= $22,896
Z (477 × 3) × $12	= $17,172
Total	= $55,332

Breakeven chart – assuming most profitable product sold first

Now we are going to assume that the products are sold in sequence in particular the most profitable product first.

To establish this sequence the contribution to sales ratio for each product should be calculated.

Product		C/S Ratio	Rank
D	($10/$16)	0.63	1
A	($4/$12)	0.33	2
Z	($2/$12)	0.17	3

Therefore Walters Plc would choose to sell D first, followed by A, followed by Z. Now in order to draw our lines on the breakeven chart we have to calculate cumulative costs and revenues.

Product	Cumulative units	Cumulative costs	Cumulative revenue
		$	$
	Nil	20,000	Nil
D (4,000 units)	4,000	44,000	64,000
A (8,000 units)	12,000	108,000	160,000
Z (6,000 units)	18,000	168,000	232,000

To draw the breakeven chart we plot cumulative units against cumulative costs and revenue

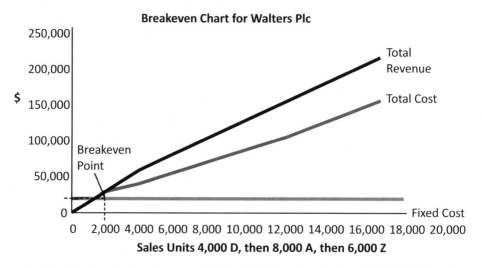

Breakeven Chart for Walters Plc

In this situation the breakeven point is at 2,000 units of sales which is 2,000 units of Product D.

 **Principle**

Drawing breakeven charts in multi-product situations

Profit volume chart for multi-product organisations

We can show the previous two approaches on a profit volume chart but instead of calculating total cost and revenues we need total profit and cumulative profit. We now will have sales revenue on the x axis and as mentioned previously both approaches can be shown on one chart.

Assuming constant sales mix:

Total revenue	= $232,000
Total profit	= $232,000 – $168,000
	= $64,000

Assuming most profitable product sold first

Product	Cumulative revenue	(Cost)/ Contribution	Cumulative profit/(Loss)
	Nil	($20,000)	($20,000)
D	$64,000	$40,000	$20,000
A	$160,000	$32,000	$52,000
Z	$232,000	$12,000	$64,000

Profit Volume Chart for Walters Plc

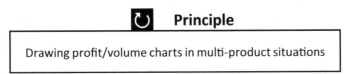

The chart shows that if Walters Plc were to sell their most profitable product first they would breakeven earlier than if they were to sell their products in a constant mix. The profit volume chart can help to identify whether a product should be discontinued or what effect a change in sales price and sales volume could have on the breakeven point and profit.

🔄 Principle

Drawing profit/volume charts in multi-product situations

7.1.9 Limitation of CVP analysis

You may be asked to discuss the limitations of CVP analysis and when asked to do this the assumptions of CVP analysis should be considered.

It makes the big assumption that sales price, variable costs and fixed costs remain constant and that it is only volume that will affect revenue and costs. This is unlikely to always be the case as economies of scale may be achieved. Also this does not consider the relationship between price and demand and also any changes in sales mix.

Assuming that fixed costs are constant also ignores the fact that they can change if output falls or increases as in reality most fixed costs are stepped costs.

Also another limitation is that CVP analysis ignores the uncertainty in the estimates of fixed costs and variable costs per unit.

Despite these limitations and assumptions CVP analysis is an important tool in helping organisations to understand the effect that changes in volume, costs and prices will have on their profit. Also by offering a graphical representation of this data make it much easier for non-financial managers to understand.

Why increase production and sales levels?

As you will have seen from the demand curve, companies can change their level of activity. As well as short term profit maximisation, there may be several reasons why sales and production might be increased

(a) Production might be increased for the following reasons:

Keep machinery running, if shutting down and restarting machinery is costly in itself

Take advantage of cheap raw materials inputs if these are available and need to be processed

Build up stocks in advance of sale, eg in anticipation of a marketing effort

Support a price penetration strategy

(b) Sales might be increased for a number of reasons, though you should remember that the person who determines a sale is the customer! However, businesses can plan an increased selling activity.

- Maximise profits in the short term, obviously
- Build market share, so that more can be sold in the long term
- To attack a competitor
- To get rid of excess stock, for example before it becomes obsolescent; there may be 'special offers' on older versions of products.

This suggests that decisions to increase production or selling are not the same. In either case, it is useful to look at the incremental costs and revenues from the increased activity. Incremental means 'in addition to'.

IE Illustrative example 7.9

A Ltd sells 150 units of X at £10 a unit, earning revenue of £1,500. If it reduces the price to £9.50, sales will increase to 200 units, earning revenues of £1,900. Overall the incremental revenue is £400. This means the extra ten units earn incremental revenues of £8 each, far less than the £10 sold for.

Now let's look at the cost side, let's assume that the cost per unit is £5. Selling 150 at (£10 - £5 costs) gives profit of £750. Selling 200 at (£9.50 - £5 costs) gives profit of £900, so the incremental profit is £150 (£900 less £750), even though the profit per unit has fallen from £10-£5 to £9.50-£5.

We can see that 50 extra units have been produced, for an increase in profit of £150 in total, or £3 per unit.

This suggests that the initiative is worthwhile.

If, on the other hand, the sale price were only to increase to £8.50: well, revenues would be £1,700 (200 x £8.50), costs would remain the same per unit, and so the profit would go down to £700 (in other words 200 x (£8.50 -£5)), meaning that A Ltd would have earned £750 from selling £150 at £10, now earns £700, a reduction of £50, with a profit of £3.5 per unit, but a loss of £1 on each extra unit sold

It is very possible that the incremental production cost will fall. After all, if the company is using more raw materials, it might be able to negotiate volume discounts. Fixed costs would be, by definition, fixed.

EG Learning example 7.4

Tool Ltd manufactures three products, X, Y and Z. The management accountant is evaluating product mix decisions with the help of breakeven analysis. Following is an extract from the accounts of three products;

	X	Y	Z
	$	$	$
Selling price	10	8	11
Direct costs	6	5	9

Total fixed costs are $100,000 per annum

At present three products are sold in the ratio of 2:1:5 respectively.

Required:

   (a) Calculate contribution to sales ratio (C/S) for each product
   (b) Calculate weighted average C/S ratio
   (c) Calculate breakeven revenue if all products are sold in their original ratio
   (d) Calculate breakeven revenue if management decides to sell the most profitable product first.

Key Learning Points

- CVP analysis is the study of the interrelationships between costs, volume and profit at different levels of activity. (B2a)
- CVP analysis focuses on marginal costing principles:

  Sales revenue − Variable cost = Contribution = Fixed cost + Profit (B2a)

- Key formulae (single-product environment):
  - Breakeven units = Fixed costs/Unit contribution
  - Target contribution = Fixed costs + Target profit
  - Target volume = Target contribution/Unit contribution
  - Margin of safety = (Budgeted sales − Breakeven sales)/Budgeted sales × 100%
  - CS Ratio = Unit contribution/Unit selling price
  - Breakeven sales revenue = Fixed costs/CS ratio (B2b)

- In a multi-product environment, it is assumed that products will be sold in a constant mix. (B2c)
- Key formulae (multi-product environment):
  - Weighted average CS ratio = Total contribution/Total sales revenue
  - Breakeven sales revenue = Fixed costs/WACS ratio
  - Breakeven mixes = Fixed costs/contribution per mix (B2c)

- Breakeven charts show costs and revenue against sales activity levels. (B2e)
- Profit volume charts show net profits against sales activity levels. (B2e)

 What's the story?

Stop and think through the 'story' of this chapter and how it links with other chapters (use the Overview to help).

Learning example solutions

EG Solution 7.1

Breakeven units	= $45,000/$30
	= 1,500 units
Units to achieve required profit	= ($45,000 + $15,000)/$30
	= $60,000/$30
	= 2,000 units

EG Solution 7.2

Firstly we need to calculate the breakeven point in units:

Breakeven (units)	= $100,000/$20
	= 5,000 units
Margin of safety (units)	= 16,000 units – 5,000 units
	= 11,000 units
Margin of safety (revenue)	= (16,000 units – 5,000 units) × $50
	= $550,000
Margin of safety (%)	= (16,000 units – 5,000 units)/16,000 units
	= 0.6875 = 68.75%

EG Solution 7.3

C/S ratio	= $16 / $40
	= 0.4 or 40%
Breakeven sales revenue	= $160,000/0.4
	= $400,000
Required revenue	= ($160,000 + $56,000)/0.4
	= $216,000/0.4
	= $540,000

EG Solution 7.4

1.

	X	Y	Z
Selling price	$10	$8	$11
Less: variable cost	6	5	9
Contribution per unit	4	3	2
÷ selling price	10	8	11
C/S ratio	40%	37.5%	18.18%

2. Weighted average C/S ratio = contribution per mix/sales revenue per mix

Assuming a standard mix of 2 units of X, 1 units of Y and 5 units of Z, the revenue and contribution earned from each mix would be as follows:

Product	X	Y	Z	Total
Units per mix	2	1	5	
Revenue	20	8	55	83
Variable cost	12	5	45	62
Contribution	8	3	10	21

Weighted Average C/S Ratio = 21/83 = 0.253 or 25.3%

3. Total fixed costs/Weighted average C/S ratio

= $100,000/25.3%

= $395,257

4. As per (a) above product X has the highest C/S ratio, therefore revised breakeven revenue using product X:

$100,000/40% = $250,000

8

Pricing Decisions

Context

It is important for any business to fully understand its costs. In order to make a reasonable profit, the business must charge an appropriate sales price to ensure that its revenues cover its costs. There are three key determinants of cost that we will consider:

- Cost-plus pricing – where the start point is the costs of the business, which then adds on a margin in order to establish the sales price.
- Market-based prices – where various pricing tactics can be adopted to ensure that customers are charged a price that they would be willing to pay for the goods.
- Demand curve theory – a theoretical method of being able to quantify the effect of price changes on customer demand levels.

The examiner will expect you to be able to not only compute possible sales prices, but also to discuss the results you have established. Therefore ensure that you are aware of how to compute prices, as also to apply the attributes of different pricing tactics to questions and scenarios.

3Q	
1.	In the cost plus pricing method, what happens if the budgeted sales volume is not achieved?
2.	What is the difference between market skimming and penetration pricing?
3.	What is the equation of the demand curve?

8.1   Pricing decisions

So far we have assumed a sales price for the goods and services being produced by the business. We will address a number of different techniques for establishing the sales price of a product.

Many of the techniques that we will develop are based on the business trying to create a sales price based on internal factors (for example by taking the costs of a business, adding on a margin in order to arrive at a sales price). Alternatively, the business may (as in target costing) identify, through its own marketing research, the price that competitors are charging and what price customers are willing to pay for the product.

Key techniques to address include:

- Cost-plus pricing;
- Marketing approached to pricing;
- Demand curve (from Economics)

8.2   Cost-plus pricing techniques

The key concept behind cost-plus pricing is that the base point of how the price is set starts **internally** to the business. A margin is then added on to internal costs in order to arrive at a sales price.

The cost base can be from:

- Total costs (production or production + non-production overhead);
- Marginal costs – the mark-up relates closely to contribution per unit;
- Opportunity costs – the relevant costs of the decision could be the basis for establishing the sales price;
- Hybrids of the above.

In summary, the steps are:

- Establish cost base of business (full cost/marginal cost/relevant cost/etc.)
- Add on an appropriate margin (on selling price) or mark-up (on cost).
- Cost plus margin = sales price

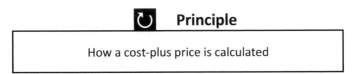

Principle

How a cost-plus price is calculated

Cost plus pricing appears to be a sensible way to set prices. It is used extensively in reality.

| IE | **Illustrative example 8.1** |

A painter when tendering for a contract will estimate the cost of paint required the cost of paying a helper to assist in the painting etc. The painter (along with most businesses!) will have a clear understanding of their costs and hence what sort of price is necessary in order to cover those costs and make a profit.

8.2.1   Potential drawbacks of cost-plus pricing

- The business may have a margin on all of the products that it sells. However if budgeted sales **volumes** are not achieved, then not enough contribution will be earned to pay off the fixed costs of a business and secure a profit.
- A **vicious circle** could arise where a business pushes prices up unrealistically high in order to try to make a profit. For example if fixed costs rose for a business:

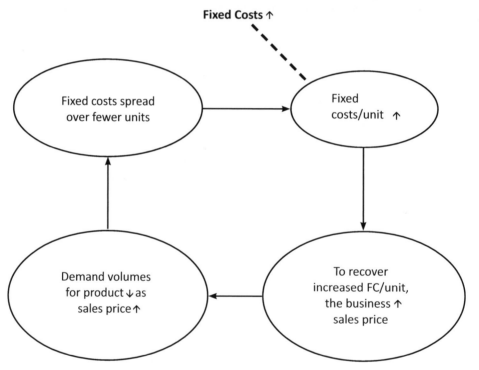

- The price charged may ignore what customers are willing to pay and what competitors are charging. It may be possible to charge a higher price, or (problematically) the business may be charging too high a price for its products/services.
- Cost plus pricing may not lead to profit (wealth) maximization for the business.

8.2.2   Uses for cost-plus pricing

- If the business has a unique product, for example in job, batch or contract costing situation. The product is very specific to the needs of the customer and the costs that the producer will incur. It is important for the customer to consider how efficient and cost-focused the supplier is. Governments will allow contract pricing on a cost-plus basis for government contract. However rigorous cost audits are often undertaken to make sure that the supplier is not overspending ('padding' costs) and trying to charge an unrealistically high price on the contract.
- In a simple cost-plus pricing environment, cost-plus pricing may be appropriate, as for a painter/decorator, fruit seller in a market and so on. These sort of business clearly understand what their products cost and will add on a fairly standard margin in order to establish a sales price.

 Principle

Advantages and disadvantages of cost-plus pricing

8.2.3   Mark-up versus margin:

It is important to distinguish between mark-up (expressed as a % of cost) and margin (expressed as a % of sales price).

If we consider a 20% mark-up or 20% margin with reference to a sales price of $100 in the following example we can illustrate this concept:

	Mark-up $			**Margin** $	
Cost	100.00	100%	Cost	100.00	80%
Mark-up	20.00	20%	Margin	25.00	20%
Sales price	**120.00**	120%	Sales price	**125.00**	100%

- **Mark-up** is expressed as a % of cost and therefore if goods cost $100.00, the mark-up must be $100.00 x 20% giving a sales price of $120.00

 Learn

- **Margin** is expressed as a % of the sales price and if (as here) we know the cost of the goods then the calculations are a little trickier:

$$\text{Margin} = \$100.00 \text{ (cost)} \times \frac{20\%}{80\%} = \$25.00$$

$$\text{Sales Price} = \$100.00 \times \frac{100\%}{80\%} = \$125.00$$

 Learn

IE Illustrative example 8.2

Superal is designing a new product, the Thrilla Winna. The following costs have been estimated:

		$
Direct materials	3 Ku @ $4.50/Ku	13.50
Direct labour	4 hours @ $7.50/hour	30.00
Variable production overhead	2 machine hours @ $4/hour	8.00
Budgeted fixed production overheads	Absorbed on a direct labour hour basis. Direct labour hours are limited to 80,000 hours in the period	$500,000
Opportunity cost of labour	Labour can earn a contribution per hour (after deducting the cost of labour) of $3.00 in another department where they are currently fully utilised.	

Compute the sales prices if Superal uses the following cost plus bases:

Marginal production cost with a contribution margin of 45%

Full production cost plus 25%

Full production cost and opportunity cost per unit plus 10%

Marginal production cost with a contribution margin of 45%

	$
Direct materials	13.50
Direct labour	30.00
Variable production overhead	8.00
Marginal production cost	51.50
	$93.64

$$\text{Sales price: } (\$51.50 \times \frac{100\%}{55\%})$$

Full production cost plus 25%

	$
Direct materials	13.50
Direct labour	30.00
Variable production overhead	8.00
Marginal production cost	51.50
Fixed Production overhead per unit:	25.00

$$OAR = \frac{\$500,000}{80,000 \text{ labour hours}} = \$6.25/\text{hour x 4 hours}$$

	$
Total absorption cost	76.50
	$95.63

Sales price: $(\$76.50 \times \frac{125\%}{100\%})$

Full production cost and opportunity cost per unit plus 20%

	$
Direct materials	13.50
Direct labour	30.00
Variable production overhead	8.00
Marginal production cost	51.50
Fixed production overhead per unit:	
	25.00

$$OAR = \frac{\$500,000}{80,000 \text{ labour hours}} = \$6.25/\text{hour x 4 hours}$$

	$
Total absorption cost	76.50
Opportunity cost per unit = (Lost contribution per labour hour + labour cost/hour) x labour hours: $3 + $7.50 = $10.50 × 4 hours	42.00
Full production cost and opportunity cost	118.50
	$142.20

Sales Price: $(\$118.50 \times \frac{120\%}{100\%})$

8.3 Marketing approaches to pricing

Marketing approaches to pricing include tactics to address:

- Product lifecycle issues – we need a more detailed understanding of the implications for pricing a product dependent upon which stage it has reached in its lifecycle.
- New product issues – particularly if the business is in the position of having a monopoly on that product in its early years of production.
- Existing product issues. For example a business may launch a new product into a market where similar products are already established.

The product lifecycle framework assumes that all products pass through distinctive phases as shown in the diagram below:

8.3.1 Product lifecycle

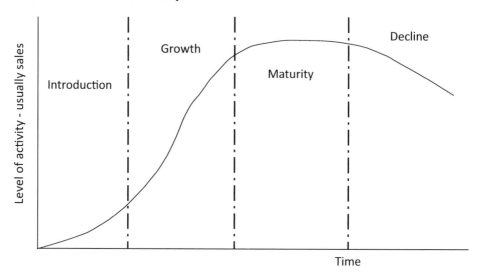

- **Introductory phase:** This is a high risk phase, where products have just been launched on to the market. The customer base is largely unaccustomed to this new product. The business may need to focus on advertising and promotion to build sales. Heavy introductory price discounts may be necessary to entice customers to try the product. If the product is highly innovative or desirable (e.g. a brand new top of the range computer game), then the price charged may be high to reflect the desirability of the product.
- **Growth phase:** As demand for the product rises, possibly due to the innovative qualities of the product, market share will grow and the product becomes (hopefully!) more profitable. Pricing will become more competitive if new competitors enter the market.

- **Maturity phase:** The product will be well established in the market. However customers will be highly knowledgeable about the product and redesign, re-packaging and re-pricing of the product may be necessary to maintain the product in the market place. This will be particularly important since competitors may compete heavily on a price basis.
- **Decline phase:** At the end of a product's life, demand may fall dramatically as it is superseded by upgraded or improved products. This is particularly noticeable in hi-tech markets. However, the decline phase may occur over many years (if at all), if the product still has a reasonable demand base.

It is interesting to identify the implications on a business's operations of the phases in the life cycle:

Introduction	Growth	Maturity	Decline
Profitability			
Low sales volumes at the point of launch = low/ negligible profits and possibly losses. This is the highest risk point in a product life cycle –a 'make or break' point	If the product is successfully launched – likely to be highly profitable. This is especially likely to occur if the business has a monopoly position. A high premium is likely to occur on price	Profits are likely to decline in the face of competition and customers switching between suppliers based on price-based decisions.	If competitors leave the market, it is possible to create a profitable niche in the market (e.g. the sales of vinyl records to collectors and club DJs). Otherwise if demand falls, the product is unlikely to be profitable to make and may be ceased.
Cash flow			
Cash flows are likely to be heavily negative due to low inflows and significant outflows such as: product launch marketing development etc	Revenue cash flows will rise, although outflows are likely to rise as well as product as enhanced and consolidated in the market (e.g. Microsoft developing new software on the back of other successful software launches). The overall cash flow position is likely to be neutral.	Considerable cash flows can be generated at this phase, even though profit margins may be quite low. If competitors are unable to gain market share, the dominant position of a business' product should be able to generate considerable positive cash flow.	Cash flows may become negative if the product's demand falls away. Product should therefore be divested. Otherwise cash is unlikely to be invested in products which are retained, but in their decline phase.

Introduction	Growth	Maturity	Decline
Strategy			
Key strategies will involve marketing and promotion in order to get market acceptance form the customer base.	The importance of building a brand and ensuring the proper functioning of a product and product range needs to be considered. For example if a successful gentleman's 3-blade razor is launched, the business may consider developing and selling 4 or 5 blade razors or similar models for the female market.	Cost control/ reduction is critical during the maturity phase. Revenue streams may be hard to manage, so in order to maintain profitability and cash flow, little will be spent on unnecessary cost areas.	The decline phase will necessitate sensible timing of when to exit a market.

8.4   New product pricing

Two main strategies can be adopted in the situation where a business may have a monopoly over the market when it launches a brand new product.

8.4.1   Market skimming (aim = high price, low volume)

With this pricing tactic, the business looks to address a small niche of a marketplace. This niche is willing to pay substantial prices to purchase a product often in its very early phases of a life cycle. This is particularly noted in the hi-tech gadget sector (e.g. mobile 'phones, computer games and software). Most of the 'market' is ignored and the top few customers, who are price *insensitive* will be willing to pay a high price to acquire the latest and most up to date products.

There are two *requirements* for such a tactic:

1. A protected monopoly needs to exist:
   - (a) A strong **brand** may help protect the monopoly position (e.g. Coca Cola)
   - (b) A **patent** or **copyright** may allow the product to be produced without competition for a period of time (e.g. a pharmaceutical company launching a new patented drug).
   - (c) The use of **technology** may cement the monopoly position of the business. For example a computer games manufacturer may launch a hi-tech games console with superior graphics. To access this technology, customers must buy both the console and the dedicated games for that console.

2. Relatively low **investment** and **low volumes** would allow this approach to work if only a small percentage of the market is being 'skimmed'.

8.4.2   Advantages of market skimming:

1. Low investment is needed and is therefore low risk. The business has only committed to addressing a small segment of the market.
2. If the launch does not work at a high price, the price can be lowered in order to increase sales volumes.
3. The business is able to build a strong brand and reputation for high quality on the market place. The business has built a reputation for supplying a high quality, innovative, premium product.

 Principle

Market skimming approach to pricing

8.4.3   Penetration pricing (aim = low price, high volume)

Penetration pricing is in essence the opposite to market skimming. The aim is to price the product low, in order to again quick and substantial market share from the launch of the product. This tactic is sometimes adopted by publishers trying to launch a brand new magazine. The danger is that the high volumes will not be achieved and that the product may make substantial losses.

Why?

1. No **barriers to entry** exist. Unlike market skimming there is no protection of a monopoly position to prevent other entrants coming into the market with an identical or similar product. Low prices may act as a barrier or deterrent to

competitors trying to enter the market. They will not be able to compete at very low prices.

2. High **initial costs** exist in the development and launch of a product. This will require the business to recover these negative cash flows as quickly as possible.

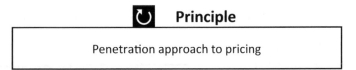

Principle

Penetration approach to pricing

8.5 Existing market

In this situation there is no obvious monopoly position. Instead a business needs to find a position amongst the competition. An example of this is the rather strangely named 'monopolistic' competition, where similar businesses compete by offering a slightly different product or service to their competitors. For example fast food restaurants may have a slightly different product range, décor and price structure to their direct competitors. However no one competitor dominates the market place.

Pricing strategies that can be followed include the following:

Average pricing

In the UK food retailers such as Tesco, Sainsbury, Asda and Morrisons are very large retailers. Because of their sheer scale, the prices that these businesses set for their products will be at or close to the industry average, since they provide a significant proportion of the whole market. Other retailers, whilst looking to sell a good number of units, have little choice but to 'follow' the prices set by the major players.

Premium pricing

If a business has attributes to its products or services that are highly valued by customers, it is possible to charge a premium price. For example in the UK, food retailers such as Marks and Spencer, Waitrose, Selfridges and Harrods provide food that are or are perceived to be of a higher quality than the industry average and therefore they can charge a higher sales price.

Discount pricing

Some retailers may aim to be profitable by selling larger volumes of units at a lower than industry price. The products sold will not necessarily be inferior, but perhaps there is less choice, not such a good perceived quality or the products are bought and sold in bulk. Food retailers that possibly follow this strategy in the UK could include Aldi and Lidl.

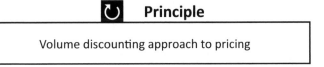

Principle

Volume discounting approach to pricing

Penetration pricing

Penetration pricing may be implemented by new entrants into a market or existing players aiming to undercut their competition. It is possible that a business may sell goods at a loss or 'loss leaders' in order to gain market share.

Complementary products

Many businesses sell products where the main product is sold at a low margin but the accessories or after-sales service required, is sold subsequently at a high margin. Therefore over the life of the product a healthy profit can be made. Examples of this might include shaving razors or electric toothbrushes where the handle is sold at a very low margin but the tailor-made replacement blades and brushes are sold at a healthy profit margin.

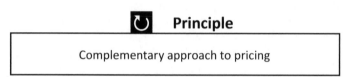

Principle

Complementary approach to pricing

Product line pricing

Some products may be sold in a range of items. For example if customers buy china crockery, then the business may price each type of chinaware (e.g. plate, cup, vegetable dish etc.) at the same margin or mark-up. Alternatively different products in the range may be sold at different margins so that a reasonable profit is made over time from an 'average' customer purchase. For example basic plates and bowls might be sold at a low margin, but customers buying these products may tend to buy a salt and pepper pot in the same range but at a much higher price and hence margin.

Principle

Product line approach to pricing

Price discrimination

Using price discrimination a business may be able to sell what is essentially the same product or service to different customers at different prices. In order to do this a business must recognise that it sells products to customers with different price sensitivities. Some customers 'tolerate' paying much higher prices than others. The key is identifying the circumstances where this happens and preventing customer from moving from a high price to a lower price paying position.

IE Illustrative example 8.3

Train companies will charge higher prices for customers travelling on weekdays to and from major cities like London early in the morning. There is little alternative form of transport to London and so the customers will pay a higher fare. When at the weekend it is much easier to travel by car, bus, bicycle, motorcycle etc. into London and also overall demand for train transport is lower, the train companies have to charge lower fares to attract weekend custom.

Bases of discrimination can include age (e.g. child fare versus adult fare on a bus), time of provision of service or even market segment (for example electricity companies may charge different rates to industrial or domestic customers).

Principle

Price discrimination approach to pricing

8.5.1   Demand-based pricing

We need to have a core appreciation of economics in terms of the relationship between the price charged for goods/services and the quantities sold of those goods/services.

We have addressed 'price sensitivity' in our earlier discussions and now need to formalise this understanding.

8.5.2   Demand functions

Demand functions can be derived for a product or service. Generally speaking if the price of a product rises, then the quantity demanded falls. This can be shown graphically as follows:

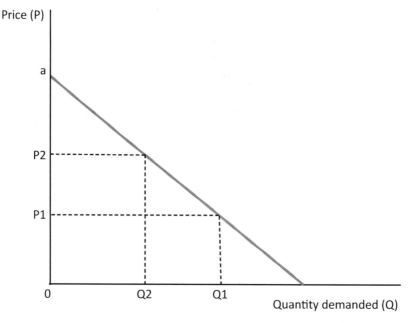

A price rise from P1 to P2 causes demand to fall from Q1 to Q2. Indeed if the price rose as far as 'a' then there would be no demand at all for the product.

The general equation of this straight line demand function is:

$P = a - bQ$

where:

$$b = \frac{\text{Change in price}}{\text{Change in quantity}}$$

a = price when Q = 0

 Given

If you need to derive a demand function in the exam it is quite straightforward given these formulae.

IE Illustrative example 8.4

The O'Reilly currently sells for $20. At this price 25,000 units are sold. If however the price is raised to $24, marketing research indicate that demand would fall to 23,000 units.

The demand function for the O'Reilly can be calculated using the following steps:

- Step one: calculate 'b'

$$b = \frac{\text{Change in price}}{\text{Change in quantity}} = \frac{\$24 - \$20}{23{,}000 - 25{,}000} = 0.002$$

- Step two: substitute 'b' into the demand function formula using either pair of quantity and price data in order to find 'a':

$P = a - bQ$: using the pair of figures \$24 and 23,000 units) and b = 0.002

$24 = a - (0.002 \times 23{,}000)$

$24 = a - 46$

$a = 24 + 46 = 70$

- Step 3: write down and verify your equation:

$P = 70 - 0.002Q$

Using the other set of figures (\$20 and 25,000 units) to check:

$20 = 70 - (0.002 \times 25{,}000)$

$20 = 70 - 50$

$20 = 20$

Therefore the answer is correct.

8.5.3   Price elasticity of demand

Definition

Price elasticity of demand (PED) measures the sensitivity of quantities demanded by customers to changes in sales price:

PED = |% change in quantity demanded / % change in sales price|

or

$$PED = \left| \frac{(Q_2 - Q_1)/Q_1}{(P_2 - P_1)/P_1} \right|$$

 Learn

Note that the PED calculation will always yield a negative result due to the inverse relationship between price and quantity demanded. However, the negativity should be ignored and the positive answer taken.

EG Learning example 8.1

A product, the Coppell, is priced at $30. At this price 100,000 units are sold. The price is increased to $35 and the demand for Coppell falls to 96,500 units.

Calculate the PED.

Interpretation of PED

Once we have calculated the PED, we need to understand what this tells us about the price sensitivity of the product. The product will fall into one of the following categories:

Price inelastic

If the **PED < 1** this means that the product is **price inelastic.** A large increase in price only leads to a small reduction in quantity demanded. This means that customers largely will pay a higher price to sustain their buying habits and patterns.

The demand function for an inelastic product would be similar to the following:

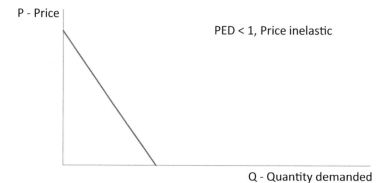

We can see from the above that a change in the price does not significantly impact the quantity.

Products which are likely to be price inelastic can include:

- Essential goods (e.g. basic food, water, power etc.)
- Products with a strong brand image (e.g. Coca-Cola)
- Products which have no substitute (e.g. petrol or diesel)

For inelastic goods, it should increase revenues and profits (generally) if prices are increased. This explains why governments will tax products such as tobacco or petrol, since there will be a large increase in revenues and only a small reduction in quantity demanded.

Price elastic

If the **PED > 1** this means that the product is **price elastic.** A small increase in price will result in a proportionately larger reduction in quantity demanded. This means that many customers are only prepared to buy the product if the price is lower.

The demand function for an elastic product would be similar to the following:

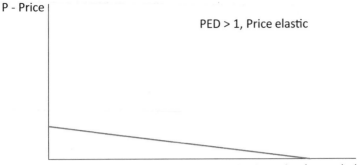

We can see from the above that a change in the price has a significant impact on quantity demanded.

Products which are likely to be price elastic can include:

- Non-essential goods (eg luxuries etc)
- Products which have ready substitutes (e.g. raspberry versus strawberry jam)

For elastic goods, it should increase revenues and profits (generally) if prices are decreased.

Unit elastic
If the **PED = 1** this means that the product is **unit elastic.** This means that is price increases by, for example, 10% then quantity demanded will reduce by the same percentage.

The demand function for an inelastic product would be similar to the following:

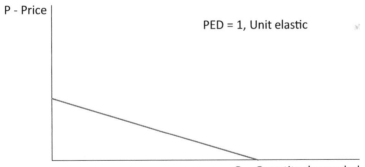

Perfectly inelastic
If the **PED = 0** this means that the product is **perfectly inelastic.** This means that a change in price does not affect the quantity demanded. The quantity demanded will always be the same, regardless of what price the company charges.

The demand function for an inelastic product would be similar to the following:

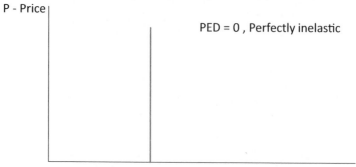

In reality, it is highly unlikely that a product would be perfectly inelastic. If the price of a product increases by a high enough percentage, there will usually always be some customers who will stop buying the product.

Products which would be the closest to being perfectly inelastic would include life-saving medicines, which people will be prepared to pay for regardless of the price.

Perfectly elastic

If the **PED = ∞** this means that the product is **perfectly elastic.** This means that demand is limitless at a particular price. However, if price is increased by even a very small amount, demand will immediately drop to 0. There is no incentive for the company to reduce the price as this would only reduce profits.

The demand function for an inelastic product would be similar to the following:

P - Price

PED = ∞ , Perfectly elastic

Q - Quantity demanded

In a perfectly competitive market, a product with be perfectly elastic. This is because if a company increased the price very slightly, the customers with perfect information would buy an identical product from another company.

 **Principle**

Interpretation of price elasticity of demand

8.6 Profit-maximising price and quantity

We have seen so far that as price decreases, the quantity of units sold will increase. Given that this is the case, is it better for a given company to sell fewer units at a high price or sell high volumes at a lower unit price? Presumably, a company wishes to select the option that is going to maximise the total profits earned.

Before we look at how the profit-maximising price and quantity are established, first we must understand a number of concepts.

8.6.1 Total revenue

Traditionally, total revenue is viewed as linear i.e. if the selling price is $50/unit then total revenue will increase by $50 every time one more unit is sold. However, we have now seen that for sales volumes to increase, the price per unit would have to be reduced.

IE **Illustrative example 8.5**

Price	Quantity demanded	Total revenue = P × Q
50	0	0
49.50	1	49.50
35	30	1,050
10	80	800

As we can see from the above, as quantity increases initially total revenue will also increase. However, if price is reduced by too much, revenue will begin to decline as the increase in quantity is outweighed by the lost revenue from price reductions.

Given this, total revenue can be shown graphically as follows:

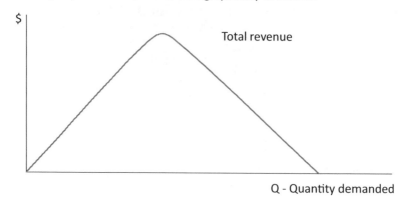

8.6.2 Marginal revenue and marginal cost

Definition

Marginal revenue is the additional revenue earned from selling one more unit. As we have seen, the selling price will decrease and quantity demanded increases, therefore marginal revenue decreases as Q increases.

IE Illustrative example 8.6

Quantity demanded	Price	Total revenue	Marginal revenue
1	$100	$100	$100
2	$90	$180	$80
3	$80	$240	$60
4	$70	$280	$40

Marginal revenue can be shown graphically as follows:

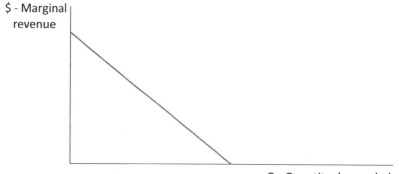

Marginal revenue (MR) can be calculated as:

MR = a – 2bQ

 Given

Definition

Marginal cost is the additional cost incurred from making one extra unit. This is usually just the variable cost/unit and for now, we will assume that this is constant. So if the variable cost/unit is $10 then it will always cost the company $10 to produce one extra unit.

We can now show both marginal cost and marginal revenue on a graph:

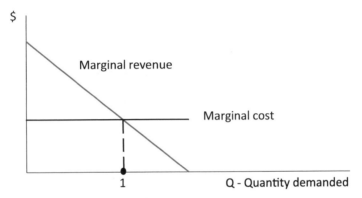

We can see from this graph that **profit will be maximised at the point where marginal revenue is equal to marginal cost.** In the graph above, point 1 therefore represents the profit-maximising quantity.

This is because if quantity of units is below point 1, then the marginal revenue is greater than the marginal cost. Therefore it would increase profits if quantity sold was increased by one unit.

However, once the quantity goes above point 1, the marginal revenue is less than the marginal cost. Therefore selling further units above point 1 would actually reduce profits.

| IE | Illustrative example 8.7 |

If we have a constant marginal cost of $8 per unit and the following revenue figures we can work out where marginal cost equals marginal revenue (or is closest).

Units	Price per unit ($)	Total Revenue	Marginal Revenue
1	20	20	20
2	19	38	18
3	17	51	13
4	15	60	9
5	13	65	5

Here we can see that marginal cost equals marginal revenue (or closest) where we sell 4 units. Does this make sense? The profit at this level of activity is $60 revenue less $32 cost (ie 4 units at $8 cost each), which equals $28. Try yourself and you'll find that 3 units makes a profit of $27 (51-24) and 5 units makes a profit of $25 (65-40), so 4 units does maximise the profit.

IE Illustrative example 8.8

A company estimates the following demand for the prices given:
Price = $7, demand = 100 units

Price = $8, demand = 60 units

The marginal cost of making each unit is $5.

To work out the number of units and price we need to find the demand curve formula P=a-bQ, work out the marginal revenue function and then set it equal to marginal cost to find the optimal quantity to sell.

Demand curve
b = change in price/change in quantity = -1/40 = -0.025

a = 7 + 0.025 x 100 = 9.5 (using and rearranging P=a-bQ)

So the demand function is P = 9.5 - 0.025Q and the Marginal Revenue function is 9.5 - (2 x 0.025 Q) or 9.5 - 0.05Q. Just learn the Marginal Revenue function if you never studied differentiation in mathematics.

If marginal cost is $5 then to maximise profit we set MC = MR:
5 = 9.5 - 0.05Q so rearranging the equation, Q = 90 and P = $7.25 from P=a-bQ

So we sell 90 units at $7.25 to maximise profit, giving a profit of $652.5 revenue less $450 costs = $202.50 profit. We can see that this is higher than 100 units where we make $7 - $5 profit on each, so $200 profit, or 60 units where we make $180 profit.

EG Learning example 8.2

A company sells 1,000 units at a price of $100 per unit, and sells 800 units at a price of $150. The variable cost per unit is constant at $50.

Required:

(a) Determine the demand function of the company
(b) Determine the profit maximising quantity and price

Key Learning Points

- Cost-plus pricing:
    - Sales price = Cost per unit + Mark-up per unit
    - Mark-up is expressed as a % of cost.
    - Margin is expressed as a % of sales price. (B4g)

- Marketing approaches to pricing:
    - New products:

        o Market skimming

        o Penetration pricing

    - Existing products:

        o Discount pricing

        o Complementary pricing

        o Product line pricing

        o Price discrimination (B4g)

- Demand curves:
    - Price elasticity of demand (PED): = % change in quantity demanded/% change in sales price

        o PED < –1 = inelastic

        o PED > –1 = elastic (B4b)

    - Demand functions:

        o General equation = $P = a - bQ$ (given in the exam)

        o b = (given in the exam)

        o a = price when $Q = 0$ (given in the exam) (B4c)

    - The profit maximising price and quantity will occur at the point where marginal revenue is equal to marginal cost, where marginal revenue (MR):

    $MR = a - 2bQ$ (given in the exam) (B4d)

 What's the story?

Stop and think through the 'story' of this chapter and how it links with other chapters (use the Overview to help).

Learning example solutions

EG Solution 8.1

$$PED = \left| \frac{(96,500 - 100,000)\Big/ 100,000}{(35 - 30)\Big/ 30} \right|$$

$$PED = \left| \frac{-0.035}{0.167} \right| = 0.21$$

EG Solution 8.2

(a)

Assuming a linear demand function $P = a - bQ$

b = change in price/change in quantity demanded

b = 50/200 = 0.25

Therefore $P = a - 0.25Q$

We know that when P = 100, Q = 1,000. Substituting these values into the demand function gives us:

100 = a − 0.25 x 1,000

Therefore a = 350

The demand function of the company will be;

P = 350 − 0.25Q

(b)

To determine the profit maximising price and quantity, we must find the point where Marginal Cost (MC) = Marginal Revenue (MR)

We know that MC = $50

And the equation for MR:

MR = a − 2bQ

So, MR = 350 − 0.5Q

To establish the profit maximising quantity, we simply let the MR equation equal to the MC value of 50:

50 = 350 − 0.5xQ

Which gives us Q = 600 profit maximising quantity

Finally, we need to calculate the corresponding price. We know from the demand function that:

P = 350 – 0.25Q

Therefore:

P = 350 – 0.25 x 600

Which gives us P = $200 profit maximising price

This tells us that in order to maximise profits, this company should set a selling price of $200 and therefore sell 600 units.

9

Decision-making Under Uncertainty

Context

So far we have assumed that we know the possible outcomes of a project with certainty. In reality this is not likely to be the case, so we need to use techniques which help to assess the uncertainties and risks surrounding a project.

Calculation of expected values is a key skill in the exam. If probabilities are neatly tabulated, it makes it much easier to work out the answer and also for the marker to assess your thought process. This is also important in the use of maximax, maximin and minimax regret techniques.

3Q

1. What is the concept of expected value?

2. Can you explain the minimax, maximin and minimax regret techniques?

3. What is the 'value of perfect information', and how would you calculate it?

9.1 Decision-making under uncertainty

As a progression from all of our previous studies, we can consider situations where we are making decisions in an uncertain environment. For example, we will still consider relevant costing principles in our decision making.

The key topic areas to be discussed are:

- Nature of risk and uncertainty
- Expected values – the calculation of weighted averages in decisions
- Other decision rules – which extend the use of expected values.

We will use 'payoff tables' to help us set out our work.

9.1.1 Risk and uncertainty

Decisions affect the future. A business is deciding today on an issue that will affect its *future* operations. For example a business is launching a new product. Will it sell? If so how well will it sell? The business cannot know exactly how well the product will perform in advance.

Although often used interchangeably, there is a subtle difference between the terms risk and uncertainty.

Risk	Uncertainty
Multiple possible outcomes exist for a particular decision being made.	Multiple possible outcomes exist for a particular decision being made.
It is possible to quantify those possible outcomes (e.g. assess the probability of good, average or poor sales arising on the sale of a new product)	It is **not** possible to quantify those possible outcomes (e.g. assess the probability of good, average or poor sales arising on the sale of a new product)

 Principle

> The difference between risk and uncertainty

IE Illustrative example 9.1

To identify risk involved, marketing research could be undertaken to identify the likely sales levels for a new product. For example, marketing research highlights the following daily sales patterns:

- High sales of 25,000 units will occur with a 30% probability
- Average sales of 16,000 units will occur with a 50% probability

Poor sales of 4,000 units will occur with a 20% probability

9.1.2   Marketing research

Marketing research can be undertaken to reduce uncertainty, and hopefully allow the possible outcomes of a decision to be quantified (i.e. assess the risk of the project).

Marketing research techniques include techniques such as:

- Questionnaires and interviews – potential customers could be asked questions in details about their likely future buying requirements and needs.
- Test marketing – prototype products are trialled in small markets. For example a food retailer may trial a new product line in 5 shops and gauge customer feedback and buying patterns.
- Online panel research – a group of individuals may have agreed to feedback on marketing research questions, for example regularly providing details of their buying patterns.
- Focus groups – a group of individuals who may meet to discuss the attributes and features of a new product.

 Principle

> How market research can be used to reduce uncertainty

9.2   Expected values (EV)

The technique of using expected values (EV) is very important in decision making involving risk and uncertainty. It involves the use of:

- Possible outcomes; and
- Their associated probabilities.

9.2.1   Probability

Probability is the measurement of possible outcomes in terms of their estimated likelihood of occurring.

The overall probability of an event must sum to 1.0 (or 100%). For example if you toss a coin there is a 0.5 (50%) probability of a head and a 0.5 (50%) probability of a tail.

The probability of throwing a head or a tail (the only two possible outcomes) is 1.0 (100%)

9.2.2   Expected value (EV)

EV measures the weighted average value of all the possible outcomes. It does not reflect the degree of risk, but simply what the average outcome would be if the event were repeated a number of times.

It is denoted as:

$$EV = \sum px$$

where:

∑ = sum of (i.e. add up!)

p = probability of an outcome

x = value of an outcome.

 Learn

IE Illustrative example 9.2

As seen in Illustrative example 9.1, marketing research highlights the following daily sales pattern possibilities for a new product about to be launched:

High sales of 25,000 units will occur with a 30% probability

Average sales of 16,000 units will occur with a 50% probability

Poor sales of 4,000 units will occur with a 20% probability

Sales level	Units (x)	Probability (p)	EV (∑px)
High	25,000	0.30	7,500
Average	16,000	0.50	8,000
Poor	4,000	0.20	800
			16,300

We can see that if the sales pattern was repeated many times, on average we would sell 16,300 units per period.

9.2.3   Issues with weighted averages

- The results that are generated are highly dependent on the accuracy of the probabilities and estimates used in the calculation of the EV. The importance of accurate marketing research is obvious here.
- If we are considering a large population or a series of results that 'repeats' frequently over time, EVs can provide useful information. Since the daily sales patterns in our example are likely to repeat over time, the 16,300 weighted average is a useful estimate of likely overall sales.
    - For example it is not unreasonable to predict that sales for a year will be 365 days x 16,300 units per day = 5,949,500 units.

- EVs however do not reflect accurately a single outcome. For example in our example if we were only trying to predict one day's sales, the only possible outcomes are 25,000, 16,000 or 4,000 units. The EV of 16,300 is not a possibility.
- The EV can be used in subsequent calculations. For example if the expected sales price is $12 per unit, we can predict that sales revenues (e.g. for a forecast Income Statement) are likely to be:
    - 16,300 x $12 = $195,600

- EV techniques however ignore the range of outcomes. We lose an assessment of the level of risk a business might face. In our example the EV is 16,300 units. However, the best outcome is 25,000 units and the worst 4,000 units. This data is lost in EV analysis.
  - This may be an issue when we consider risk attitudes:

    1. A **risk seeker** is interested in the best possible outcomes that can be achieved (25,000 units).

    2. A **risk avoider** is focused on the worst possible outcome that can occur (4,000 units).

    3. An individual with a **risk neutral** attitude is concerned with the most likely outcome (16,000 units).

 Learn

IE Illustrative example 9.3

Marketing research highlights the following daily sales pattern possibilities for a new product about to be launched:

High sales of 25,000 units will occur with a 30% probability

Average sales of 16,000 units will occur with a 50% probability

Poor sales of 4,000 units will occur with a 20% probability

The expected sales price is $12 if sales are at the average level, but are estimated to be 10% higher if demand levels are poor and 15% lower if demand levels are high. Calculate the expected revenue for a 30 day month of sales.

Sales level	Units (x)	Probability (p)	EV units (Σpx)	Estimated unit sales price	Expected revenue $
High	25,000	0.30	7,500	$12.00 x 85% = $10.20	76,500
Average	16,000	0.50	8,000	$12.00	96,000
Poor	4,000	0.20	800	$12.00 x 110% = $13.20	10,560
		Expected daily sales units	16,300	Expected daily revenue	$183,060

30 day revenue = 30 days x $183,060/day = $5,491,800

9.3   Simulation techniques

Elaborate computer software exists which can help a business model complex problems involving probabilities. For example a programme could be run which assigns random numbers to the particular outcomes of a project weighted by the probabilities of those outcomes. The computer can then simulate the possible outcome of that project many times over so that the management team can identify the patterns of returns they could expect on that project.

9.3.1   Other decision criteria

As an extension of EVs, we can consider other techniques which particularly focus on different attitudes towards risk that investors may have:

- **Maximax**: This decision criterion focuses on the **risk seeker** attitude to risk. Risk seekers look to **maximise** the **maximum possible return (best possible outcome)** that can be achieved ('best of the best') – i.e. the focus is on the upside risk.
- **Maximin**: This decision criterion focuses on the risk averse attitude to risk. Risk averse investors seek to **maximise** the **worst possible return (best possible outcome** of the **worst options)** that can be achieved ('best of the worst') – i.e. the focus is on the downside risk. Sometimes the best of the worst options is to do nothing if all the worst options are negative
- **Minimax regret**: This decision criterion focuses on the **opportunity cost approach** attitude to risk. This approach seeks to **compare** the return achieved against the best possible outcome. This is sometimes known as the **sore loser** defence. The aim is to **minimise** the **maximum opportunity cost.**

 Learn

In tackling questions, you will have to tackle a situation where you have a 'decision' followed by an 'outcome'. In the example below we have to **decide** how many cases to order before he knows the **outcome** (i.e. how many cases are sold).

IE Illustrative example 9.4

Mr Byornbye is a greengrocer (food seller). He buys a product for $20 per case. He can sell the product for $40 per case on his stall. The product is perishable and it is not possible to store any food, instead any cases unsold at the end of the day can be sold off as scrap for $2 per case.

Purchase orders must be made before the number of sales is known. He has kept records of demand over the last 150 days.

Demand/day	Number of days
10	45
20	75
30	30

Required:

(a) Prepare a summary of possible net daily margins using a payoff table.

(b) Advise him:

(i) How many cases to purchase if he uses expected values.

(ii) How many cases to purchase if he uses maximin or maximax.

(iii) How many cases to purchase if he uses minimax regret.

Again it is worth noting how Byornbye needs to make a decision (how many cases to order) before he knows the outcome (demand levels). In this scenario the decision directly affects the costs concerned (buying cases) and the outcome directly affects the revenues earned (either through sales to customers or scrap proceeds).

We also in this scenario need to compute the probabilities associated with each outcome:

Demand/day	Number of days	Probability
10	45	$\dfrac{45}{150} = 0.30$
20	75	$\dfrac{45}{150} = 0.50$
30	30	$\dfrac{30}{150} = 0.20$
Totals	150	1.00

We will solve all problems using expected values by using 'payoff tables'. This involves setting up a matrix which covers all possible outcomes.

We can (in this scenario) **decide** to purchase 10 or 20 or 30 cases in a day. Similarly, **the outcomes** will be sales of 10, 20 or 30 units.

		Decision (purchases)			
Profit		10	20	30	
Outcome	10				
	20				
(sales)	30				

We could also (if necessary) set up appropriate workings to help us identify the possible combinations of decisions and outcomes. This could be necessary if the question is particularly complicated. For this scenario we get:

Decision (how many purchased): Outcome (how many sold)	Workings	Margin
10:10	(200) + 400 =	200
10:20	(200) + 400 =	200
10:30 *	(200) + 400 =	200
20:10**	(400) + 400 + 20 =	20
20:20	(400) + 800 =	400
20:30	(400) + 800 =	400
30:10***	(600) + 400 + 40 =	(160)
30:20	(600) + 800 + 20 =	220
30:30	(600) + 1200 =	600

It is necessary to be quite clear as to what your computations are. It is easy to make a silly mistake.

In our example:

* if we order 10 cases yet demand is 30 cases. We spend 10 x $20 = $200, yet can only sell 10 cases for $40 each (i.e. $400 in total) even though demand is for 40 cases. Overall margin is $400 - $200 = **$200.**

** if we order 20 cases yet demand is only 10 cases. We spend 20 x $20 = $400, yet only sell 10 cases for $40 each (i.e. $400 in total). The remaining 10 cases are sold for scrap at $2/case (i.e. $20 in total). Overall margin is $400 + $20 - $400 = **$20.**

*** if we order 30 cases yet demand is only 10 cases. We spend 30 x $20 = $600, yet only sell 10 cases for $40 each (i.e. $400 in total). The remaining 20 cases are sold for scrap at $2/case (i.e. $40 in total). Overall margin is $400 + $40 - $600 = **$(160)** – a loss.

It helps us to understand what is happening if we ensure that the key information that we have computed is slotted into a payoff table. This allows us to organise our numbers and may be computed straight away without the detailed workings previously undertaken:

(a) Summary of possible net daily margins:

		Decision (purchases)			
Profit		10	20	30	
Outcome	10	200	20	(160)	
	20	200	400	220	
(sales)	30	200	400	600	

We can now assess how to calculate the remainder of the question contained in part (b)

We can now use the payoff table in order to calculate the expected values associated with each purchase level. Remember the probabilities relate to the outcomes (demand). We are trying to calculate the expected value of our decision (i.e. how many cases to order).

		Decision (purchases)			
Profit		10	20	30	Probability
Outcome	10	200	20	(160)	0.30
	20	200	400	220	0.50
(sales)	30	200	400	600	0.20
Expected values					

The expected value of purchasing 10 cases can be computed:

Outcome (sales)	Margin	Probability	Expected value
10	200	x 0.30 =	60
20	200	x 0.50 =	100
30	200	x 0.20 =	40
		Total	**200**

The expected value of purchasing 20 cases can be computed:

Outcome (sales)	Margin	Probability	Expected value
10	20	x 0.30 =	6
20	400	x 0.50 =	200
30	400	x 0.20 =	80
		Total	**286**

The expected value of purchasing 30 cases can be computed:

Outcome (sales)	Margin	Probability	Expected value
10	(160)	x 0.30 =	(48)
20	220	x 0.50 =	110
30	600	x 0.20 =	120
		Total	182

Therefore the final table becomes:

		Decision (purchases)			
Profit		10	20	30	Probability
Outcome	10	200	20	(160)	0.30
	20	200	400	220	0.50
(sales)	30	200	400	600	0.20
Expected values		200	286	182	

Conclusion:
We can use the various decision criteria that we have at our disposal:

EXPECTED VALUES:
On an expected value basis, we would seek to maximise the expected margin and would order in quantities of 20, since this maximises expected returns ($286).

		Decision (purchases)		
Profit		10	20	30
Outcome	10	200	20	(160)
	20	200	400	220
(sales)	30	200	400	600
Expected values		200	**286**	182

MAXIMAX

Using the maximax decision criteria, we choose the order quantities based on 'the best of the best' basis. This involves looking at each decisions level and identifying the best possible outcome at each level. Once this has been performed, we select the best of these best values. We seek to maximize the maximum possible return:

		Decision (purchases)		
Profit		10	20	30
Outcome	10	200	20	(160)
	20	200	400	220
(sales)	30	200	400	600
Best outcome at each decision level		200	400	600
Maximax decision – select the 'best of the best'.				600

The decision is therefore to order 30 cases, since by doing this we get the best possible return of the maximum possible returns under each possible decision level. This approach would be adopted by a risk seeker.

MAXIMIN

Maximin focuses on the worst outcomes of each decision level. We then choose the order level which will maximise these 'worst' outcomes:

		Decision (purchases)		
Profit		10	20	30
Outcome	10	200	20	(160)
	20	200	400	220
(sales)	30	200	400	600
Worst outcomes at each decision level		200	20	(160)
Maximin decision – select the 'best of the worst'.		200		

The worst outcomes have been identified for each level. The pessimistic investor, or risk-averse investor, will seek to get the best possible return, given these worst possible outcomes for each decision level. Clearly that is where 10 units are ordered. We can make a minimum return of $200 at that level. It is possible in contrast to make a loss of $I60 if 30 cases were ordered, so we choose the option which maximises the returns given the worst possible position at each decision level.

MINIMAX REGRET

Minimax Regret takes an opportunity cost approach to the problem. We compare each outcome with the best possible outcome at that outcome level. The aim is minimise the maximum possible opportunity cost at each level.

Calculation of opportunity costs

The first step is for each outcome to identify the best **outcome** and then see how each decision level return compares to that best outcome.

OUTCOMES: SALES = 10 CASES

		Decision (purchases)		
Profit		10	20	30
Outcome	10	200	20	(160)
(sales)				

For example if we consider sales levels of 10 cases. The best possible return is $200 and is obtained of we order in quantities of 10 cases. There is no lost opportunity if we order in quantities of 10 cases (i.e. we obtain the best possible return if demand is 10 cases by ordering 10 cases).

Had we ordered 20 cases we would have only made $20. We get a return some $180 ($200 - $20) lower than we would have got had we ordered 10 cases. We therefore 'regret' that we have ordered 20 cases –there is an opportunity cost of $180.

Had we ordered 30 cases we would have made a loss of $(160). We get a return some $360 ($200 - $(160)) lower than we would have got had we ordered 10 cases. We therefore 'regret' that we have ordered 30 cases – there is an opportunity cost of $360.

We need to show these opportunity costs in our table.

		Decision (purchases)					
Profit		10		20		30	
Outcome	10	200		20		(160)	
(sales)	Opportunity						
	cost		nil		180		360

OUTCOMES: SALES = 20 CASES:
If we now consider outcomes of 20 cases being sold:

		Decision (purchases)		
Profit		10	20	30
Outcome				
(sales)	20	200	400	220

The best possible return is $400 and is obtained of we order in quantities of 20 cases. There is no lost opportunity if we order in quantities of 20 cases (i.e. we obtain the best possible return if demand is 20 cases by ordering 20 cases).

Had we ordered 10 cases we would have only made $200. We get a return some $200 ($400 - $200) lower than we would have got had we ordered 20 cases. We therefore 'regret' that we have ordered 10 cases –there is an opportunity cost of $200.

Had we ordered 30 cases we would have only made $220. We get a return some $180 ($400 - $180) lower than we would have got had we ordered 20 cases. We therefore 'regret' that we have ordered 30 cases –there is an opportunity cost of $180.

We need to show these opportunity costs in our table.

		Decision (purchases)						
Profit		10		20		30		
Outcome								
(sales)	20 Opportunity cost	200	200	400	nil	220	180	

Outcomes: sales = 30 cases:
IF WE NOW CONSIDER OUTCOMES OF 30 CASES BEING SOLD:

		Decision (purchases)			
Profit		10	20	30	
Outcome					
(sales)					
	30	200	400	600	

The best possible return is $600 and is obtained of we order in quantities of 30 cases. There is no lost opportunity if we order in quantities of 30 cases.

Had we ordered 10 cases we would have only made $200. We get a return some $400 ($600 - $200) lower than we would have got had we ordered 30 cases. We therefore 'regret' that we have ordered 10 cases (opportunity cost of $400).

Had we ordered 20 cases we would have only made $400. We get a return some $200 ($600 - $400) lower than we would have got had we ordered 30 cases. We therefore 'regret' that we have ordered 20 cases (opportunity cost of $200).

We need to show these opportunity costs in our table (shown in **bold**)

		Decision (purchases)					
Profit		10		20		30	
Outcome (sales)	20 Opportunity cost	200	**400**	400	**200**	600	**nil**

Summary and calculation of minimax regret
A summary table of the above

		Decision (purchases)		
Opportunity cost		10	20	30
Outcome	10	nil	180	360
(sales)	20	200	nil	180
	30	400	200	nil
Maximum opportunity cost at each decision level		400	200	360
Minimisation of maximum opportunity cost			200	

We can see that the largest opportunity cost at each decision level can be identified (reading down the table). It is key to note that with the Minimax Regret approach, the aim is to minimize these opportunity costs. Therefore we will order 20 cases at a time, since it is at this level that we only ever stand to lose $200 maximum if the demand is not as we would like!

 Principle

> Making a decision using the expected value, maximax, minimax and minimax regret criteria

EG Learning example 9.1

A sandwich selling shop sells vegetarian sandwiches near a temple. Demand varies depending on weather conditions which affect number of people going to worship. Selling price per sandwich is $2 and cost of each sandwich is $1. Any unsold sandwiches left at the end of the day are sold at a price of $0.50 per sandwich.

The following are the probabilities of weather conditions and demand levels for the next quarter based on past experience.

Good weather	0.4	10,000 units
Poor weather	0.6	4,000 units

The owner has to decide from one of the levels of volume to produce sandwiches.

Required:

(a) Create a payoff table showing all possible profits.
(b) Decide the level of sandwich production on the basis of following decision rules

   (i) Maximax

   (ii) Maximin

   (iii) Expected value

9.4 Value of perfect information

So far in this chapter we have looked at what decisions we would make when there is doubt and uncertainty in our information. However now we will look at what an organisation would do if there was no uncertainty in the information and it could be used to predict the future with 100% accuracy.

The information that we have considered so far is imperfect information as it cannot predict the future with 100% accuracy. Although it is imperfect it is better than no information at all as an organisation needs to make decisions however, due to its inaccuracy it could lead to wrong decisions being made.

Perfect information eliminates all uncertainty in a situation and mean that the decision made by managers will be the optimum course of action.

The value of the perfect information is calculated as the difference between the expected value (EV) of profit with perfect information and the EV of profit without perfect information.

 Learn

9.4.1 EV of profit without perfect information

When we do not have perfect information we would need to make a choice between several courses of action and one way we can do this is to use expected values. We would choose the course of action with the highest expected value of profit. We know that this may not always be the best course of action as it is based on probabilities and what happens in reality may be very different.

9.4.2 EV of profit with perfect information

If we had perfect information then the best course of action would always be chosen. So for each outcome we will identify what the best course of action would be and use this information to calculate our expected value. Although we know what is going to happen with perfect information we still require the probability to calculate an expected value as this relates to the frequency that the outcome will occur. For example if we had an outcome of 100 with a probability of 0.5, with perfect information we know the outcome will be 100 but it will still only happen 50% of the time.

9.4.3 Value of perfect information

The value of perfect information is the difference between the two expected values. It calculates how much an organisation should be prepared to pay to acquire the perfect information. An organisation would not be prepared to pay more than this as it would lower the overall expected profit.

 Principle

How to calculate the value of perfect information

EG **Learning example 9.2**

Using the previous example of Mr Byornbye calculate the value of perfect information.

9.5 Decision trees

A decision tree is a diagram which is used to make decisions by illustrating the choices and possible outcomes of a decision. They can be used to deal with much more complex probability questions to ensure that all data is taken into consideration.

There should be nothing that is new in terms of knowledge within this topic area as you will still be calculating expected values to make a decision. However, this time we will be presenting and evaluating the information in a diagram format.

9.5.1   Drawing the decision tree

The decision tree should be drawn from left to right. Try and make the decision tree as big and as neat as possible and label it clearly. This will help the examiner to see what you have done and award marks.

The following symbols should be used when drawing the tree:

A square is used to represent a decision point. At a decision point the decision-maker has a choice of which course of action he wishes to undertake.

A circle is used to represent an outcome point. The alternatives from here are always subject to probabilities.

 Learn

Then lines, or branches, will be drawn from each decision point and outcome point which will represent the different choices and alternatives.

The tree will start with a decision point and the branches for each decision will be drawn. Label the branches with the decision and any cost associated with it. For example:

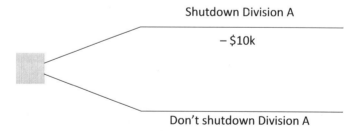

Shutdown Division A

− $10k

Don't shutdown Division A

If the outcome of the decision is certain then the branch does not need to continue. However if the outcome of the decision is uncertain and has various possible outcomes then an outcome point will be inserted at the end of the branch. Each possible outcome will then be shown as a subsidiary branch from the outcome point. The probability of the outcome should be labelled on the branch. For example:

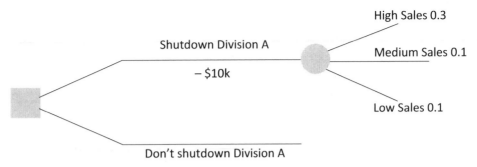

In some situations there will be more than one outcome point or more than one decision point and we can look at how we deal with this and how to evaluate the decision trees using the examples below.

More than one outcome point

This can be understood using the following example:

IE ## Illustrative example 9.5

A fruit company is trying to decide whether or not to advertise an outdoor market. The sales of groceries is dependent on the weather. If the weather is poor it is expected that 5,000 items of fruit will be sold without advertising, which will give a loss of $2,000. There is a 60% chance that the weather will be poor. If the weather is good it is expected that 10,000 items of fruit will be sold without advertising, which gives a profit of $9,000. There is 40% chance that the weather will be good.

If the market is advertised and the weather is poor, there is a 70% chance that the advertising will stimulate further demand and fruit sales will increase to 7,000. This level of sales gives a profit of $3,500. If the weather is good there is a 25% chance the advertising will stimulate further demand and fruit sales will increase to 13,000. This level of sales gives a profit of $15,000.

The cost of advertising is $1,500 and has not been included in the calculation of profit

It is important to read the scenario carefully and establish the following information:

- What is the decision to be made?
- What are the outcomes?

In the scenario above the decision to be made is whether to advertise or not to advertise. There are two outcome points, firstly the weather being poor or bad. This outcome will happen whether the company advertises or not. The second outcome point is there being further demand or not but this outcome will only happen if the company choose to advertise.

Once we have established this information we can now draw and label the decision tree.

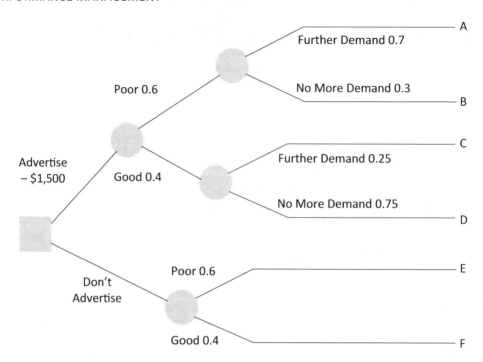

Now the tree has been drawn we need to evaluate the tree to find the expected value of each decision. Once we have calculated this a decision can be made based on the highest expected profit.

One way that the expected value of each decision can be calculated is by evaluating each branch at the end of the tree. In order to do this joint probabilities will need to be calculated. This is calculated by multiplying all the probabilities along the branch together. For example if we decide to advertise and the weather is poor, the joint probability would be 0.6 x 0.7 = 0.42.

Once each branch has been evaluated the branches under each decision should be added together to give the expected value and then the decision should be made based on this expected value. Make sure you clearly state what your decision is in your answer.

Point	Units of Fruit	Profit (x)	probability (p)	px
A	7,000	3,500	0.42	1,470
B	5,000	(2,000)	0.18	(360)
C	13,000	15,000	0.10	1,500
D	10,000	9,000	0.30	2,700
		Less: Advertising cost		(1,500)

Point	Units of Fruit	Profit (x)		probability (p)	px
		EV of Advertise			3,810
E	5,000	(2,000)	0.6		(1,200)
F	10,000	9,000	0.4		3,600
		EV of Don't advertise			2,400

Therefore the company should advertise as it generates the highest expected profit.

Multiple decision points and outcome points

Let us understand this concept with an example:

IE | **Illustrative example 9.6**

Sindha Services has a new product and currently the company has two possible courses of action, to test the product or abandon it.

If the company tests it, the cost will be $50,000 and the results could be positive or negative with probabilities of 0.7 and 0.3. If the result is positive the company could either abandon the product or market it.

If it markets the new product, the outcome might be low, medium, or high demand, and the respective net gains/(losses) would be –$100,000, $100,000 or $500,000. These outcomes have probabilities of 0.1, 0.6 and 0.3 respectively.

If the result of the testing is negative and the company goes ahead and markets the product, estimated losses would be $300,000. If, at any point, the company abandon the product, there would be a net gain of $25,000 from the sale of scrap.

Using a decision tree evaluate whether Sindha Services should test market the product or abandon.

Firstly we need to establish the decision to be made which is whether to test the product or to abandon it.

Secondly we need to establish if there are any outcomes of these decisions and these are whether the test will be whether the test is positive or negative. For the abandonment decision there are no further outcomes or decisions.

After this outcome we need to establish if there are any further decision or outcome points. In this case there is a further decision point which is to decide whether to go ahead and market the product or to abandon it. This decision will be made whether the test is positive or negative.

Finally there is one last outcome point which is the demand which will only occur if they test the product, it is a positive result and then they go ahead to market the product.

Now we have interpreted the information we can now draw the tree.

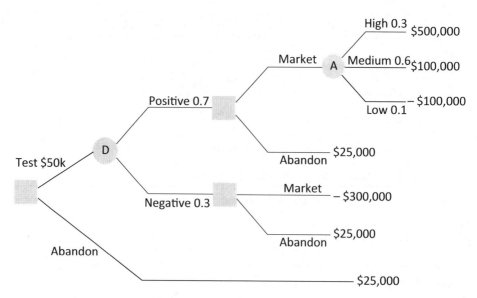

Now we need to evaluate the tree and this time we will use the other approach which is to evaluate the tree from right to left which is sometimes known as 'rollback analysis'.

At each decision point you choose the option which gives the best expected value. At each outcome point you calculate the expected value which could be revenue, cost or profit.

We will now evaluate the above decision tree using this method.

Point A
This is an outcome point and so the expected value should be calculated.

EV = ($500,000 × 0.3) + ($100,000 × 0.6) + (−$100,000 × 0.1)

= $150,000 + $60,000 − $10,000

= $200,000

Point B
This is a decision point and therefore the option that has the highest expected value should be chosen. Therefore this will be the option to market the product as it gives the expected profit of $200,000 which is higher than the option to abandon, which is $25,000.

Point C
This is a decision point and again the option with the highest expected value should be chosen. This will be to abandon the product as this gives an expected profit of $25,000 which is higher than the option to market which is − $300,000.

Point D
This is an outcome point and therefore the expected value should be calculated.

EV = ($200,000 × 0.7) + ($25,000 × 0.3)

= $140,000 + $7,500

= $147,500

Point E

This is a decision point and is the overall decision to be made, whether to test the product or to abandon it. The decision with the highest expected profit should be chosen which is to test the product with an expected profit of $97,500. ($147,500 less the cost of testing $50,000).

 Principle

How to draw and evaluate a decision tree

 Key Learning Points

- Expected values are calculated using:

  $EV = \sum px$ where:

  p = probability of an outcome

  x = value of an outcome (B6b)
- Maximax: Maximise the maximum possible return ('best of the best'). (B6d)
- Maximin: Maximise the worst possible return ('best of the worst'). (B6d)
- Minimax regret: Minimise the maximum opportunity cost. (B6d)
- Value of perfect information is the difference between expected value of profit with perfect information and the expected value of profit without perfect information. (B6f)
- Decision trees are an illustrative approach to making decisions under uncertainty. You should be able to draw and evaluate decision trees. (B6e)

 What's the story?

Stop and think through the 'story' of this chapter and how it links with other chapters (use the Overview to help).

Learning example solutions

EG **Solution 9.1**

(a) Pay off Table:

Possible outcome		Decisions to produce		
		10,000		4,000
		$		$
Good weather 10,000	W1	10,000	W3	4,000
Poor weather 4,000	W2	1,000		4,000

W1:

Sales	$2 x 10,000 units = $20,000
Costs	$1 x 10,000 = (10,000)
Profit	10,000

W2:

Sales	($2 x 4,000 + $0.50 x 6,000) = $11,000
Costs	$1 x 10,000 = (10,000)
Profit	1,000

W3:

Sales	$2 x 4,000 units = $8,000
Costs	$1 x 4,000 = (4,000)
Profit	4,000

(b)

Possible outcome	P	Decisions to produce			
			Px		px
		$	$	$	$
Good weather 10,000	0.4	10,000	4,000	4,000	1,600
Poor weather 4,000	0.6	1,000	600	4,000	2,400
Expected value Σpx			4,600		4,000

    (i) Maximax

Maximum profits	10,000	4,000
Choose the best	10,000	

Therefore the owner should choose to produce 10,000 units

    (ii) Maximin

Minimum Profits	1,000	4,000
Choose the best		4,000

Therefore the owner should choose to produce 4,000 units.

    (iii) Expected value

Expected values have been calculated above, and decision rule is to choose the higher expected value of the outcome which is 4,600. Therefore the owner should choose to produce 10,000 sandwiches.

EG Solution 9.2

EV of profit without perfect information

When the expected value of each decision was calculated the option that was chosen was to purchase 20 cases. This gave an expected value of **$286.**

EV of profit with perfect information

Outcome	Best decision	Profit	Probability	EV
10	Purchase 10	$200	0.3	$60
20	Purchase 20	$400	0.5	$200
30	Purchase 30	$600	0.2	$120
				$380

Value of perfect information	= $380 – $286
	= $94

Provided that the information does not cost more than $94 to collect, it would be worth having this information.

Budgeting

Context

This exam invariably contains a number of questions on performance evaluation and budgeting. It is important to be able to not only compute whether a manager or a division has reached a predetermined target but also to understand and explain why this might not be the case or why there may be significant flaws in the current performance management system.

This chapter contains very useful material to help you to assess the adequacy of a business's ability to set meaningful targets to its staff.

You may be required to assess the adequacy or otherwise of a business's budgetary control system. What the examiner is not usually looking for is a 'textbook' answer. You must try to apply and illustrate good budgetary practice to the scenario.

3Q

1. Do you know what 'principal budget factor' is?

2. What are the different types of budgets?

3. Why do most major supermarkets employ non-participatory budgeting?

10.1 Budgeting

Budgeting has been addressed to some degree at the Management Accounting paper. We need to build our understanding of budgeting from there. The key topics that we will address are:

- **Budgeting types** – different budgetary mechanisms
- **Budgeting controls** – particularly (later in our studies) the use of standard costing and variance analysis, and
- **Forecasting** – how do we *derive* some of the figures used in budgets.

Each will be addressed in turn in depth.

10.1.1 Budget

A budget...

- is a forward thinking plan. Some elements of the plan will be more detailed and frequently prepared than others. For example a cash forecast may be prepared to plan ahead one week, one month or one quarter. This is particularly important for companies who carefully need to assess and manage their cash flow.
- is quantifiable, expressed in both financial ($) and non-financial terms. The business will want to know about how *many* units it has sold (a non-financial quantifiable amount) as well as how *much* it has sold them for (standard sales prices and budgeted total revenue – financial measures).
- is not an open ended forecast, it will be prepared for a finite period of time – often one year. This allows the budget to coincide with the preparation of the financial statements, however more usefully, many businesses are seasonal and would expect their sales and cost patterns to fluctuate over a year. A High Street retailer for example will expect a significant proportion of its annual sales to occur in the month leading up to a big festival such as Christmas.

10.1.2 Objectives of the budgeting process:

The purposes of budgeting types can be summarised in a mnemonic PCCCEMA. It is important to note how any budgeting system that a business is adopting should address one or more of the following:

- **P**lanning – a business needs to map ahead how it intends to operate in its environment. By planning, management are forced to think and plan ahead as to how their business is to operate, compete and grow.
- **C**ontrol – by setting up a budget a business uses standard cost cards. These set out the expected sales price to achieve for goods sold, the expected resources that each unit should consume and at what cost.
- **C**ommunication – the budget is a formal part of the businesses reporting channels, often reflecting the hierarchy of responsibility in the business. The budget may reflect and indeed dictate the intended activities of the business. Senior management for example may, through the budget, set targets for junior management to achieve in terms of sales volume and activity.

- **Co**-ordination – in large organisations especially, it is hard to ensure that all departments are working towards common aim and objectives. For example it is critical that if the sales department are aiming to sell 1,000 units, his must be communicated through the budget to the production department so that they know how many units they are expected to make. The production department will need (via budgets) to communicate with the purchasing department to ensure that enough components are purchased to cope with the production of 1,000 units and so on.
- **Evaluation** – budgeting can allow the business to have a benchmark in order to assess the performance of individual departments, functions or indeed managers within a business. This is a very commonly examined area and is dealt with in later sessions.
- **Motivation** – If a departmental manager is given a budget, it acts as a target for that manager to aspire to. If by achieving that budget the manager is rewarded, the budget acts as an incentive to the manager. If all managers achieve their targets (and are rewarded for doing so) then the business as a whole should achieve its aims and objectives.
- **Authorisation** – budgets can act as a tool to authorise junior management to undertake a particular action. For example if Manager X has $45,000 included in their budget to recruit two new members of staff, then the manager has in essence been authorised to undertake the recruitment and spend a set amount of money doing so.

The above mnemonic can be applied to many exam style scenarios.

 Principle

What is a budget and why is it prepared

10.1.3 The budgeting process

The budgeting process is importantly not just a numerical but also a human communication and interaction exercise. The budgetary process reflects this:

- **Budget committee meets:**
  - The budget committee is usually made up of senior management/directors overseeing the **overall strategy** and **main objectives** of the business. For example the business may have a five-year plan. The annual budgets, in particular its profit forecasts need to map out how the business is to meet the **business aims**.
  - The budget committee may also be concerned with **secondary business objectives** (customer retention levels, achieving industry awards, productivity levels, levels of Research and Development expenditure).
  - The individual department managers will have to prepare their own departmental budget. To ensure that all budgets are prepared in a consistent manner, there will be **underlying assumptions** about core issues such as:

    o Inflation

- o   Interest rates

- o   Exchange rates

- o   Sales growth rates etc...

- The budgetary information will be prepared using **standard documentation** that best meets the organisation's needs.

- **Identify the principal budget factor**
  - The principal budget factor is the limiting factor for the activity of the business. For most businesses this is **sales demand levels** and sales growth that can be achieved. In the short-term there may be restrictions such as labour hours or machine capacity (as we have seen already in limiting factor analysis). For a NFP (Not-For-Profit organisation such as a mutual Building Society, local government department or Trades Union), the principal budget factor may be levels of funding that the NFP can raise.

- **Prepare the sales budget**
  - Assuming Sales is the principle budget factor; the Sales Budget is prepared in **volume** and **sales price** terms.
  - This is a difficult process involving extensive sales and marketing research and assessment of the business's product life cycle. The sales budget is critical to be as accurate as possible. If not, then the budgets that are all driven from the sales budget are likely to be inaccurate as well.

- **Prepare the functional (or departmental) budgets**
  - Although the overall sales targets are likely to be identified by the budget committee, departmental managers will not appreciate having a large amount of their own budgets (on which they are likely to be assessed) imposed on them.
  - Effective budget setting is likely to be **participatory** ('bottom-up'). Each manager will be expected to prepare a budget for their own department.
  - Budgets prepared by departmental managers should be more accurate, since local managers have **good local knowledge.**
  - Additionally local managers will be more motivated if they have **ownership** of that budget. Local managers will be more **motivated** to achieve targets that they have created themselves.
  - Significant dangers of **'bottom-up'** budgeting are:

    - o   local managers may pursue their own objectives which may conflict with overall business aims (e.g. local managers may seek rapid sales growth by reducing sales prices, damaging the company profitability overall).

    - o   Local managers may set targets that are easy to achieve and hence make their overall performance look impressive (possibly in seeking big bonuses at the end of the period). This is **budgetary slack.**

- **Negotiation process**
  - Senior managers and junior managers will review the budget prepared by the junior manager in detail and discuss/negotiate whether the budget is reasonable to both parties. Ideally the targets set need to be fair but not too tough.
  - It is important that the human skills of **compromise** and **negotiation** are utilised. If local managers feel that targets are being imposed on them they will fell demotivated. Similarly, if senior management do not ensure that local targets are in line with corporate plans there will be a lack of **goal congruence**. (Goal congruence occurs when individual and corporate goals dovetail).
  - The negotiation process must end with the **genuine agreement** of all parties.

- **Review process**
  - The whole budgetary process is reviewed and all the subsidiary budgets (e.g. departmental costs and revenues) are consolidated into an overall master budget (e.g. overall business Income Statement).
  - If at this stage a lack of co-ordination between departments is discovered this must be rectified. The budget is checked for **feasibility** – will it work?
  - The budget needs to be compared back to the budgetary aims at the start of the process. Only if the original budgetary aim (e.g. with respect to overall profit) is met, will the master budget (and detailed subsidiary budget) be **acceptable** to the directors and the business. The directors must be careful at this stage if they request (say) further cost cuts to ensure that the original targets are being met, since this may undermine the credibility of the budget process and demotivate junior managers.

- **Formal acceptance of the budget**
  - If the budget committee and the junior managers accept the budget, then any budgetary spend has effectively been **authorised.**
  - Junior managers will then be expected to achieve the targets that they themselves have (hopefully!) set!

 Principle

> The steps involved in the budgeting process

Element in hierarchy	Role of budgets
Strategic planning	Most strategic plans are supported by budgets and plans, at least to give some financial understanding of the implications of the strategy. This will be concerned with resource allocation between departments, and where the claims of competing projects can be assessed. A strategic budget projects revenues and expenses in the future.
Tactical/management control	Budgets are a key management tool, and are used to compare and predict performance. Many firms might prefer to compare with last year for performance issues. They are set annually but typically reviewed monthly for management accounting purposes.
Operational control	Budgets are a basis for establishing the bases for variance analysis, for example actual versus budget costs. These are critical in determining forecast cashflows. These are set annually.

10.1.4   Changing a budgetary system and the types of budget used

For many organisations, a budget is a regular, routine, labour intensive exercise in which sales, production and other departments are all involved. All submit their plans and requirements according to the agreed timetable. Information is gathered in standard formats, there are negotiations to and fro, and there is a set timetable. These budgets may be communicated outside the organisation, eg to bankers.

A budgeting system provides a common language for running the business. A large organisation's accounting data is also structured by a chart of accounts, which sets up coding systems, cost centres. In many systems, standard reports are produced.

Moving from one type of budget or budgetary system to another can cause some problems, depending on the nature of the change.

(a) If this involves changing the chart of accounts or standard reports, then many legacy IT systems will not be able to cope.

(b) Reclassifying and reformatting information can create errors or anomalies.

(c) The old classifications of costs and revenues may not be suitable for the new system. It will therefore be hard to make comparisons or budget to prior year unless 'actuals' are modified also to the new format. Comparing budget performance with prior year, when the budget is being prepared, actual will not be comparing like with like.
New reports and cost classifications may be needed. For example, an organisation moving to Activity Based Budgeting (ABB, see later), will need to identify cost pools, and classify transactions costs accordingly.

(d) A lot of organisational learning will be necessary, not just in the finance department

(e) A radical change to a budgeting system – eg to Zero Based Budgeting (ZBB, see later) in which every activity (and job) has to be justified from the ground up, has to have a significant disruptive effect, and may be a significant organisational change. The costs of change may not be warranted by the budgetary improvements delivered.

Not all changes are quite so radical. Moving from an annual exercise to a 12-month rolling budget may spread the effort over the year and provide more stability

10.2 Types of budget

There are different types of budgets and means of setting budgets.

10.2.1 Incremental budgeting

This is a common, 'simple' and cheap method of creating the figures for use in a budget. Incremental budgeting essentially uses this year's budget as a basis for the next year's budgetary figures.

Next Year's budget = This year's budget ± adjustments.

Adjustments would be needed for factors which may change such as:

- Inflation.
- Known cost increases (e.g. known rent review rises).
- Volume changes (e.g. sales volumes are expected to rise by 3%.
- Planned changes in product mix (e.g. new products that will be introduced and old products withdrawn from the product portfolio).

We therefore accept that current in/efficiencies are acceptable and that only the adjustments to this year's budget require formal acceptance in the budgetary process. The business needs to be careful that budgetary slack does not become engrained in the targets for the business.

 Learn

10.2.2 Periodic budgeting

Budgets are usually prepared separately for one year (e.g. 12 months to 31 December 20X4) from the budget that has been prepared for a previous year (e.g. 12 months to 31 December 20X3). Although 20X4's year's budget may have been prepared incrementally, the **entire** budget (and not just adjustments) will usually require authorisation from the budget committee.

Periodic budgets work well in situations where the underlying environment is very **stable** and predictable (for example a newsagent selling newspapers and confectionary).

 Learn

10.2.3 Participatory budgeting

As we have already seen, active participation from junior management is beneficial in achieving goal congruence.

10.2.4 Comparative budgeting methods:

We can compare the above methods with budgets that are prepared with a different focus in mind:

Incremental budgeting	versus	Zero Based Budgeting (ZBB)
Periodic budgeting	versus	Continuous (rolling) budgets
Participatory budgeting	versus	Non-participatory budgeting

10.2.5 Zero-based budgeting (ZBB)

ZBB are an improvement on incremental budgets.

ZBB involves the simple idea of preparing a budget from a 'zero base' each period (like a 'clean sheet of paper'!). There is no expectation that current activities should continue from one period to the next. ZBB is unlikely to be used frequently in manufacturing industries, where the **manufacturing** processes are likely to be identical or very similar year-on-year. Therefore there is little point in redrafting the entire budget from scratch. The manufacturing process largely dictates how costs are incurred.

ZBB is normally found in **service** industries where costs are more likely to be **discretionary.** There is more flexibility to adapt the service provided from one period to the next to better fit in with (say) customer expectation.

IE Illustrative example 10.1

LSBF could in one year provide students with:

- Tuition Days
- Revision Days
- Study Text Book
- Revision Kit
- Study Notes
- Revision Notes
- Practice Exams

All of these products and services will have their own associated costs. If however student demand is such, or there is a major selling opportunity, LSBF can undertake ZBB and decide to alter their course structure and provision dramatically.

For example LSBF can alter course structure in length and timings, change its course material, run courses from new locations, offer new products (such as video lectures and discussion board) etc. As a service business it is much easier to adapt the mode of delivery of its 'product' and previous budgets will bear little resemblance to future activities (i.e. there is little scope for incremental budgeting).

Organisations considering using ZBB would need to consider the four basic steps to follow:

1. **Prepare decision packages**
   Identify all possible **services** (e.g. courses offered by LSBF) and **levels of service** (e.g. length of course) that may be provided and then cost each service or level of service. These are known individually as **decision packages.**

IE Illustrative example 10.2

LSBF can consider a wide variety of methods of delivering courses. Each possible service or level of service (decision package) needs to be costed (e.g. printing cost of a textbook) and assessed for the likely benefit (e.g. number of students attracted to LSBF courses) it will bring to the organisation.

2. **Rank the decision packages**
   Each decision packages is ranked in order of importance, starting with the mandatory requirements of a department.

IE Illustrative example 10.3

LSBF **have** to provide a tuition and revision course for each paper. These are essential services which must be funded by the business. Other decision packages can then be considered. LSBF may then consider updating its course study notes as being the next most 'value-added' activity. After that the next most important decision packages are ranked. This forces the management to consider carefully what their aims are for the coming year and importantly their priorities.

3. **Funding**
   Identify the level of funding that will be available to the business. This may relate to the amount of cash LSBF has available, its lines of credit with its bankers etc.

4. **Utilise**
   These funds are then used up in the order of the ranking at step 2, until exhausted. The highest ranked decision packages are financed. Allocation of funding continues until it is exhausted (say at the 12th ranked decision package). Any lower-ranking decision packages, being less of a priority to the business may not be funded and are 'shelved' (e.g. the 13th ranked decision package onwards). If however more funding becomes available, then the business can select the next decision package (the 13th) and undertake that decision package.

The key with ZBB is that if focuses the business's attention on where its money must be spent to best effect. It helps the business to prioritise where it should invest, without being dependent on a previous year's budget (as with incremental budgeting). It is a **considered allocation of resources.**

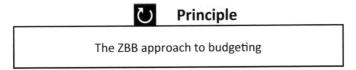

Principle

The ZBB approach to budgeting

Advantages of ZBB (as opposed to incremental budgeting)

1. Emphasis on future need not past actions. ZBB focuses on future plans and is not 'swayed' by what was in last year's budget. The strategies that worked well in the past are no guarantee of future success.
2. Eliminates past errors that may be perpetuated in an incremental analysis. Any inefficiencies or mistakes in previous budgets under incremental budgeting are perpetuated (and often magnified) in future budgets. ZBB eliminates these errors (although the possibility of new errors being introduced cannot be eliminated).
3. A positive disincentive for management to introduce slack into their budget. Decision packages containing budgetary slack are more likely to have low priority when the decision packages are ranked. It is quite possible that these project will not be allocated funds at all (increasing costs > benefit of decision package).
4. A considered allocation of resources. The business does not automatically carry on the projects that they have always performed in the past.
5. Encourages cost reduction. The business may continue projects that it has undertaken in the past, but a close review of costs will have been undertaken.

Disadvantages of ZBB

1. Can be costly and time consuming. ZBB techniques will take a lot of time in terms of training managers in the required techniques and more time and effort in preparing each decision package.
2. May lead to increased stress for management. Managers may become nervous that their decision packages may not be accepted. It is possible that the manager may worry about redundancy if they have too few decision packages that are approved. It is conceivable that managers may put forward unrealistic decision packages to ensure that they are accepted.
3. Only really applicable to a service environment. It is not applicable in a manufacturing environment where the production process dictates how the production is undertaken.
4. May 're-invent' the wheel each year. It is quite conceivable that if ZBB is undertaken each year, the same decision packages are accepted. This is an inefficient approach to budgeting.
5. May lead to lost continuity of action and short-term planning. The business may alter its activities and plans year by year, causing a lack of consistency and possible drift from its strategic aims. For example if LSBF decided one year to run its courses entirely online and the next year purely in the classroom, it would antagonise students and have serious repercussions for resource allocation and

usage (for example having to find and kit out premises and recruit tutors at very short notice).

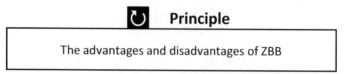

Principle

The advantages and disadvantages of ZBB

10.2.6   Continuous budgeting ('rolling' budgets)

As we have seen, in a periodic budgeting system the budget is normally prepared for one year, a totally separate budget will then be prepared for the following year. In the example below, a separate budget is prepared for 20X3 and then another separate budget for 20X4 (although 20X4 may be prepared on an incremental basis from 20X3's figures). This works well in a stable environment, although if the environment does change then the budget can become out-of-date quickly.

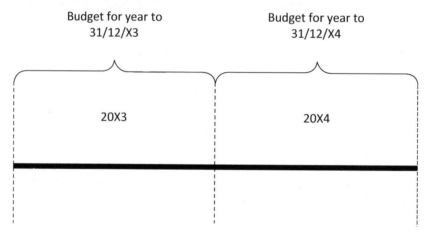

In continuous budgeting the budget from one period is 'rolled on' from one year to the next. It operates when the environment in which the business operates is **dynamic** or changing on an ongoing basis.

Typically the budget is prepared for one year, only the first quarter in detail, the remainder in outline. After the first quarter's results are known and any changes in the environment are assessed, the budget is revised for the following three quarters based on the first quarter's actual results. Additionally a further quarter is budgeted for.

This means that the budget will again be prepared for 12 months in advance. This process is repeated each quarter (or month or half year). In the diagram below the budget is set for the year to 31/12/X3. At the end of the first quarter (Q1) in 20X3, the budget is prepared again for the year to the end of the 1st quarter in 20X4. The budget is prepared in detail to Q2 in 20X3 and in outline for the remaining 9 months to the end of Q1 20X4.

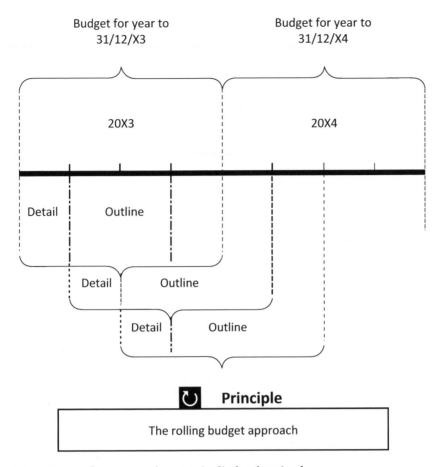

Budget for year to
31/12/X3

Budget for year to
31/12/X4

20X3

20X4

Detail

Outline

Detail

Outline

Detail

Outline

↻ **Principle**

The rolling budget approach

Advantages (compared to periodic budgeting)

- The budgeting process should be more accurate. The business is able to adapt its plans in order to reflect the changing environment in which it operates.
- Much better information upon which to appraise the performance of management. This should make performance assessment fairer and more reasonable. For example if a restaurant changes its menu part way through a year and now cooks using organic ingredients, the budget and standards would need to change in order to reflect the higher costs that are likely to be involved in the meals served.
- The budget will be much more 'relevant' by the end of the traditional budgeting period. With periodic budgeting, if the budget becomes out of date and unrealistic, the budgetary system will lose credibility quickly. Managers will be demotivated if they feel they are being assessed against unrealistic targets.
- It forces management to take the budgeting process more seriously.

Disadvantages

- More costly and time consuming. Budgets are assessed and redrafted every 3 months.

- An increase in budgeting work may lead to less control of the actual results. The business may be in danger of spending too much time focusing on budgeting and not enough time on the day-to-day running of the business (for example, managing customer relationships).

 **Principle**

> Advantages and disadvantages of rolling budgets

10.2.7 Non-participatory budgeting

Some organisations may not require junior management to participate in the budgetary process. This may be because of security or more likely due to centralised nature of the company. For example major supermarkets often have a highly centralised:

- pricing structure,
- selling and display policy,
- buying strategies etc...

Advantages

- Saves time and money. This method is clearly inexpensive and quick.
- Individual wishes of senior management will not be diluted by others' plans. This is important to ensure that the corporate goals are met. For example, if the business is in crisis, central management may have to force their plans through and impose the plans on divisional managers.
- Reduces the likelihood of information 'leaking' from the company. For example, confidentiality may be very important. If a brand new patented product is about to be launched, only Senior Management and divisional managers directly affected by the new product will be informed of its launch. Secrecy is vital!

Disadvantages

- Essentially the advantages of participatory budgeting are a mirror image of the disadvantages of non-participatory budgeting.

 **Principle**

> Issues with non-participatory budgeting

10.2.8 Activity-based budgeting (ABB)

Clearly ABB is closely related to activity-based costing (ABC). ABC provides four key points with reference to ABB:

- ABC focuses on overhead costs
- ABC should provide accurate product cost information

- Overheads are accumulated into cost pools relating to key activities within the business
- Overheads are absorbed from cost pools on the basis of an appropriate cost driver (absorbed on a cost driver rate).

Applicability of ABB (and ABC):

ABB/ABC is used in environments with the following criteria:

1. Complex manufacturing environment.
2. Wide range of products.
3. High proportion of overhead costs.
4. Competitive market.

Benefits of ABB

- Planning – better budgetary planning should arise through ABB:
    - more accurate overhead cost allocation should occur giving a better understanding of how overhead costs are incurred.

- Control – better cost control could accrue:
    - Through a better understanding of costs and cost drivers, management get a clearer picture of how to control costs and the incidence of the use of costs drivers.
    - For example production set-up costs are incurred on the basis of the number of batches processed. If production runs can be extended (i.e. more items processed per batch), then the number of cost drivers reduces and hence the production set-up cost should fall. The key is not to concentrate on the cost itself but on the activity that **drives** the cost.

Key point

Whenever discussing ABB in an exam context a balance must be drawn between the better information that is provided against the high cost of implementation and maintaining an ABB system.

 Principle

Activity-based approach to budgeting

10.3 Budgetary control

Budgetary Control is often key to any exam question. Often the budgetary control systems being operated are inappropriate or demotivating to divisional managers. For example, a divisional manager will be highly demotivated if he/she is assessed against an unrealistic budget. This will be worsened if the manager misses out on a profit-related bonus or promotion because of an inappropriate budget against which their performance has been assessed.

Budgetary control therefore involves the use of budgeted data for control purposes. The budget is used as the benchmark or yardstick against which the actual results may be compared. Any differences can then be investigated and appropriate action taken. Budgetary control is closely related to **responsibility accounting** because it gives individual managers the responsibility to achieve results.

An overview of the budgetary process is set out on the next page:

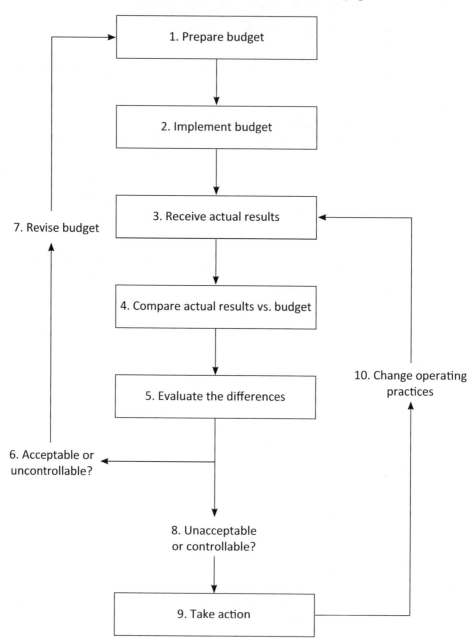

10.3.1   The steps

1. Prepare **budget:** Once the corporate aims and objectives of the business have been established, the targets that the business has to achieve in the budget period will be established. The divisional and master budgets will be prepared.
2. **Implement the budget:** The divisional budgets will be put into action by the divisional managers.
3. **Receive actual results:** The actual results (e.g. sales levels, sales revenues, costs, profit levels etc...) will be periodically received (e.g. monthly) by the divisional managers and consolidated into overall results for the Board of Directors to consider.
4. **Compare actual results vs. budget:** Both the divisional managers (local level) and the Board of Directors (business-wide level) will compare the actual results achieved and measure against budgets and standards. It is at this stage that variance analysis and other performance measurement techniques (e.g. increase in market share, reduction in wastage levels etc...) can be assessed.
5. **Evaluate the differences:** the managers/directors need to assess whether that differences are due to factors that are possible to operationally correct or whether the targets/budgets will need adjusting for the future.
6. **Acceptable/uncontrollable?:** The factors leading to the differences at steps 4 & 5 may be outside the business's control. For example, power cost variances may be highly adverse because of a rise in the world oil price. There is little that the business can do about this in the short term and so this factor is outside of the responsibility of the local managers. In variance analysis these are known as *planning variances.*
7. **Revise budget:** The natural step after deciding that a difference is outside the business's control is to revise future budgets to give more accurate benchmarks. This is highly subjective (see later – budget padding, slack and games) but may be necessary if divisional managers are not going to be demotivated by being assessed against targets that are unrealistic and unattainable. Similarly the business can only gauge its progress against reasonable targets and benchmarks.
8. **Unacceptable or controllable?:** The factors leading to the differences at steps 4 & 5 may be within the business's control. For example material price variances may be highly adverse due to poor negotiation and buying strategies with suppliers. In variance analysis these are known as *operational variances.*
9. **Take Action:** The managers must therefore take corrective action to alter the current operating practices of the business. The cost of materials purchased here is within the control of the managers and the business.
10. **Change operating practices:** The actual operations of the business will need adjusting if the differences are unacceptable and/or controllable. In the example at step 9 local managers will need to ensure that purchasing managers are

negotiating more rigorously with suppliers in order to save the business money overall. This should then impact future operating results.

 **Principle**

Steps in the budgetary control process

EG Learning example 10.1

Selhurst division has the following budgeted and actual information:

	Units	Cost
Budget	1,000	$20,000
Actual	1,200	$22,500

Required:

(a) Has the division performed better or worse than expected?
(b) If we are now told that $10,000 of budgeted costs are variable, the remainder being fixed: are we able to tell whether the company has done better or worse than expected?

EG Learning example 10.2

Complete a budgetary control statement using a flexible budgeting approach:

	Original budget	Actual results
Sales units	1000	1200
	$	$
Variable costs:		
Direct material	10,000	12,500
Direct labour	15,000	17,000
Variable overheads	25,000	27,000
Sub-total	50,000	56,500
Fixed overheads	25,000	33,500
Total cost	75,000	90,000

EG Learning Example 10.3

The take-up of beyond budgeting by businesses has been reasonably slow. Think of reasons why this might be so.

10.4 Behavioural aspects of budgeting

It is important to appreciate that budgeting is largely a **human** exercise and many exam questions are based around areas where a manager's performance may be assessed against unfair or unreasonable budgets. We not only need to consider **why** the budget is unreasonable, but also to consider **what** the effect is likely to be on the manager's behaviour and attitudes.

It is very easy for the budgetary process to cause **dysfunctional** activity. For example, if junior management believe that a budget imposed upon them is unattainable, their aim may well be to ensure that the budget is not achieved, thereby proving themselves to be correct. This behaviour is unlikely to motivate the manager and will certainly not contribute towards the business meeting its aims and goals.

Budgets need to be set at a level that is tough enough to challenge the manager, but be attainable so that the manager will feel motivated to achieve it (particularly if the budget is linked to the business's reward schemes).

10.4.1 Promoting goal congruence

Goal congruence exists when the personal aims and goals of individual manager coincide with the corporate goals of the business. This is summarised well in the following model:

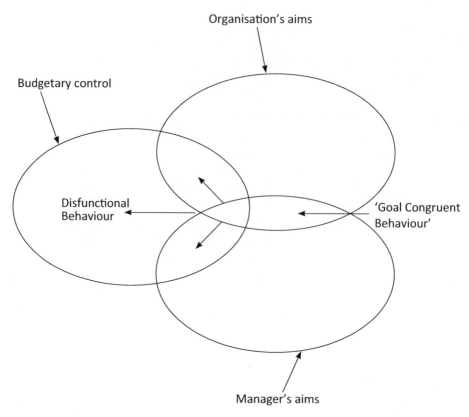

The key to recognise here is that the aims of the manager and the organisation will only overlap in certain areas. For example, the manager may be interested in overall profitability, if he holds shares in the business. However there will be many aims of the business (e.g. development of new products or marketing policies in another part of the business) that the manager will have no interest in.

Similarly the organisation's aims may coincide with the manager's aims in areas such as capital expenditure budgets granted in the manager's area of control. However the manager may have personal aims which the business is not interested in (for example, reducing his or her golf handicap).

The key is to try to ensure that there is better overlap between these two sets of aims (denoted by the **grey** arrows on the diagram). This is where the business tries to promote **goal congruence.** The business can attempt to get a budgetary control system to assist in this process. The budgetary control system (particularly if linked to a rewards system such as bonuses, promotion etc.) can encourage the manager to work harder and smarter, so the manager's aims move closer to the business, and the business's aims closer to the manager.

Dysfunctional behaviour can occur often due to unforeseen circumstances. This is behaviour that is desired by neither the manager, nor the company, but arises because inappropriate budgetary control systems have been applied.

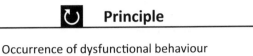

Principle

Occurrence of dysfunctional behaviour

Examples of dysfunctional behaviour include:

- **Budgetary slack (or padding)** – the manager may prepare budgets with inherent inefficiencies built in. This will make the budget easier to achieve and possibly earn a bonus.

 Learn

- **Gaming** – the manager sets targets that are not over ambitious. If for example a manager sets a growth target for sales of just 3%. If that target is achieved this year, next year's target should not be too strenuous. Next year's target may only be another rise of (say) 3%.

 Learn

- **Management 'fraud'** – management may deliberately manipulate the accounts or underlying business activities in order to achieve targets. If, for example, a business is underachieving on its sales budget, the sales manager may lie to customers, warning them of a likely price rises early next year. The sales manager may encourage customers to stockpile goods now to protect themselves from the price rise. This will boost the manager's sales and hence the sales manager will achieve a bonus. From the business's perspective, customers may stop purchasing from the business when they subsequently discover that they have been duped.

 Learn

- **Conflict** – managers may benefit from the misfortunes of others in the business. For example the manager in Branch A of a retail shop chain may have bought too much of a perishable good. The manager in Branch B may only agree to buy this excess stock from Branch A at an unrealistically low price, thus exploiting the Branch A's poor buying decision.

Learn

- **Short-termism** – managers may make decisions to ensure that the budget is made this year, without considering future years. For example, often a 'discretionary' expense could be a business's training budget. If this is cut, this year's profit target may be reached but at the expense of the future development of the business.

 Learn

10.4.2   Participation of employees in negotiating targets

Benefits

- Targets are likely to be more realistic, based on what an employee can actually achieve
- Targets are likely to be more motivating if an employee has participated in target setting
- Whilst participating in the target setting process, the employee will be able to identify resource needs which can be brought into discussions
- Dependencies will be revealed in the process, for example if an employee relies on another department for support in reaching a target

Drawbacks

- Some employees will set targets they think they can achieve, not 'stretch' targets that management might prefer
- There will be a high incentive to set 'easy' targets, to make it easy to earn a bonus.
- The target-setting process may not be linked to the real performance of the business: an individual may only be effective as a member of the team. The employee will only focus on the target not the wider context of the team.

10.5   Behavioural aspects and beyond budgeting

Traditional budgeting has been criticised as bureaucratic and the control systems that it uses are said to stifle businesses. Also, it looks backwards at previous years and doesn't consider the changes that are happening in the business that may be affecting the future of the organisation. Traditional budgeting is predictable but it takes up a lot of time and may not be right for a fast-moving organisation.

10.5.1 Criticisms of traditional budgeting are that it:

1. fixes the company's thinking and how it reacts to new events,
2. takes into account the previous year's reality only, ignoring the cost drivers of the organisation and not challenging non-value-added costs,
3. ignores many future issues and complexities,
4. is time-consuming and expensive, using a lot of finance staff and the time of operational management, so adds little value,
5. is subject to internal bargaining between divisions and managers, as managers try to obtain as easy a budget as possible,
6. looks internally far more than externally,
7. may make managers complacent.

 Learn

10.5.2 In response to this, the 'beyond budgeting' approach has been developed. What this means is the following:

- Rolling budgets, updated on a regular basis, even monthly, are produced.
- These rolling budgets will be based on key performance indicators (KPIs).
- The budgets produced will compare the performance of the parts of the organisation to external comparisons more than past performance.

 Learn

These all mean that the management of future results is more important than what has previously happened to the organisation. It allows managers to react to external changes and be more innovative to try to succeed.

We have seen many situations where there are major changes in businesses and managers need to react quickly. Examples include supermarkets and high street shops, which have been affected by the emergence of online shopping, taxis, which have been affected by apps such as Uber, and publishers which have been affected by e-books and the large amount of readily available information on the Internet. Businesses have to change quickly and those that haven't changed have often disappeared.

Beyond budgeting:

1. is motivational as it makes managers think and challenges them to do well,
2. is team-based, as no one person can achieve everything by themselves,
3. focuses organisations on what most consider to be the key stakeholders of a business: their customers,
4. is reliant on good information systems on the organisation,
5. helps to free resources for new areas of business that become apparent.

 Learn

This all leads to a focus on competitive success based on current issues rather than internally and past issues.

This makes a lot of sense for knowledge-based organisations, as they are often subject to rapid change, though it is relevant to most organisations. There is likely to be improved information systems in organisations using beyond budgeting, and high quality staff in order to make beyond budgeting work well.

Key Learning Points

- Budgeting process:
    - Budget committee – overall responsibility
    - Identify principal budget factor
    - Set sales budget
    - Draw up functional/departmental budgets
    - Negotiation with junior management
    - Review

- Types of budget: attributes and advantages vs disadvantages
    - Incremental vs zero-based budgeting
    - Periodic vs continuous
    - Participatory vs non-participatory
    - Activity-based budgeting (C1e)

- Budgetary control
    - Differences between actual and budgeted results
    - Acceptable/uncontrollable vs unacceptable/controllable
    - Fixed vs flexible/flexed budgets (C1d)

What's the story?

Stop and think through the 'story' of this chapter and how it links with other chapters (use the Overview to help).

Learning example solutions

EG Solution 10.1

(a) At a high level we can perform a 'variance analysis' between budgeted and actual costs:

	Activity (units)	Cost	
Budgeted costs	1,000 units	$20,000	
Actual costs	1,200 units	$22,500	
Variance		$2,500	Adverse

This clearly shows that the division has underperformed, spending $2,500 more than expected (an 'adverse' variance).

This is a reasonable comparison if the costs are entirely fixed. Fixed costs should not vary with activity levels and the divisional manager appears to have overspent.

If however a significant proportion of the costs are variable this is **not** a reasonable comparison. The divisional manager is likely to be highly demotivated if being assessed against an unrealistic or unflexed budget. For example if we assume that the cost per unit is $20/unit. We would **expect** costs to rise with activity levels. We would expect costs to rise to 1,200 units x $20/unit = $24,000 if the costs are variable.

Our variance now becomes:

	Activity (units)	Cost	
Budgeted costs	1,000 units	$20,000	
'Flexed' budget cost	1,200 units x $20/unit	$24,000	
Actual costs	1,200 units	$22,500	
Variance		$1,500	Favourable

The manager has now spent wisely and should be rewarded for delivering a favourable position, spending $1,500 less than expected (a 'favourable' variance).

FIXED BUDGETS
The problem is that we do not know from the information given whether the underlying costs are indeed fixed or variable. In this situation the business has prepared a **fixed budget**. We only know the budgeted cost base at a single level of activity with this fixed budget. We are unable to perform detailed budgetary control without more detailed information about the division's cost behaviour.

(b) In this situation we are given more budgetary cost details and are in a position to more accurately assess actual costs against a reasonable target.

FLEXED BUDGETS

A budget prepared with the costs classified as either fixed or variable can be adjusted to reflect actual output activity. This will allow us to perform **meaningful** budgetary control. The budget may be prepared at any activity level and can be **'flexed'** or changed to the actual level of activity for budgetary control purposes.

We can summarise how costs are expected to behave activity levels differ from budget:

Cost	Expected to rise if activity rises?
Variable costs	**Yes**
Fixed costs	**No**

In our example we can now prepare a more sophisticated budget vs. actual comparison:

Using the information available we can now assess from the information given, that:

	Activity level	
Total budgeted costs	1,000 units	$20,000
Total variable costs		$10,000
÷ budgeted units		1,000 units
= variable cost/unit		$10/unit
Variable costs @1,200 units **(a flexed budget)** 1,200 units x $10/unit		$12,000
Total budgeted costs –		$20,000
Total variable costs =		$10,000
Fixed costs		$10,000

Actual costs versus a flexed budget becomes:

Original budget	Flexed budget	Actual cost $	Variance $
Variable costs	10,000	12,000	
Fixed costs	10,000	10,000	
Flexed budget for 1,200 units	22,000	22,500	**500** adverse

We now have a more reasonable overall comparison of the division's performance.

EG Solution 10.2

We can note from the table that the actual level of activity (1,200 units) is greater than budgeted (1,000 units). Therefore we must flex the variable costs to reflect that the actual level of activity is higher than the budgeted level of activity.

It is important to calculate the unit variable costs to be able to flex the original budget effectively to the actual activity level of 12,000 units:

	Unit variable cost	Flexed budget for 1,200 units
Direct materials	$\dfrac{\$10,000}{1,000 \text{ units}} = \$10/\text{unit}$	1,200 units x $10/unit = **$12,000**
Direct labour	$\dfrac{\$15,000}{1,000 \text{ units}} = \$15/\text{unit}$	1,200 units x $15/unit = **$18,000**
Variable overheads	$\dfrac{\$25,000}{1,000 \text{ units}} = \$25/\text{unit}$	1,200 units x $25/unit = **$30,000**

The fixed costs are not expected to change with activity levels and are not flexed!

Our budgetary control statement becomes:

	Original budget $	Flexed budget $	Actual cost $	Variance $
Direct materials	10,000	12,000	12,500	500 A
Direct labour	15,000	18,000	17,000	1,000 F
Variable overheads	25,000	30,000	27,000	3,000 F
Sub total	50,000	60,000	56,500	3,500 F
Fixed overheads	25,000	25,000	33,500	8,500 A
Total costs	75,000	85,000	90,000	5,000 A

A = adverse variance (actual costs > flexed budget cost)

F = favourable variance (actual costs < flexed budget cost)

We can see that the business has spent $3,500 less on variable overhead than expected when the actual variable costs incurred are compared to a flexed budget. The detailed variances explaining this have been seen in your earlier studies and will be re-visited in later sessions.

Unfortunately the business has significantly overspent on fixed overheads and will need to take corrective action accordingly. Either the budget is unrealistic or the operational cause of the fixed costs needs investigating.

EG **Solution 10.3**

Possible reasons for slow uptake of beyond budgeting include:

- Organisations are reluctant to remove existing internal systems, due to the cost of doing so and the inertia of staff.
- Organisations that operate in slow-moving environments may not feel the need to use beyond budgeting.
- Many other organisations may feel that there will not be enough changes in a year to warrant using it.
- Using rolling budgets brings more work, if budgets need to be revised each month, say.
- Enough allowance can be made at the end of each budgeting period if there have been environment changes, even within a fast-moving environment, to warrant not making the switch to beyond budgeting.

Quantitative Aids to Budgeting

Context

This chapter emphasises the ability of data analysis to provide information in a manner that allows for forecasting or predicting future results.

There is no shortcut to learning the techniques illustrated here. Make sure in particular that you are able to forecast using whatever technique is present in the question. The learning curve appears to be the most popular question area over time.

3Q

1. Can you explain the high–low method of separating fixed and variable costs?

2. Can you draw and describe a learning curve?

3. In your exam, what are the two steps you would use in a learning curve application question?

11.1 Estimating a straight line cost relationship

We need to be able to separate the costs into fixed and variable elements and be able to forecast those values at a range of activity levels.

11.1.1 Theory reminder

Fixed cost	Variable cost
A cost which remains constant regardless of the level of activity within the relevant range of activity.	A cost which varies proportionately with activity. Variable costs per unit will remain constant on a per unit basis.

11.1.2 High-low method

A simple method to separate fixed costs from the variable costs by using only two pairs of data. Given a range of pairs of data only the high and low level of activities are picked with their associated costs. From these two values we can then calculate the variable cost per unit and the fixed cost in total

Level of activity = LofA

$$\text{Variable cost/Unit} = \frac{(\text{Cost at the high LofA} - \text{Cost at the low LofA})}{\text{high LofA} - \text{low LofA}}$$

 Learn

Fixed cost = Total cost − Variable cost

 Learn

EG Learning example 11.1

A process has the following recorded costs for the past four months:

Month	Level of activity (units)	Cost ($)
1	1,500	12,000
2	2,400	15,500
3	3,000	16,500
4	2,000	14,800

Required:

Analyse the cost into

    (a) Variable cost per unit

    (b) Fixed cost in total

    (c) Predict the cost at a level of activity of 2,800 units

11.1.3   Problems with the high-low method

The high-low method is a simple technique that suffers from two significant weaknesses:

1. Only two pairs of data are used even if there is more data available.
2. The pairs of data used are at the extreme values which may not be representative of the overall data.

11.1.4   Reminder

The dependent variable is y and must always be on the vertical axis.

Independent variable is x and always goes on the horizontal axis.

The equation of the line of best fit is **Y = a + bx.**

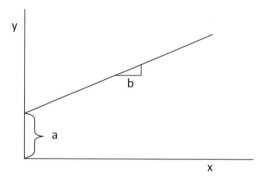

The key is to calculate the values for a and b using the estimating formulae. If we have these values we have our best fit equation that can then be used for forecasting purposes.

The estimating formulae are as follows

$$b = \frac{n\Sigma xy - \Sigma x\Sigma y}{n\Sigma x^2 - (n\Sigma x)^2}$$

$$a = \frac{\Sigma y}{n} - b\frac{\Sigma x}{n}$$

11.2   Learning curve

A statistical relationship relating to learning of a complex operation, that labour time per unit falls as a complex task is repeated. As workers become more familiar with the production of a new product or task, average time (and average cost) will decline and exhibit a statistical relationship. It can be stated as follows:

"As cumulative production doubles from the first unit, the cumulative average time per unit falls by a constant percentage."

 Learn

11.2.1   Application of learning curve

Whenever you are using the learning curve the meaning of the sentence above cannot be over emphasised. In particular the fact that we always start from the first unit and any calculation must commence from that unit. If that is understood and always acted upon then any learning curve calculation should not present a problem.

To start with the illustration will show how the learning curve works by doubling the production, This technique is not very helpful in more complex computations but is often examined.

IE   Illustrative example 11.1

If the first unit requires 100 hours and the learning curve rate is 80%, calculate the following cumulative and incremental data.

Cumulative units	Average time per unit	Cumulative total time	Incremental (additional) units	Incremental (additional) total time	Average time per unit
1 unit	100 hours × 0.8	100 hrs	1 unit	100 hrs	100 hrs
2 unit	80 hours × 0.8	160 hrs	1 unit	60 hrs	60 hrs
4 units	64 hours × 0.8	256 hrs	2 units	96 hrs	48 hrs
8 units	51.2 hours	409.6 hrs	4unit	153.6 hrs	38.4 hrs

Graphical illustration

The relationship can be illustrated on a graph, after a certain point the learning curve effect will cease. At that point the time taken per unit is described as being in a steady state.

The y value will represent the cumulative average time per unit and the x value will represent the cumulative units produced.

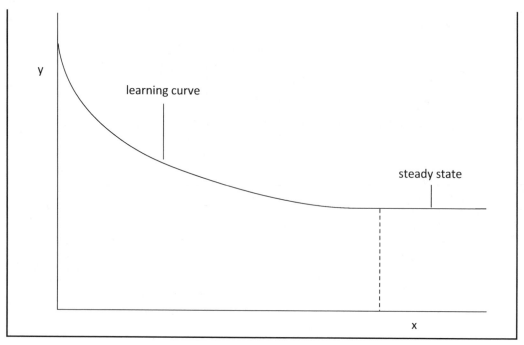

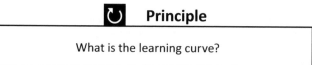 **Principle**

What is the learning curve?

Formula

The graphical relationship can be described by a formula which is given by the examiner with a full description of what each element means. All you need to know is how to apply the formula

$y = ax^b$

Where

y = average time (or average cost) per unit

a = time (or cost) for first unit

$b = slope = \dfrac{\log r}{\log 2}$ (r = rate of learning)

x = cumulative output

b – the learning curve coefficient

 Given

The b value may be required to be calculated. This is not difficult so long as you possess a scientific calculator. Make sure that you are able to calculate the following values.

Learning curve rate	b – learning curve coefficient
90%	log 0.9/ log 2 = - 0.152
80%	log 0.8/ log 2 = - 0.322

Note: Both 90% and 80% are popular rates with examiners but if you can apply this calculation you can calculate the learning curve coefficient for any rate.

Application of the learning curve formula

Remember the key is to understand that we always calculate cumulative values using the learning curve therefore always do the questions in two steps:

1.   Use the learning curve to calculate the appropriate cumulative values needed;

2.   Apply the information to the specific needs of the question which may mean an incremental value has to be calculated, see below how this works.

EG Learning example 11.2

If the first unit requires 100 hours and the learning curve rate is 80%, calculate the following cumulative and incremental data.

Time taken for

   (a) 2nd unit
   (b) 3rd unit

After seeing how the formula works now we can consider more complex requirements. Note that many questions focus on batches of units rather than units of production when considering cumulative production. Always make sure that you understand the relationship between units and batches when looking at exam questions.

Also note that learning curve relates to labour and labour related costs. This means that if variable overheads are absorbed on labour hours then they too will be affected by the learning curve.

IE Illustrative example 11.2

A company is introducing a new product that is produced in a labour intensive environment. The first batch of 100 units is expected to take 20 hours. A 90% learning curve rate is expected to apply.

Each labour hour costs $12/hour and the variable overhead rate per hour is $20/hour. A steady state is expected to be reached after 10,000 units. The budgeted production per month is 4,000 units. Production commences at the beginning of the month.

Required:

Calculate the labour time for the first 3 months in which the product is produced.

Learning curve working

What cumulative production values are needed?

We need the value for the end of each month (4,000, 8,000, 10,000) but note that the learning effect finishes at 10,000 units. If a steady state is reached we need the time taken for the last unit during the learning effect, in this case the 10,000th unit. All units produced thereafter will take this time per unit.

Remember that the learning curve relates to batches and not units. Therefore it makes sense to convert all the unit information into batches.

Units	Batches
4,000	40
8,000	80
10,000	100

Note that we need to calculate the time taken by each unit at steady state production. This is done by taking the total time taken for 100 batches less the time taken for 99 batches. This will give us the time taken for the 100th batch which is the point at which steady state production begins.

Applying the learning curve

$b = \log 0.9 / \log 2.0 = -0.152$		Cum ave time per batch
X = 40	$y = 20 \times 40^{-0.152}$	= 11.416 hours
X = 80	$y = 20 \times 80^{-0.152}$	= 10.274 hours
X = 100	$y = 20 \times 100^{-0.152}$	= 9.932 hours
X = 99	$y = 20 \times 99^{-0.152}$	= 9.947 hours

Now interpret the information in the manner needed to answer the question

Month 1	Total hours	
Total time for the first 40 batches		
40 batches x 11.416 hours per batch	456.64 hours	
Month 2		
Total time for batches 41 to 80		
Total time for 80 batches		

Month 1	Total hours	
80 batches x 10.274 hours per batch	821.92 hours	
Less Total time for 40 batches		
(see above)	(456.64 hours)	
		365.28 hours

Month 3 (remember that learning curve ceases at 10,000 units and so some of the batches will be at steady state)

Total time for batches 81 to 100		
Total time for 100 batches		
100 batches x 9.932 hours per batch	993.2 hours	
Less total time for 80 batches		
(see above)	(821.92 hours)	
		171.28 hours
Steady state production batches 101 to 120		
Time taken for 100th batch		
100 batches		
(see above)	993.20 hours	
99 batches		
99 batches x 9.947 hours/ batch	984.75 hours	
	8.45 hours	
X 20 batches	x 20 =	169.0 hours
Total time taken in the 3rd month		340.28 hours

Note to get the labour related cost we must add the labour rate of $12/hour to the variable overhead cost per hour of $20/hour.

 Principle

How to apply the learning curve to labour cost calculations

The application of the learning curve is important and can be found in questions involving:

1. pricing;
2. budgeting;
3. standard costing; and
4. decision-making.

11.2.2   Determining the learning rate

How should managers determine what learning rate to apply to a new product?

(a) They can get data from similar products in the past, and plot the learning rate against this.

A simple way is, from the historic data, to identify how long it took to double production on similar products, or to conduct research. If the process is more complicated, they may want to look at it, as more complex processes over more potential for learning.

IE   Illustrative example 11.3

Example using very simple data

Production of a unit doubled from four to eight units

Units produced	Time
4 units	4200
8 units	7560

The learning rate can be crudely estimated as (7,560 – 4,200)/4200 = 80%.

You might be given production schedules that have more than doubled on a number of occasions. How do you estimate the learning rate from this?

IE   Illustrative example 11.4

To calculate 'r' the rate of learning, let's use another example

Units produced	Time per unit (hours)
1 unit	60 hours
2 units	You don't have data
4 units	45.1 hours

Here, production has doubled twice, from one to 2 units, and from 2 to 4 units, so you know that

- 60 x the learning rate = time for 2 units
- Time for two units x the learning rate is 45.1

Therefore 45.1/60 = the learning rate squared

So the learning rate is the square root of [45.1/60], or approximately 87%

If production had doubled again, and you were given 8 units, you could have to apply the square root twice.

IE | **Illustrative example 11.5**

Let us assume we have 64 batches, which cumulatively took 10.3125 hours per batch, but the first batch took 25 hours.

Remember, to get to 64 from 1 by doubling production, we double production from 1 to 2, from 2 to 4, from 4 to 8, from 8 to 16, from 16 to 32 and from 32 to 64, in other words five times

Apply learning curve formula, where y is the time to produce the batch in question, a is the first batch, x is cumulative output and b is the slope, which the log r/log 2, with r being the rate of learning. So let's start:

$y = ax^b$

$10.3125 = 25 \times 64^b$

$64^b = 10.3125/25$

Using logarithms, and some simple algebra:

$b \log 64 = \log(10.3125/25)$

$b = \log(10.3125/25) / \log 64$

However, we know that b = log (Learning Rate)/log 2

So log r (ie log of the learning rate) = log (10.3125/25) x log 2/log 64 = -0.212922

So Learning Rate = 10 ^ -0.212922 = 0.8628 = 86.27%

11.3 Spreadsheets in budgeting

Spreadsheets are used as modelling and decision making tools and are very versatile. In a budgeting process, the finance department might typically send out a 'budget pack' showing the required format for submissions.

11.3.1 Benefits of using spreadsheets in budgets

- Most managers know how to use spreadsheets at a basic level
- Spreadsheets offer high-level modelling tools which some accounting processing systems do not possess: using spreadsheets makes it easier to do sensitivity and another analyses on budget figures.
- It is easy to aggregate spreadsheet submissions if in a common format.
- The accounting system may be organised on a functional basis, eg most companies have a common payroll system.
- Spreadsheets may be easier to use for budget submission by staff who do not use the accounting software.
- Spreadsheets enable data to be organised in different ways.
- If the transaction processing system is primitive or inflexible, spreadsheets may be used routinely in management reporting anyway, and it is therefore natural to extend their use to budgeting.

The drawbacks are the downside of their main virtue, which is flexibility.

- The more complex the spreadsheet model, the riskier it is to error or manipulation. Even one mistake in a formula, or a shift in a decimal point, can affect many other cells in a spreadsheet.
- Many people can use them at a basic, not sophisticated level, and there might be human error in the input data.

The way to deal with risks is through control over the formats used and proper training.

 ## Key Learning Points

- The high-low method is used to separate out total cost into the fixed and variable components where:
  - Variable cost/unit = Change in total cost/Change in level of activity
  - Fixed costs = Total cost – Variable cost per unit × Level of activity (C3a)

- The learning curve looks at the relationship between the average time taken to produce units of product and the number of units produced. Learning curve defines the relationship as: When production doubles, the average time per unit will decrease by a fixed percentage. (C3b, C3c)
- The learning curve equation is $y = ax^b$ (given in the exam) where:
  - y = average time per unit
  - x = number of units
  - a = time taken for the first unit
  - $b = \log r/\log 2$ where r = learning rate (C3b, C3c)

 ## What's the story?

Stop and think through the 'story' of this chapter and how it links with other chapters (use the Overview to help).

Learning example solutions

EG Solution 11.1

High LofA (month 3) = 3,000 units	$16,500
Low LofA (month 1) = 1,500 units	$12,000

(a) $$\frac{\text{Variable cost}}{\text{Unit}} = \frac{(\text{Cost at the high LofA} - \text{Cost at the low LofA})}{\text{high LofA} - \text{low LofA}}$$

= ($16,500 - $12,000) / (3,000 units - 1,500 units)

= $4,500/ 1,500 units

= $3/ unit

(b) Fixed cost = Total cost - Variable cost

At High LofA = $16,500 - ($3 x 3,000 units)

= $7,500

(c) Predicted costs at 2,800 units

	$
Variable cost	
($3 x 2,800 units)	8,400
Fixed cost	7,500
Total cost	15,900

EG Solution 11.2

Learning rate = 80%	b = -0.322

2nd unit

First apply the learning curve formula

$$y = ax^b$$
$$= 100 \times 2^{-0.322}$$
$$= 80.0$$

This is the average time taken by each of the first two units

Then interpret what is needed

2nd unit	hours
2 units (80 x 2)	160
- Less 1 unit	(100)
	60

3rd unit

Apply the learning curve formula

$y \qquad = ax^b$

$= 100 \times 3^{-0.322}$

$= 70.2$

This is the average time taken by each of the first three units

Then interpret

3rd unit	hours
3 units (70.2 x 3)	210.6
- Less 2 units (see above)	(160)
	50.6

Variance Analysis (Basic)

Context

Variances are simply the difference between expected or standard levels of performance and actual results. You need to have an in-depth understanding of all aspects of variance analysis.

It is absolutely critical to learn the key proformas and methods to calculate detailed variances. This will enable you to quickly and accurately calculate variance. More importantly, the basics learnt here will be of critical importance when studying advanced variance analysis.

3Q

1. Do you know some applications of variance analysis?

2. How does quality of material create price variance?

3. What are the possible reasons for fixed overhead variances?

12.1 Standard costs

For some organisations, the actual costs incurred may differ from budget.

> **IE** **Illustrative example 12.1**
>
> A publisher might budget to spend £1m on printing each year for a given volume of books. The actual cost may be different as a result of price changes (and paper prices are notoriously volatile), changes in usage (if books are longer), changes in quality (if the paper is better or worse). Later in this chapter we will look at standard mixes.
>
> Having a standard cost enables a business to focus on what causes a change in what has been budgeted, and to identify where variances come from.
>
> But where do the standards themselves actually come from?

12.1.1   Price

- The external market price. Where there is a widely traded external market price for a commodity (eg paper), the standard cost can use this as a benchmark. (This is similar to the way that oil contracts are quoted, in Brent crude.) The external market price of an input at a particular time can be used.
- An estimate of the future market price. If it looks likely that the price will go up, a company can adopt a future price. It is perhaps worth noting that organisations can, by buying futures or options contracts, reduce the volatility to which they are subject.
- Last year's price, adjusted for any volume discounts available, as informed by the organisation's procurement department.
- For labour, the budgeted hourly rate (if hourly paid): this is what the organisation plans to pay per hour or per unit, so this might as well be the standard cost.

12.1.2   Usage of materials and labour

- For materials, last year's actual usage, if this were stable; however, this might change if new machinery or new production initiatives are brought into line, and materials are used more efficiently.
- Similar considerations apply to variable labour costs and time. For example, call centres have a standard time per call to deal with customers.

12.1.3   Learning curve and life cycle effects

As a company becomes more experienced in making products, the unit cost will fall. In setting out standard costs for a period, the stage of the product on the life cycle might be considered. Products made at launch phase in small quantities will be more expensive per unit than those made when the product is well established.

12.2   Variances

A variance is simply a difference. We are calculating the difference between the original standard cost that we prepared as part of the budgeting process and the actual results achieved.

By comparing these values we can identify the degree to which the costs or revenues are out of control. An important aspect of variance analysis is that we can break up the overall total difference into individual differences.

For example instead of just knowing that we spent more or less on material we will know that we used more or less of the material – the usage variance - or that we spent more or less per kilo of material – the price variance.

12.2.1   Application of variance analysis

1. **Cost control.**
   By separating each cost element from each other it should make it possible for the company to better understand where problems with cost control are occurring and hence how to control costs.

2. **Reconciliation between budgeted and actual profit (or contribution or cost).**
   By calculating all the cost and revenue variances we are able to reconcile from the budgeted levels to the actual levels of profit, contribution or cost.

3. **Variances may quantify the value of a known difference.**
   In the event that there is a problem in a process the use of variance analysis will allow the company to calculate the value of that error or problem.

12.2.2   Performance appraisal

The key use of variance analysis is to measure the performance of processes and the management within that process. The performance of a manager may be identified by separating variances by responsibility. There will always be a problem however regarding variances that may be the responsibility of more than one manager. Additionally, by attempting to achieve favourable individual variances, a manager may take actions that adversely affect the business as a whole.

You need the ability to prepare variances for the following elements:

- materials;
- labour;
- variable overheads;
- fixed overheads;
- sales.

Please note that materials, labour and variable overheads are all variable costs and as such they will all be treated similarly.

 **Principle**

What variances are and when they are used

IE Illustrative example 12.2

Ponty Ltd uses a standard costing system. The standard cost card for one product is shown below:

		$
Direct material	2 lt at $5 per lt	10
Direct labour	2 hours at $6 per hour	12
Variable overhead	2 hours at $4 per hour	8
Total variable cost		30
Fixed overhead	2 hours at $5 per hour	10
Total product cost		40
Standard selling price		50
Standard profit margin		10

The budgeted output and sales was 500 units. Actual production and sales for the period was 600 units. Actual cost and revenue were as follows:

		$
Direct material	1,250 lt, costing	6,700
Direct labour	1,100 hours, costing	6,100
Variable overhead		4,500
Fixed overhead		5,350
Sales revenue	600 units at $48 per unit	28,800

Required:

Calculate all possible variances.

We will use this illustration to prepare all further examples when introducing basic variances. Please refer to this example to understand where the information we are using is taken from.

12.3 Material variances

If we take the appropriate information from Illustrative example 12.2 we find the following:

Standard cost		
Direct material	2 lt at $5 per kg	
Actual results		
Actual output		600 units
Materials purchased and used	1,250 Kg, costing	$6,700

Note

If we remember back to the budgetary control work we did in budgeting we can prepare a flexed budget for material to reflect that, due to its variable nature, as the output rises or falls then the need for material will also change.

Flexed budget: 2 lt x $5 x 600units=$6,000

This value is the expected or standard cost of material of the actual level of activity or output because of the variable nature of the cost.

Now we can look at the proforma

SQSP (standard quantity × standard price)

 Learn

2lt × $5 × 600units=$6,000

Whenever we see standard quantity (or hours) this means standard quantity of actual output because of the variable nature of the cost. Please note it is vital in any exam question that you pick up the levels of activity, actual production and budgeted production.

AQSP (actual quantity × standard price)

 Learn

1,250lt × 5=$6,250

These numbers should always be easily available from the question, actual quantity of the material used and standard price per unit of the material. Make sure you can identify them in the original question.

AQAP (actual quantity × actual price)

 Learn

$6,700

This value is normally given, the multiplication of actual quantity by actual price will give you the total actual cost.

Note

In the exam you will not need to do any more than pluck the numbers from the question and place them directly in the pro forma in the manner shown below:

SQSP

2lt x $5/lt x 600units = $6,000

AQSP

1,250lt x $5 = $6,250

AQAP

= $6,700

To calculate the variances all we have to look at is the proforma broken down into two:

SQSP AQSP	Comparing the first two components the standard price is the same and the only thing that differs is the quantity or usage. Therefore by comparing the first two elements we know whether we have used more or less material than expected -a usage variance.

 Learn

QSP AQAP	Comparing the second two comparators the actual quantity is the same and the only thing that differs is the price. Therefore by comparing the second two elements we know whether we have paid more or less material than expected -a price variance

 Learn

To calculate cost variances all you need to do is take away the bottom figure from the top figure, if it is positive it is good or favourable and if it is negative it is bad or adverse.

12.3.1 Variances

SQSP			
2lt x $5 x 600units	=$6,000		
		Usage Variance	$250 Adverse
AQSP			
1,250lt x $5	=$6,250		
		Price Variance	$450 Adverse
AQAP	=$6,700		
		Total Variance	$700 Adverse

12.3.2 What does this mean?

Here we can see that:

1. We have used more material in making 600 units than expected. Hence the material usage variance is adverse. We have used 1,250 lt to make 600 units, yet we expected (per the standard cost card) to use 1,200 Kg. The material usage variance values the difference of 50lt at the standard material cost per lt of $5/lt.
2. We have spent $450 more however than expected purchasing these 1,250lt (the material price variance).

The **total material variance** is the difference between the flexed budget material cost and the actual cost of material. More simply, it is the sum of the usage and price variance – i.e. $250A + - $450A = **$700 adverse.**

 Learn

Possible reasons

When looking at variances in exam question be aware that your examiner is likely to give you a lot of information regarding why the variances have occurred, therefore it is very important that you read the question carefully. If we were to look more generally for the sort of reasons why we could include the following:

12.3.3 Price variance

Quality of material

If the quality of the material is better or worse than that originally in the standard this will affect the price and hence the variance. This is an obvious problem when assessing the performance of a manager in charge. If the variance is substantially favourable it would suggest that they are buying poorer material to benefit them at the expense of usage and the eventual quality of the product.

External factors

The price of a material is not to be taken in isolation from the economy as a whole. The unexpected movement in inflation or exchange rates can easily produce a substantial variance. This is best illustrated by considering the often dramatic movements in the commodity prices such as oil.

12.3.4   Usage variance

Quality of material

As discussed already the purchasing policy on material will have an effect on the usage in process, any lower quality of material leading to an adverse variance.

Motivation and skill level of labour

The skills and motivation of the labour force will determine how careful they are and hence the usage of material.

Theft

It is possible at any point in the process that theft may occur leading to an adverse variance.

 **Principle**

Understand possible causes of material variances

12.4   Labour variances

Standard cost	
Direct labour	2 hours at £6 per hour
Actual results	
Actual output	600 units
Hours paid and worked	1,100hours
Labour cost	£6,100

The pro forma for labour will be the same as for material except for the fact that instead of talking about quantity we talk about hours and instead of price we talk about rate.

SHSR

                         Difference = Efficiency variance

AHSR

                         Difference = Rate variance

AHAR

 Learn

Note the calculation of the values should be exactly the same as before, note two points:

1. When we talk of standard hours we mean the standard or expected hours of actual production;
2. When calculating the values always start at the bottom because it is easier!!

SHSR	
2hrs/unit x 600 units x $6/hr =	$7,200
AHSR	
1,100hrs x $6 =	$6,600
AHAR	$6,100

Once we have the values then we simply take the top from the bottom to get the variances!

SHSR $7,200		
	Efficiency	=$600 Favourable
AHSR $6,600		
	Rate	=$500 Favourable
AHAR $6,100		

Here we can see that:

1. We have used less labour in making 600 units than expected. Hence the labour efficiency variance is favourable. We have used 1,100 hours to make 600 units, yet we expected (per the standard cost card) to use 1,200 hours. The labour efficiency variance values this difference of 100 hours @ standard labour cost/ hour of $6.
2. We have spent $500 less than expected paying the workforce (the labour rate variance).

Possible reasons
Your examiner is particularly interested in labour variances because of the motivational impact of increasing or decreasing salary on employees.

12.4.1   Efficiency variance

Motivation of employees

Any process where employees have a major impact on the quality or quantity of the output will be affected by the positive or negative motivations of the workforce

Quality of employee or materials

Obviously a drop in quality in any of the inputs can lead to a fall in the efficiency of labour simply due to the longer time it may take to rectify problems associated with poor quality inputs.

12.4.2   Rate variance

Wage inflation

The amount paid to employees will not be known for certain when the standard is prepared and can be affected by many factors such as the wider economy or the shortage of a specific skill level of labour.

Overtime/Bonuses

Overtime is paid at a higher rate per hour normally and would lead to a higher average rate per hour, likewise a bonus would uplift the hourly rate.

 Principle

Understand possible reasons for labour variances

12.5   Variable overhead variances

Standard cost
Variable overhead 2 hours at £4 per hour

Actual results	
Actual output	600 units
Hours worked (from above)	1,100
Variable overhead cost	£4,500

When considering variable overheads we will use exactly the same proforma as labour but it is normal to call the rate variance an 'expenditure' variance. Otherwise the calculation of the variances is exactly the same as we have already done with both labour and materials.

Note: When we write standard hours we mean the standard hours of actual output

SHSR		
2hrs/unit x 600 units x $4/hr =	$4,800	
	Efficiency	
AHSR		$400 Fav
1,100hrs x $4 =	$4,400	
	Expenditure	
		$100 Adv
AHAR	$4,500	

 # Learn

12.5.1   Possible reasons

Efficiency variance

Similar to labour efficiency, it is likely that the efficiency is based on labour hours. As such, any impact on labour will have a further effect on variable overhead.

Expenditure variance

Variable overheads are made up of many different overhead cost elements; to identify reasons for the variance we would need to analyse all elements separately.

EG Learning example 12.1

Katch			$
Direct material	4kg at $4	per kg	16
Direct labour	1.5 hrs at	£10 per hour	15
Variable overhead	1.5 hrs at	£2 per hour	3
Total variable cost			34

The budgeted output and sales was 2,000 units. Actual production and sales for the period was 1,600 units

Actual cost and revenue were as follows:

		$
Direct material	6,000 kg, costing	24,450
Direct labour	2,500 hrs, costing	26,250
Variable overhead		5,000

12.6 Fixed overhead variances

We have computed variable cost variances. If we extend our analysis, we can also compute fixed cost variances. We need to be careful here. The manner in which they are calculated is dependent on the costing method that is used, absorption costing or marginal costing.

12.6.1 Absorption costing

We know by now that in absorption costing all (production) costs are charged to the product or cost unit. This means that included in that total cost will be the fixed overhead costs of production. When calculating variances we must consider not only whether we have spent more or less than expected, but also whether we have absorbed or recovered as much as originally expected or budgeted.

Initially we will work all examples based on absorption costing principles

12.6.2 Marginal costing

Under marginal costing techniques, we make no attempt to absorb fixed production overheads into cost units. Instead the entire overhead is written off as incurred to the Income Statement. Fixed production costs here are a period cost. In this situation all we need to concern ourselves with is whether we spent more or less than originally budgeted.

We will consider the use of marginal costing later after considering sales variance

12.7 Fixed overhead variances – absorption costing

The overall total variance in an absorption costing environment is similar to under/ over absorption of overhead. This is because we are comparing the overhead absorbed (the standard cost of actual output) to the overhead incurred (actual overhead incurred.

12.7.1 Total variance

SCAP – standard fixed overhead cost of actual production
(similar to overhead absorbed)

Total fixed overhead variance

ACAP – actual fixed overhead cost
(similar to overhead incurred)

Of course this variance only tells us what the difference is and not the reason why. To consider why the difference has occurred we must break the total into sub-variances:

- the expenditure variance – did we spend more or less than expected;
- the volume variance – did we absorb or recover more or less than expected.

12.7.2   Expenditure

The key is to remember that we are considering a fixed cost, ie a cost which is not expected to change as the level of activity changes. This means that when looking at expenditure we do not need to flex the budget. All we do is compare the actual to the original budget.

12.7.3   Comparison

SCBP – budgeted cost

(Note – the standard cost is per unit but links to the budgeted level of activity because we do not expect it to change)

ACAP – actual cost

This is normally the most important variance within fixed overheads because it relates to cashflow and as such will have a direct impact on the health of the business. It can also be argued that this variance is the only fixed overhead variance over which the production director is likely to have any direct control

 **Principle**

What the expenditure variance measures

12.7.4   Volume variance

When considering the volume variance we look at whether we have absorbed or recovered more or less overhead than we expected to recover in the budget. The recovery of the overhead is based upon how many units are produced and valued at the standard fixed overhead cost per unit.

12.7.5   Comparison

SCAP – Standard cost of actual production

SCBP – Budgeted cost

Note the only difference between these two are the number of units. We are comparing the amount we originally expected to absorb (budgeted cost) with the amount we actually absorbed based on the actual level of activity.

In addition, the actual level of activity will be determined in the main by sales and would probably be beyond the control of the production director. As such the volume variance could be argued to be uncontrollable and be used solely as a reconciling item.

↻ Principle

> What the volume variance measures

12.7.6   Overall pro forma

SCAP – standard cost of actual output

> Difference = Volume variance

SCBP – budgeted cost

> Difference = Expenditure variance

ACAP – actual cost

Learn

Let's go back to the original illustration and consider how the numbers work.

IE   Illustrative example 12.3

Fixed overhead:

2 hours at $5 per hour   10

The budgeted output and sales was 500 units. Actual production and sales for the period was 600 units

Actual results were as follows:

Fixed overhead $5,350
Labour hours   1,100 hours

SCAP - $10/unit x 600 units   =$6,000

> Volume variance $1,000 Fav

SCBP - $10/unit x 500 units   =$5,000

> Expenditure variance $350 Adv

ACAP – actual cost $5,350

Note, if we know our proforma then we have no problem calculating the numbers.

Further analysis of fixed overheads:

It is normal to absorb the overheads based on labour (or machine) hours, this means that we are able to further analyse the variances to take account of the hours involved. Please note that we have already seen a lot to do with labour hours in labour and variable overhead variances. It is always useful to remember the similarities rather than highlight the differences in techniques that we must use.

If we consider the hours we are able to break the volume variance into two sub-variances:

- The efficiency variance – whether we work more or less hours than expected producing the actual output (similar to labour efficiency or variable overhead efficiency variances)
- The capacity variance – whether we work more or less hours than originally expected in the budget, a new variance.

 Principle

Know what the efficiency and capacity variances measure

How does this work? Let's use the numbers from the illustration to see how it works. Please note the importance of the standard hour, it is a measure of output. We can multiply the actual production by the standard hours to get standard hours and by budgeted production to bet budgeted hours.

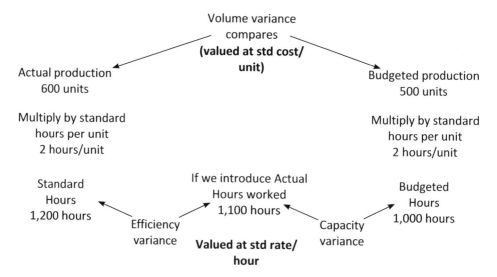

The key is that you are able to calculate the variances quickly and accurately, to do this you need the following proforma:

SHSR –   Standard cost

                                        Efficiency variance

AHSR –   Actual hours at the standard rate per hour

                                        Capacity variance

BHSR –   Budgeted cost

                                        Expenditure variance

AHAR –   Actual cost

 Learn

| IE | **Illustrative example 12.4**

Fixed overhead   2 hours at $5 per hour $10

The budgeted output and sales was 500 units. Actual production and sales for the period was 600 units. Actuals were as follows:

Fixed overhead: $5,350

Labour hours: 1,100 hours

SHSR	2hr x 600 units x $5	=	$6,000		
				Efficiency variance	$500 Fav
AHSR	1,100hrs x $5	=	$5,500		
				Capacity variance	$500 Fav
BHSR	2hr x 500 units x $5	=	$5,000		
				Expenditure variance	$350 Adv
AHAR		=	$5,350		

Possible reasons:

Efficiency variance – as per labour or variable overhead efficiency

Capacity variance – simply the fact that we have worked more or less hours than budgeted, this is likely to be due to factors beyond the control of the production director, such as higher or lower demand than expected leading to more or less hours being worked.

> **Expenditure** – as already commented upon this variance relates to cashflow and is of critical importance from the perspective of controlling cost

IE Illustrative example 12.5

Fixed overheads	Budget	Actual
Units	1,400	1,530
Hours	3,500	3,846
Cost	$9,625	$10,780

Required:

Calculate the fixed overhead variances in as much detail as possible

To understand the question a bit better it is useful to calculate the standards from the information given. The standards will be related to the budgeted information.

Standard hours/ unit	= 3,500hrs/1,400 units	= 2.5 hours/unit
Standard rate/ hour	= $9,625/3,500hrs	= $2.75/hour

SHSR 2.5 hrs x 1,530 x $2.75 = $10,519

Efficiency variance $57 Adv

AHSR 3,846 hrs x $2.75 = $10,576

Capacity variance $951 Fav

BHSR 3,500 hrs x $2.75 = $9,625

Expenditure variance $1,155 Adv

AHAR = $10,780

Please note the difference between the standard hours (based on actual output) and budgeted hours (based on budgeted output), this should not be difficult but is a common area of confusion.

Possible reasons for fixed overhead variances		
Expenditure variances	**Efficiency variances**	**Capacity variances**
Incorrect budget/standard cost card. For example the allocation and apportionment of overhead may have been inaccurate.	*Incorrect budget/ standard cost card.*	*Incorrect budget/ standard cost card.*
Further analysis of individual components – fixed overheads include many different types of cost (e.g. factory rent, machine depreciation etc.) These would need to be analysed individually to see if they have cost more or less than expected. In our example the fixed overhead appears to have been used less economically than expected.	Same *reasons* as labour efficiency variances! Fixed overhead is absorbed on a labour hour basis therefore issues will arise with respect to: *Labour skill level; Motivation; Idle time.*	*In our example, we have a favourable capacity variance. Labour has worked more hours than budgeted. This may be due to overtime being worked or an extra shift pattern being arranged to cope with production needs. More hours were worked than budgeted to be available.*

 Principle

> Possible reasons for fixed overhead variances

12.8 Sales variances

Sales variances arise when:

* We sell more or less units than budgeted – the **sales volume variance.** This is favourable if we sell more units than budgeted.

- The actual sales price achieved was higher or lower than the standard sales price - **sales price variance.** This is favourable if we sell goods at a higher or lower sales price than expected.

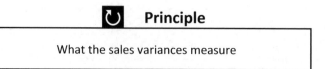

Principle

What the sales variances measure

Importantly, we must recognise that we have dealt with ALL differences between actual and expected production costs in the cost variances. We are only now concerned with sales volumes and sales prices.

12.8.1   Sales volume variance

This variance is calculated by comparing actual and budgeted sales quantities in units- have we sold more or less units than budgeted? Each unit we sell will generate an extra 'margin' per unit sold – the difference between the standard unit sales price and the standard unit cost.

12.8.2   Absorption costing

If we are adopting an **absorption costing system** then we assume that every unit sold will incur:

- The standard sales price (difference between actual and standard sales prices are dealt with in the sales price variance); and
- The standard unit absorption cost (differences between actual and standard costs/usages having been dealt with in the cost variances).

Standard unit sales price:	X
Less standard absorption cost/unit	(X)
Standard profit margin/unit	X

The sales volume variance may be written as a formula:

(AS – BS) x SPM

Learn

ie the comparison of the actual and budgeted sales units valued at the standard profit margin.

12.8.3 Sales price variance

The difference between the actual sales price achieved and the standard or expected selling price.

The sales price variance is calculated using the following formula:

(ASP –SSP) x AS

☞ Learn

Standards	
Total product cost	40
Standard selling price	50
Standard profit margin	10

The budgeted output and sales was 500 units. Actual production and sales for the period was 600 units.

Sales revenue	600 units at $48 per unit	28,800
Sales volume variance		
(AS - BS) x SPM)		
(600units – 500units) x $10/unit		=$1,000 Fav
Sales price variance		
(ASP - SSP) x AS)		
($48/unit - $50/unit) x 600units		=$1,200 Adv

Note: the formula helps you to calculate it correctly, a negative value is adverse and a positive value is favourable. To achieve this we start with actual values because we are looking at revenue and the higher the actual revenue the better.

12.8.4 Reasons for sales variances

In our example we had:

Sales price variance: $1,200 adverse

Sales volume variance: $1,000 favourable (absorption)

Possible reasons for sales variances	
Sales price variances	**Sales volume variances**
Incorrect budget/standard cost card.	Incorrect budget/standard cost card.
Sales drives/advertising/demanding customers. In order to sell more units (as per the sales volume variance), the sales price was dropped.	Market conditions. If economic or competitive conditions were poor, demand may be lower.
Product quality. The quality of the product was poor and so the sales price had to be cut in order to sell it.	Production difficulties/efficiencies. In our example, we have made more units than expected, possibly due to the efficiency of labour.

 Principle

Possible reasons for sales variances

EG Learning example 12.2

Budgeted data

Output	1,000 units
Revenue	$200,000
Std profit margin	$40/unit

Actual data

Output	1,035 units
Revenue	$217,350

Required:

Calculate the sales variances

12.9 Reconciliation of budget and actual profits

As stated earlier that by reconciling the budgeted profit using all the variances it should be possible to calculate the actual profit. If we look at the illustration we can quite easily calculate the actual profit directly as a check against the reconciliation.

IE Illustrative example 12.6

Actual data

		$
Sales revenue	600 units at $48 per unit	28,800
Direct material	1,250 lt, costing	6,700
Direct labour	1,100 hours, costing	6,100
Variable overhead		4,500
Fixed overhead		5,350
Sub-total the cost		(22,650)
Actual profit		6,150

12.9.1   Using variances in assessing business performance

In the examples of variance analysis in this and the previous chapter, we have seen that there are a number of explanations given for each variance, and we have ended up discussing as to whether the standard itself needs to be revised. The focus on variances has been operational and forensic, but as they focus on actual, as opposed to planned or expected performance, they can be a helpful guide to the performance of a business.

Benchmarking with similar institutions

Variances can be used in benchmarking exercises, to assess how an organisation has performed against similar organisations. For example, in the UK, universities have similar cost structures, and therefore it makes sense to compare them with each other. For example, some may spend more on information technology than others. The sector average can be used as a standard: there may be perfectly good reasons why expenditure might vary.

Review of past performance

Variance analyses are prepared against a plan or standard which, at time of preparation, aim to control future performance. A budget, is almost by definition forward looking, as a statement of expected revenues and costs.

However, it ought to be easy to use variance analysis to look at past performance, for example by doing variance analysis on current and prior reporting periods or years.

This can have two approaches:

(a) The company can understand what has changed, and go for a forensic view of revenues and costs. In effect, past performance 'stands in' for the budget or plan in the variance process. You could imagine market size and market share variances being tracked across two different years to see if this has an impact.

The variance can be tracked across multiple periods against the original strategy. There might be a difficulty in aligning variance analysis with product strategies if, for example, the product mix has changed but the cost of the components (joint and by products or services) cannot be allocated.

Furthermore, there may well be a time lag in variances. An increase in materials defects in one year, which is suggestive of lower quality, could indicate poor sales in later years, if quality is an important determinant. Or again, a change in business operations might lead to an increase in fixed overheads in the future.

(b) The company can also assess its planning effectiveness, and its ability to budget and set standards accordingly. For example, if many of the variances are put down to planning variances, this suggests either that managers are successfully gaming the system or that the standard setting process is permanently ineffective.

Improving future performance

All variances do is compare actual data versus a plan, prior year or standard.

Given variances cover both costs and revenues, they can indicate important facts about the organisation, at an operational level. Variances do dissect the income statement in a way that other performance measures, being focused on aggregate corporate performance, or purely balance sheet ratios do not.

The management task is therefore to use the variance analysis and to learn the right lessons from it, but this depends on their overall priorities.

Sales variances	Can generate a discussion about: • Sales mix • New product development, if products are performing badly • New marketing strategies • The position of a poorly performing product on the product life cycle • The impact on profitability
.Labour variances	These can generate discussions about • Training and skills • Efficient working • Outsourcing • Quality standards
Materials variances	These can generate discussions about • Just in time supply • Product quality • Product redesign, if the same product can be made with fewer materials

It is also possible that the 'wrong' lessons might be learnt from variance analysis. For example, if the purchasing function buys cheaper materials, it might score positively on the price variance. If these materials are lower quality, then the manufacturing department might score negatively on the reject variances, as well as on labour variances as the work has to be redone. This might also affect the sales variance.

A business should not use variance analysis as its guidance mechanism, on its own, especially as variances are related. It does provide evidence to inform the debate as to how an organisation should conduct its operations in future.

➡ Key Learning Points

- All variable cost variances have a standard proforma, learn them and be able to calculate them as second nature:

Material variances

SQ × SP

Difference = Usage/efficiency variance

AQ × SP

Difference = Price/rate variance

AQ × AP

Labour and variable overhead variances

SH × SR

Difference = Efficiency variance

AH × SR

Difference = Rate/Expenditure variance

AH × AR

Fixed overhead variances

SH X SR

Efficiency variance

AH X SR

Capacity variance

BH X SR

Expenditure variance

AH X AR

Note: In marginal costing there are no efficiency or capacity variances.

Sales variances

Sales volume variances	(AS – BS) × SPM – absorption costing
	(AS – BS) × SCM – marginal costing
Sales price variances	(ASP – SSP) × AS

 ## What's the story?

Stop and think through the 'story' of this chapter and how it links with other chapters (use the Overview to help).

Learning example solutions

EG Solution 12.1

Material variances

SQSP

4kg x $4/kg x 1,600units =
$25,600

AQSP	**Usage variance**	**$1,600 Fav**

6,000kg x $4=$24,000

AQAP	**Price variance**	**$450 Adv**

= $24,450

Labour variances

SHSR

1.5hr x $10 x 1,600 units =
$24,000

AHSR	**Efficiency variance**	**$1,000 Adv**

2,500hr x $10 = $25,000

AHAR	**Rate variance**	**$1,250 Adv**

= $26,250

Variable Overhead Variances

SHSR

1.5hr x $2 x 1,600units = $4,800

AHSR	**Efficiency variance**	**200 Adv**

2,500hrs x $2 = $5,000

AHAR	**Rate variance**	**Nil**

= $5,000

EG Solution 12.2

(AS – BS) x SPM	
(1,035 units – 1,000 units) x $40/unit	= $1,400 Fav
Sales price variance	
(ASP – SSP) x AS	
($210/unit - $200/unit) x 1,035units	= $10,350 Fav

Note to calculate the actual and standard selling prices

Use actual data	
ASP = $217,350/1,035units	= $210
Use budgeted data	
SSP = $200,000/1,000units	= $200

13

Variance Analysis (Advanced)

Context

This chapter deals with advanced variance analysis, building on the foundation laid in the previous chapter. The application of variance analysis is likely to be examined in every examination. The emphasis of every written question is likely to be split about 50/50 between computation and discussion. The examiner is likely to include some complex variance work each time, which needs in-depth knowledge of how to apply the appropriate technique.

You must know your basic variances and have the ability to apply the techniques with ease before you learn advanced variances. To achieve that, the key is to learn and understand the proformas and practise using them again and again.

To deal with the discussion parts of the question consider carefully past exam questions in this area to understand the link that the examiner makes between numbers and narrative in the questions.

3Q

1. Do you know the use of variance analysis?

2. What are the two components that traditional variances are broken into, and why?

3. Is a budget revision arising out of an increase in labour hours per product due to inadequate employee training acceptable?

13.1 Advanced variance analysis

Variance analysis is used to separate costs and revenues into controllable elements (eg material, labour etc) in order that we can compare expected (standard) performance with actual results. Advanced areas simply increase the degree to which the variances may be sub-analysed: This is done to reflect specific management accounting environments or issues arising from the manner in which the budgeted information is prepared. There are three specific techniques that must be prepared for and in addition there is the need to be able to analyse in-depth what the variances we calculate mean. The four basic techniques are:

1. Planning and operational variances;
2. Material mix and yield variances;
3. Sales variances;
   (a) Mix and quantity;
   (b) Market share and market size;
4. Excess idle time variances.

13.2 Planning and operational variances

This is where traditional variances that we already know are broken up into two components, a planning element and an operational one.

Issue:

The reason for doing this is because the standard that we originally prepared is considered out-of-date when it comes to comparing it to the actual result.

Remembering back to the preparation of standards we said that they were probably prepared at the beginning of the budgeting process because they are normally a key building block of the production budgets.

This means that there could easily be a delay of over a year between when the standards are prepared and when they compared to the actual result.

Problem:

If the standard is out-of-date this means that the variance calculated may be due to one of two reasons:

1. Planning error – differences arising from changes over time because the original standard is out-of-date;
2. Operational factors - differences arising due to the actions taken by operational management that have either improved or damaged the performance of the organisation.

Solution:

Revise the standard to reflect the fact that things have changed. The revised standard will reflect the best estimate of what is an appropriate standard given the change in market conditions or the production process. This will allow us to separate the planning errors from the operational factors.

Please note that this revision will be open to abuse and manipulation by operational management. This is because the easier the revised standard is made, the more likely the operational variance will be favourable. It is likely that any exam question will highlight this point.

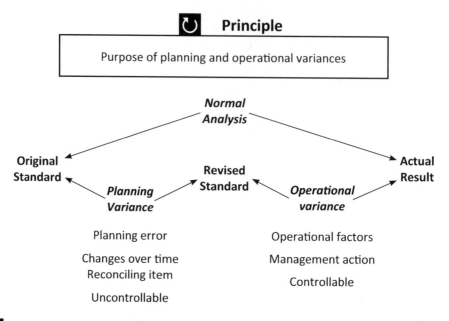

⟳ Principle

Purpose of planning and operational variances

Normal Analysis

Original Standard → Revised Standard → Actual Result

Planning Variance

Operational variance

Planning error

Changes over time

Reconciling item

Uncontrollable

Operational factors

Management action

Controllable

IE Illustrative example 13.1

A company expects to pay a standard price of £2/kg. During the period it actually used 1,000 kilos at a total cost of £2,600.

After further consideration of the market for the raw material it has been found that the general market price of the material has risen by 20% due to exchange rate movements.

Required:

(a) Based on normal variance analysis, has the purchasing manager done a good or bad job?

(b) Is your conclusion changed as a result of sub-analysing the variance into planning and operational elements?

Please note that we are only looking at material price variances and nothing else, this may be a feature of a planning and operational variance in the exam.

Basic analysis

Price variance

AQSP	$2,000		
(1,000kg x $2/kg)		Price variance	$600 Adv
AQAP	$2,600		

Based on this analyse the purchasing manager has done a very poor job with a substantial adverse variance that amounts to 30% of the standard (600/2,000).

Planning price variance

To separate out the planning from the operational variance the key is to understand what we are comparing. If you look at the diagram above you notice that the original variance compares standard to actual whereas the planning variance compares standard to revised standard.

What we do is substitute **the actual with the revised standard** to change from the standard proforma to the planning proforma. (Please note that in this situation the quantity will not change because there is no planning variance for quantity or usage.

AQSP	$2,000		
(1,000 x$2/kg)		Planning price variance	$400 Adverse
AQRSP	$2,400		
(1,000 x$2/kg x 1.2)			

Comment

Most of the adverse variance is due to planning error. This is essentially uncontrollable and cannot be related to the responsible manager. Here the price has risen substantially due to external market forces. This variance is more of a reconciling factor than anything else because it will not lead to control action.

Operational price variance

Once the planning variance has been calculated all we have to do is to compare the revised variance with the actual result. Again let us start from the original proforma.

We can substitute the original standard with the actual result

AQRSP	$2,400 (from above)		
		Operational price variance	$200 Adverse
AQAP	$2,600 (from above)		

Comment

The operational variance is still adverse but substantially less than before. This variance is solely due to operational decisions made by the responsible manager and should be used as part of their appraisal. At less than 10% of the revised standard (200/2,400) this variance is certainly of less concern than the original analysis.

Please note as suggested earlier that the setting of the revised standard is difficult to do and it may be set at a level too high or low to be realistic.

Developing the analysis

When considering both components of a material price variance, price and usage then we use exactly the same idea as before:

Basic proforma		Planning	Operational
		(substitute actual with revised standard)	(substitute standard with revised standard)
SQSP		SQSP	RSQRSP
	Difference = Usage		
AQSP		RSQSP	AQRSP
	Difference = Price		
AQAP		RSQRSP	AQAP

 Learn

EG Learning example 13.1

Standards

A manufacturing process uses 6lt/unit costing $3/lt.

Actual

Output	2,500 units
Usage	16,000 lt
Cost	$45,500

Required:

Prepare the variances using basic variance analysis and assess whether the purchasing manager and production manager individually have done a good or bad job.

IE Illustrative example 13.2

After solving Learning example 13.1, we are now told that standards should be revised to reflect that the market for the material input is depressed and a good purchasing manager should be able to buy the material at 10% less than originally thought. Also due to a change in the production process to improve output quality, it is now expected that every unit of output requires an additional 0.5lt per unit material input.

Revised standards

Price $3/lt x 0.9	= $2.7/lt
Usage 6lt + 0.5lt	= 6.5lt
6.5lt/unit for $2.7/lt	= $17.55/unit

Prepare an analysis of variances into both planning and operational elements and assess the performance of the purchasing manager and the production manager individually.

Planning variances (substitute the actual with the revised standard)

SQSP $45,000

(6 x 2,500 x 3)   Usage variance $3,750Adv

RSQSP $48,750

(6.5 x 2,500 x 3)   Planning variance $4,875Fav

RSQRSP $43,875

(6.5 x 2,500 x 2.7)

Comment
Planning variances are due to planning error, change over time and not due to the performance of managers. It is a reconciling item and no more.

OPERATIONAL VARIANCES

RSQRSP $43,875

(from above)   Usage variance $675Fav

AQRSP $43,200

(16,00 x 2.7)   Price variances $2,300Adv

AQAP $45,500

Comment

The usage variance is favourable suggesting that production manager has done a good job. The size of the variance is relatively low in relation to the standard at about 1.5% (675/43,875).

The price variance is adverse suggesting that the purchasing manager has done a poor job. Also the magnitude of the variance suggests a real problem with performance in the purchasing department at above 5% of standard (2,300/43,200).

EG Learning example 13.2

A company, Horitch Ltd, has the following information regarding the performance of its labour department:

Standards

It takes 0.5hours/unit costing $12/ hour.

We are now told that standards should be revised to reflect that the production process has changed. This has led to a reduced need for labour input by 20%. At the same time the process now needs labour to be of a higher skill level, at a higher rate of pay of $14/hour.

Actual

Output	80,000 units
Usage	33,000 hours
Cost	$447,500

Required:

Prepare the variances for both planning and operational factors and assess whether the purchasing manager and production manager individually have done a good or bad job.

It is possible that the changes included in the revisions to the standard have not yet had an opportunity to work their way through to the actual results, particularly with regard to efficiency gains with a new process.

13.3 Budget revisions

When using planning variances a key consideration is who should set the budget revisions and in what circumstances.

13.3.1 Setting budget revisions

The budget revision must be set, when at all possible, by a senior manager who does not have a direct link to the area concerned. As stated earlier there is potential for manipulation of results if the revision is made by the responsible manager because they may be inclined to set the revised standard at a less efficient value than originally and hence increase the chance that favourable operational variances are achieved.

When we say a senior manager, it is normal for budget revisions to be authorised at board level on the recommendation of the appropriate director, reflecting the importance placed on the original budget and any changes to it.

13.3.2 Appropriate circumstances for budget revisions

The budget should only be revised in a situation where there has been a step change in the value of the standard, wholly beyond the control of the operational management. If operational management had any reasonable opportunity or capability to influence the standard then the budget revision must be refused.

Examples of revisions that are or are not acceptable include:

Acceptable	Unacceptable
Substantial step changes in commodity prices that could not be reasonably forecast	General rises in prices that could have been forecast by a competent operational manager
Substantial increase in the need for labour hours per unit due to new health and safety guidelines being introduced without prior warning	An increase in the labour hours per unit required due to poor training and inadequate staff skills
Liquidation of an existing supplier without warning leading to an increase in the material cost per unit	Loss of a key supplier after continued problems over a number of years without any consideration of a back-up source

The key with any exam question is to make sure that you argue both sides of any situation, as the marks are predominantly awarded for the argument rather than the conclusion.

 Principle

> When planning and operational variances should
> be calculated

13.4 Mix and yield variances

Mix and yield variances may be prepared given a specific manufacturing environment where:

1. Two or more material inputs go into to making the product; and
2. The material inputs are inter-changeable to some degree. It is only likely that materials are inter-changeable in a process costing environment where it is possible to end up with the same product using different combinations of material inputs. An example would be any form of food manufacture (eg soup)

where the quality of the material input which differs from season to season may be compensated for by the mix and yield.

 **Principle**

> Situations where mix and yield variances would be calculated

When considering this variance the key is to remember that it is simply a further development of the material variances. To make it as easy to calculate as possible let's focus solely on the additional information needed. The mix and yield variances are a sub-analysis of the usage variance, the price variance is unaffected.

To separate the mix from the yield a further calculation is needed, we need to calculate the actual quantity at the standard mix at the standard price.

SQSP

Difference = Yield

Usage divides into mix and yield   AQ(SM)SP

Difference = Mix

AQSP

 Learn

IE Illustrative example 13.3

Akram produces 50 kg bags of fertiliser by mixing three material inputs, A, B and C, and the following standards apply:

Standard proportions		Standard cost per bag
	%	$
X	70	0.4
Y	20	0.6
Z	10	1.0

During the process of mixing, a process loss of 10% is regarded as the standard.

During the week, 920 bags of the fertiliser were produced and inputs were as follows:

Actual inputs		Actual prices	Actual cost
	Bags	£ per bag	$
X	680	0.45	306
Y	190	0.62	117.8
Z	130	0.95	123.5
	1,000		$547.3

Calculate the price mix and yield variances.

To answer this question it is very useful to prepare a proforma. There is a substantial amount of calculation so a formal step by step approach is needed.

Steps

1. Prepare a proforma using the analysis discussed above, leaving space for individual and total values

2. Work methodically through each calculation from the bottom to the top.

3. Sum the total of each row

4. Calculate the variances (top minus bottom)

Notes on calculations

AQSMSP

The only new calculation is line 2. To calculate the actual quantity at standard mix the key is to take the total actual quantity (the sum of all the material inputs) and then split them in the standard proportions. The reason for starting at the bottom of the analysis is because it may help with information for line 2.

SQSP

In this type of question it is common for a loss factor to arise. We are told that there is a standard process loss of 10%, that means that for every 10 bags input we expect to lose 1 bag and only have 9 bags of good output.

If we are given the output (920 bags) then we can work backwards by multiplying by 100 over 90 to get the standard or expected usage of that output.

Variances

We have only calculated the mix and yield variances in total terms because if calculated individually they may lead to misleading information. The price variances are calculated individually because they provide better information in this manner.

Material inputs	X	Y	Z	Total $	Variance
	$	$	$		$
1. SQSP	286.2	122.7	102.2	511.1	
X 920 x 0.7 x 100/90 x 0.4					Yield
Y 920 x 0.2 x 100/90 x 0.6					variance
Z 920 x 0.1 x 100/90 x 1.0					11.1 Fav
2. AQ(SM)SP	280	120	100	500	
X 1,000 x 0.7 x 0.4					Mix
Y 1,000 x 0.2 x 0.6					variance
Z 1,000 x 0.1 x 1.0					16 Adv
3. AQSP	272	114	130	516	
X 680 x 0.4					
Y 190 x 0.6					
Z 130 x 1.0					
4. AQAP	306	117.8	123.5	547.3	
Price variance					
(Line3-Line4)	34 Adv	3.8 Adv	6.5 Fav	31.3 Adv	

Comments

Price variance

The materials X and Y are both adverse suggesting that the company is trying to source those materials in a more competitive market, this may have lead the company to substitute those materials with the third material Z.

Mix variance

In total terms we have an adverse variance, this is because we have used less of material X and Y, and more of material Z. Material Z is more expensive leading to a higher average cost per bag for the mix than standard.

This may lead to an improved quality of product, which will both help yield and also the quality of the end product to the customer.

Yield variance

The overall yield is slightly higher than expected. This could be due to good management of the process or due to environmental factors working in our favour.

Overall

The process appears to be broadly under control.

 Principle

> Steps in calculating all material mix, yield and price variances and interpretation of material variances

IE, Illustrative example 13.4

Dev produces malt extract by mixing two material inputs, malt and feed, and the following standards apply:

	Standard proportions	Standard cost per tonnes
	%	$
Malt	20	240
Feed	80	110

During the week, 540 tonnes of malt extract were produced and inputs were as follows:

	Actual inputs tonnes	Actual prices $ per tonne	Actual cost $
Malt	120	230	27,600
Feed	440	105	46,200
	560		73,800

Calculate the price mix and yield variances.

Material inputs	Malt	Feed	Total	Variance
	$	$	$	$
1. SQSP	25,920	47,520	73,440	Yield
Malt (540 x 0.2 x 240)Feed (540 x 0.8 x 110)				variance
				2,720 A

Material inputs	Malt	Feed	Total	Variance
2. AQ(SM)SP	26,880	49,280	76,160	Mix
Malt (560 x 0.2 x 240)				variance 1,040 A
Feed (560 x 0.8 x 110)				
3. AQSP	28,800	48,400	77,200	
Malt (120 x 240) Feed (440 x 110)				
4. AQAP	27,600	46,200	73,800	
Price variance (Line3-Line4)	1,200 F	2,200 F		

13.4.1   Issues in changing materials mix

One way of responding to a price variance is to change the mix of materials. These materials may be cheaper or different. (You will have encountered this if you have to buy print cartridges.)

(a) The cost may go down if the same quantity is used, and it is cheaper. However, if more is needed there might be a higher wastage rate

(b) If the quality is poorer, there are likely to be more rejects. If this affects the performance of the product, this will appear in more complaints or possible litigation.

This is not likely to be picked up immediately in the production department, but could have long term implications for the product and the reputation of the organisation. For example, customer complaints take up time and resources, replacement products and so forth.

(c) Poorer quality materials may give an unusually favourable price variance. However, they may need more processing, and so if this is the case, they will impact on other cost bases in production.

Switching to materials that are poorer than specified can have implications for performance management

13.4.2   Controlling production processes

There are many types of production, for example making cars, which require assembly of components, oil refining (a continuous process with possible joint products), to production of a specific contract.

Production can be managed in different ways:

	Control issues
Produce for stock	Stock holding costs must be taken into account. Cost per unit might be lower in manufacturing but stock holding costs will increase
Produce for demand	If the product is simple to manufacture, make no items for stock but manufacture in advance.

13.5 Further analysis of sales variances

Your examiner has shown a willingness to look at sales variances in a variety of ways. In particular you must be able to sub-analyse your sales volume variance into the following:

1. Sales mix and quantity variances;
2. Sales market share and market size variances.

13.5.1 Sales mix and quantity variances

In much the same way the sales variances may be further analysed to better understand how inter-related products may be performing. To do so the volume variance is separated into a mix element and a volume element

The inter-relationship between the products could be that they are **complimentary**, sold together (printer and ink cartridge) or **substitute**, sold in competition to each other.

Approach

Again the basic proforma that we already know is used as a starting point.

13.6 Sales volume variance

(Actual sales − budgeted sales) × standard margin

(AS − BS)SM

This can also be illustrated in this way.

(ASSM − BSSM)

The sales variance may be calculated using either standard profit or standard contribution margin.

What we need to do is to introduce a standard mix to the analysis.

Revised analysis

ASSM

Difference = Mix variance

AS(Std Mix)SM   Total = Volume variance

Difference = Yield variance

BSSM

 Learn

IE Illustrative example 13.5

Budget and standards

Sales	Units	Standard price	Standard cost
Zain	1,500	$50	$40
Meen	2,500	80	$60
Actual results			
Sales	Units	Price	
Zain	2,000	$55	
Meen	2,250	$83	

Calculate the sales mix and quantity variances

Material inputs	Zain	Meen	Total	Variance
	$	$	$	$
ASSM Zain (2,000 x (50 - 40)) Meen (2,250 x (80 - 60)	20,000	45,000	**65,000**	Mix Variance 4,063 A
AS(SM)SM Zain (4,250 x 15/40 x 10) Meen (4,250 x 25/40 x 20)	15,938	53,125	**69,063**	Quantity Variance 4,063 F
BSSM Zain (1,500 x 10) Meen (2,500 x 20)	15,000	50,000	**65,000**	

Comment

Mix variance

We are selling more of Zain at a lower standard margin and less of Meen at a higher standard margin. This may be due to the fact that the products are too similar, allowing customers to get what they want for less with the cheaper model.

Quantity variance

We have sold more units overall than expected leading to a greater than expected profit for the company. This could be due to the market growing more than expected or the overall product line being more popular than originally thought.

 Principle

Interpretation of sales mix and quantity variances

13.7 Market share and market size variances

Another way to analyse the sales volume variance is to consider it in relation to the wider market for the product. By doing so, more information can be established for whether the market itself is growing or shrinking and the degree of penetration of the product within that wider market.

Again we start the sales volume pro forma:
(AS – BS) SM or ASSM – BSSM

To consider the impact of the market size we need to calculate a revised budgeted sales volume (RBS) based on the change in the volume of the overall market

Proforma

ASSM (actual sales at standard margin)

Difference = Market share variance

RBSSM (Revised sales at standard margin)

Difference = Market size variance

BSSM (Budgeted sales at standard margin)

 Learn

IE **Illustrative example 13.6**

Below are the budgeted, standard and actual data for the product Mo:

Budget and standards

Sales	units	standard price	standard variable cost
Mo	10,000 units	$15	$8

Actual result

Sales	units	price
Mo	8,800 units	$16

The budgeted total market for the Mo is 1,000,000 units. However, the actual sales for this market was only 900,000 units

Required:

Sales market share and market size variances.

Let us first do the revised sales working

Budgeted sales × Actual total market/budgeted total market

10,000 units × 900,000 units/1,000,000 units = 9,000 units

ASSM	$61,600		
8,800 units x $7		Market share variance	$1,400 A
RBSSM	$63,000		
9,000 units x $7		Market size variance	$7,000 A
BSSM	$70,000		
10,000 units x $7			

Comment

The performance of the company is poor. In a declining market the sales have been lower than expected due to a loss of market share. The sales price variance is not asked for but notice that we have sold at a higher price than expected which could explain the loss of market share and may be a good move in a declining market if we are concerned with falling profitability. It could however lead to a lack of competitiveness in the longer term.

 Principle

Interpretation of market size and market share variances

13.8 Behavioural aspects of standard costing

13.8.1 Variances in a JIT and TQM environment

Variance analysis as practised is best served by setting standard quantities at standard prices. A possible dysfunctional effect is that a manager might be motivated, on variance analysis alone, to make the highest number as quickly and efficiently as possible, without looking at the bigger picture.

Merely looking at quantity and price ignores the stockholding and working capital impact of production for items which are stored and not sold.

- Units of production are stored in warehouses, and the cost of this storage is not found in classical variance analysis.
- As well as the direct cost of warehousing, the labour and materials are paid for, and working capital is tied up in stock
- Overheads are a 'given'.

JIT production requires that companies minimise stockholding, and hence manufacture only when needed for sale or upstream. If sales demand is volatile, then production will be as well. Variance analysis as practised above does not reflect this reality, as it does not capture all the costs.

TQM requires attention to quality, being fitness for use with errors designed out of the system. TQM identifies a range of quality costs and overhead.

- In standard costing, overheads are a 'given'. TQM suggests that overheads related to quality control and rectification are affected by the quality of output, and are not captured by non-TQM related costing systems
- There should be minimal wastage or defects in a TQM system.
- Some standard costing systems allow for 'standard waste', but the TQM approach is that this is inherently efficient.
- The culture of TQM requires continuous improvements to processes. If standard costing is used as a planning and performance monitoring tool, this does not promote the culture

13.8.2 Rapidly changing environments

A rapidly changing environment will offer challenges to firms

Overall demand may be very volatile and hard to plan for	Standard
Consumers may want different things quickly. There may be rapid changes of product specification as a result of changing consumer requirements	Speed to market and other measures may be more important measures of business success
Prices may increase or fall rapidly	Inflation, especially if it varies, can mean that standard costs would have to be changed

Standard costing of itself becomes less relevant in these environments, as firms need to measure themselves on flexibility and responsiveness.

IE Illustrative example 13.7

An example is the clothing chain Zara. This firm pioneered 'fast fashion'. This means changing product lines very quickly. Zara is able to respond very quickly and bases its manufacturing operations close to where they are sold, rather than importing from China, which takes longer. Clearly a different set of measures – speed to market, speed of manufacture, low stock (as fashions change quickly) bringing out small quantities of new clothes very quickly - are more important to the business.

13.8.3   Impact of variances on staff motivation and action

Variances are used to analyse the impact of variables on a budget – price, quantity, time and mix. Control action is taken as a result. This control action can impact on people, and the effect of variances as motivators or demotivators will depend on how the standards are set in the first place (realistic) and they are implemented, eg as punishments or to reward performance

(a) Price

For example, if high raw material prices cause a price variance, there might be two outcomes:

-   Negative outcome: reduce quality, by corner cutting which may damage the reputation of the brand
-   Positive outcomes: buy more effectively, redesign the product

If variances are monitored crudely, the motivation will be to reduce quality Food safety examples (horsemeat sold as beef in the UK, rats sold as chicken in China) show the impact on badly managed performance measures on product quality.

(b) Labour: either encourage inefficiency or can support a culture of continuous improvement.

If a labour variance is positively exceeded:

-   Negative outcome: employees will revert to the 'standard', for fear of giving too much away to management, if they feel they are not rewarded for the hard work
-   Positive outcome: a culture of continuous improvement where embedded process improvements are celebrated and rewarded

(c) Sales variances

Many sales forces are highly motivated by regular commission.

The risks are that there may be a rush to book sales by the month- or period-end when performance is measured. This can lead to misdirected effort

- Sales to customers who are lower credit risks, in order to hit sales targets
- Extra discounts taken early, reducing the overall profit

➡ Key Learning Points

- The material usage variance can be sub-analysed into the material mix variance and the material yield variance
  - Mix variance: Measures the quantity of each individual material used to produce output, compared with the standard mix.
  - Yield variance: Measures the output from production, taking into account the inputs used. (C5a)

- Sales volume variance can be sub-analysed into the sales mix and quantity variances, where the company sells more than one different product:
  - Mix variance: Measures the mix of products sold compared to the standard mix.
  - Quantity variance: Measures the volume of units of each product sold compared to the standard. (C6a)

- Planning and operational variances make a distinction between the part of the variances which can be controlled by management (operational) and the variances which are not controllable by management (planning).
  - Planning variances: These are calculated by comparing the original standards with the revised standards taking into account uncontrollable factors such as market price movements for materials.
  - Operational variances: These are calculated by comparing the revised standards with actual results. (C7c)

What's the story?

Stop and think through the 'story' of this chapter and how it links with other chapters (use the Overview to help).

Learning example solutions

EG Solution 13.1

SQSP	$45,000	
(6 x 2,500 x 3)	Usage variance	$3,000Adv
AQSP	$48,000	
(16,000 x 3)	Price variance	$2,500Fav
AQAP	$45,500	

According to the basic analysis the purchasing manager (price variance) is doing a good job but the production manager (usage variance) is doing poorly.

EG Solution 13.2

Planning variances (substitute the actual with the revised standard)

SHSR			
(0.5x80,000x12)	$480,000		
RSHSR		Efficiency variance	$96,000 Fav
(0.5x0.8x80,000x12)	$384,000		
RSHRSR		Rate variance	$64,000 Adv
(0.5x0.8x80,000x14)	$448,000		

Comment
These variances change over time, no control significance.

Operational variances

RSHRSR	$448,000		
(from above)		Efficiency variance	$14,000 Adv
AHRSR	$462,000		
(33,000x14)		Rate variance	$14,500 Fav
AHAR	$447,500		

Comment
The production manager has performed well in overall terms as the total variance is positive ($500 Fav). There have been savings in the rate paid per hour that are off-set by the slightly lower efficiency than expected.

14

Performance Management

Context

This exam has been described by the examiner as a performance measurement paper rather than a management accounting paper. There is some truth in this inasmuch as the emphasis of many of the questions has been about performance measurement together with other elements of the syllabus.

3Q

1. Can you describe the balanced scorecard?

2. According to the building block model, what are the three areas into which performance measurement is divided?

3. How would you measure the performance of a not-for-profit organisation?

14.1 Performance measurement

When considering measuring performance the nature of the business will determine how it is done and what measures are appropriate. There are two basic measurement areas to explore:

1. Financial performance measures;
2. Non-financial performance measures.

Note that the 'controllability principle' says that managers should be held responsible just for what they can control. Hence if it isn't a manager's decision as to which materials are bought and used in their production then they shouldn't be assessed on the cost of those material in their financial performance measures. Similarly if a manager is affected by a freak storm or a general strike then the manager shouldn't be held responsible for the effect of these on any non-financial performance measures.

14.1.1   Financial measures

Financial performance measures are what most accounting systems focus on They have the advantages of being quantitative, can be expressed in numbers, comparable, everything is expressed in the same monetary unit and reconcilable and we can make sure that the numbers add up.

All traditional management accounting performance measurement systems are based on financial measures. It also links very nicely to financial accounting to which the management accounting department is likely to be closely linked.

Financial measures can be used to measure the following three areas of performance:

1. Profitability
2. Liquidity
3. Risk

Profitability

The basic measure of performance is profit. The measure of profit that is used is normally related to operating profit or PBIT (Profit Before Interest and Tax), this being the measure that is within the control of operational management.

When assessing performance of a manager it is important to only assess the manager on a profit measure that is within the control of the manager. This means that any costs or revenues that are outside the control of the manager should be excluded.

In practice the obvious uncontrollable cost for a division would be apportioned head office costs, on the basis that the incurrence of cost is controllable by head office and is charged in an arbitrary manner to the division.

Return on capital employed (ROCE)

$$\text{ROCE} = \frac{\text{Profit before interest and tax} \times 100}{\text{Capital employed}}$$

 Learn

This is also called return on investment (ROI) and is the most commonly used measure of overall profitability, this is because it assesses the performance of the business from an operational perspective before financing costs but including all operational costs such as cost of sales and operating expenses.

By comparing to the capital employed we are able to consider how well the resources are being used (the capital) in relation to the profit earned

IE Illustrative example 14.1

A company has four divisions operating within a single industry. The following financial data has been identified for past three years:

Division		North	South	East	West
Capital employed ($000s)					
Year	1	250	300	4,000	600
	2	350	400	3,800	630
	3	600	410	3,600	660
Profit (PBIT)					
Year	1	50	70	300	100
	2	70	50	300	105
	3	110	55	330	110

Discuss the performance of the four divisions.

When answering a question like this always consider the following basic ideas before developing your answer.

1. Size – what is the overall size and relative importance of the divisions;

2. Percentage performance – how has each division performed in relation to capital employed;

3. Change – what changes over time?

Once these issues are understood then a deeper analysis can be attempted

Analysis	ROCE				
Division		North	South	East	West
Year	1	20%	23%	8%	17%
	2	20%	13%	8%	17%
	3	18%	13%	9%	17%

Comments

Division East is by far the largest division in both turnover and profit which are greater than the combined performance of all other divisions. Division West comes a distant second and the other two divisions are relatively small. It is possible the Division's North and South are relatively new and are in the growth phase whereas as the other two are in mature markets.

Divisions North and West both appear to be generating a substantial return year on year. East is performing at a lower level but is generating consistent return that will be acceptable if they cover the financing costs of the business. South appears a more volatile performer maybe due to the nature of its specific market.

In relative terms North division has performed very well, this is particularly impressive given the substantial growth that this division has achieved whilst still maintaining a good return. The return has fallen by two percentage points, suggesting that margins are under pressure.

 **Principle**

Steps in assessing financial performance

The ROCE may be sub-analysed into two further profitability measures:
The performance pyramid

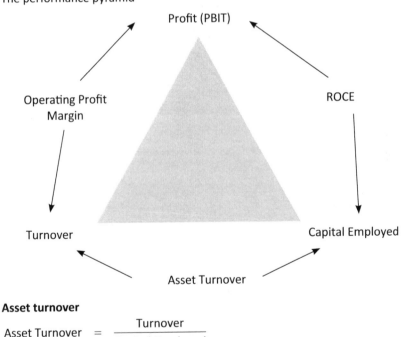

Asset turnover

$$\text{Asset Turnover} = \frac{\text{Turnover}}{\text{Capital Employed}}$$

Learn

A measure that considers the level of sales in relation to the capital employed. The asset turnover will depend very much on the type of industry, manufacturing would be likely to have more assets relative to sales than a retail operation.

When used to compare one company with another within the same industry then the measure may highlight the difference between a wholesaler or high volume retailer with high turnover rather than a specialist retailer with relatively low turnover.

IE Illustrative example 14.2

A company has four divisions operating within a single industry. The following financial data has been identified for past three years.

Division		North	South	East	West
Capital employed ($000s)					
Year	1	250	300	4,000	600
	2	350	400	3,800	630
	3	600	410	3,600	660
Turnover					
Year	1	1,000	600	20,000	3,000
	2	1,600	700	21,000	3,000
	3	3,000	750	19,000	3,000

Discuss the performance of the four divisions.

Division		North	South	East	West
Asset turnover					
Year	1	4x	2x	5x	5x
	2	4.6x	1.7x	5.5x	4.8x
	3	5x	1.8x	5.3x	4.5x

Comments
Asset turnover illustrates how well the assets are being utilised. South has a substantially lower turnover than the other divisions which may suggest that their sales are more difficult to generate or require greater input in time than other divisions. All other divisions seem to have similar asset turnovers of around 5x.

The asset turnover of North may suggest that the division is becoming increasingly efficient with making and servicing sales, possibly due to streamlining services as they grow larger. The opposite holds true of West whose turnover is progressively falling, which may be a cause for concern.

 Principle

Interpreting asset turnover

Operating profit margin (OPM)

$$OPM = \frac{Profit\ (PBIT) \times 100}{Turnover}$$

 Learn

This measure considers the profit generated as a proportion of the selling price. The profit margin again is highly dependent on the industry type, from our own experience we can understand that the profitability of one unit relative to another will differ.

Reasons for differences between profitability within the same industry sector may include:

1. Perceived quality or brand;
2. Amount of marketing or product awareness;
3. Underlying quality;
4. Scarcity of the product.

EG **Learning example 14.1**

Division		North	South	East	West
Turnover					
Year	1	1,000	600	20,000	3,000
	2	1,600	700	21,000	3,000
	3	3,000	750	19,000	3,000
Profit (PBIT)					
Year	1	50	70	300	100
	2	70	50	300	105
	3	110	55	330	110

Discuss the performance of the four divisions.

Principle

Interpreting operating profit margin

Liquidity

A company must have sufficient funds to operate. If a company runs out of cash it does not matter how profitable the company is, it will risk becoming insolvent and failing. There are two measures of liquidity:

1. Current ratio;
2. Quick (acid test) ratio.

Current ratio

$$\text{Current ratio} \quad = \quad \frac{\text{Current assets}}{\text{Current liabilities}}$$

 Learn

By comparing current assets to current liabilities the current ratio assesses how much of the current ratio is funded short-term (using current liabilities) and how much is funded on a more permanent basis.

The more of current assets funded permanently the better and less risky that is for the company. Current liabilities such as overdraft facilities may be withdrawn as a source of finance at any time. Therefore from a risk perspective the higher the current ratio the better.

At the same time if the current ratio is too high this may mean that the company is being inefficient by holding too high a level of current assets in relation to current liabilities.

The traditional safe level of current ratio is 2 times which means that current assets equal twice the value of current liabilities or half of the current assets are funded by current liabilities and the other half is funded on a permanent basis.

Quick ratio

$$\text{Quick (acid test) ratio} \quad = \quad \frac{(\text{Current assets} - \text{Inventory})}{\text{Current liabilities}}$$

 Learn

The quick ratio is a more immediate measure of the ability to pay bills as they fall due.

By comparing the liquid assets (inventory is the only illiquid current asset) to the current liabilities it is possible to see how well the current liabilities are covered if they all fell due immediately.

The traditional safe measure is 1 times which means that even if all the current liabilities fell due tomorrow the company is in a position to cover them with the liquid assets available.

Risk (Gearing)

$$\text{Gearing} = \frac{\text{Equity}}{\text{Debt} + \text{Equity}}$$

 Learn

A key measure of risk relates to the manner in which the company is funded. A company may be funded either using equity (share capital) or debt. If a company is financed solely by equity then there is no financing risk. This is because if a company has a poor year it may not earn any profit. When funded by equity this is not critical because the return paid to the shareholders in the form of a dividend may be stopped.

If a company is funded by debt there is a legal obligation to pay the interest on that debt.

Failure to do so risks company failure. The level of debt that a company may hold is dependent on a number of factors such as:

1. **Industry type** – some industries generate more volatile profits than others. If profits are highly volatile then the level of debt financing will have to be relatively low.
2. **Company size** – Smaller companies tend to have a higher risk of company failure and so should be more circumspect in their financing.
3. **Economic conditions** – If the economy is very healthy then banks are far more likely to be in a position to lend and be willing to lend. If the economy is in recession then funding is more difficult to source.

14.1.2   Problems with financial measures

Although it is important to measure the impact on financial performance there are problems with relying too much on solely financial measures. These include the following areas:

1. Short-termism;
2. Ignoring qualitative data;
3. Ignoring key performance areas;
4. Internal focus.

Short-termism
Financial results tend to be prepared around an annual cycle. Therefore any performance measure will be based around the same timeframe. If managers are being appraised on these measures this means that they may be inclined to work towards a short-term goal which could adversely affect the long-term performance.

Qualitative data
Some key issues for the company cannot be quantified. Examples may include experience and skills of staff or the perception of the brand by the customer. By attempting to measure everything in financial terms it is possible that key measures that cannot be quantified in this way are downplayed and ignored.

Key performance areas

The use of financial measures tends to mean that measures are restricted to the limited ratios illustrated above or such things as variance analysis. This means that areas of performance such as efficiency and utilisation are heavily emphasised at the expense of other critical areas such as flexibility and quality which are ignored.

Internal focus

Financial analysis is concerned with our internal financial performance. It ignores the relationship between our performance and that of our competitors which is critical to the ongoing success of the business

 Principle

Issues with focusing on financial performance only

14.1.3 Non-financial performance measures

More recently there has been an emphasis on introducing non-financial measures to augment, and in some cases, replace the financial measures traditionally used. The use of non-financial measures is intended to address some of the problems highlighted with financial measures, particularly relating to qualitative issues, wider performance areas and internal focus.

A weakness of non-financial measures is that they cannot be easily reconciled or linked together meaning that we have a wide mix of unrelated measures. There is no easy way to avoid this.

There are two models that we may use to understand the scope of non-financial measures. Note both of them have an overall financial measure included within them highlighting the fact that overall financial health is of course still important. The difference is that the supporting detailed performance measures is non-financial rather than financial. The model are:

1. The balanced scorecard (Kaplan and Norton)
2. The building block model (Fitzgerald)

The balanced scorecard

The balanced scorecard forces managers to look at the business from four important perspectives. The idea being that all of the perspectives are linked and critical to the business.

It links performance measures by requiring firms to address four basic questions:

1. How do customers see us? – Customer perspective.
2. What must we excel at? – Internal perspective.
3. Can we continue to improve and create value? – Innovation & learning perspective.
4. How do we look to shareholders? – Financial perspective.

 Learn

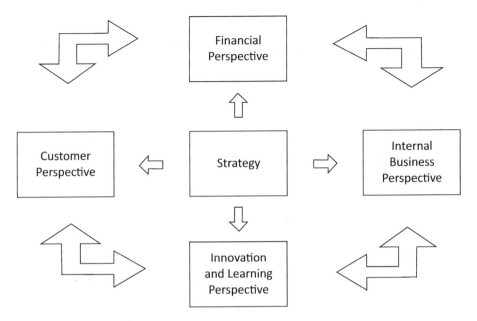

Customer perspective

- How do customers perceive the firm?
- This focuses on the analysis of different types of customers, their degree of satisfaction and the processes used to deliver products and services to customers.
- Particular areas of focus would include:
  - Customer service.
  - New products.
  - New markets.
  - Customer retention.
  - Customer satisfaction.

 Learn

Internal business perspective

- How well the business is performing.
- Whether the products and services offered meet customer expectations.
- Activities in which the firm excels?
- And in what must it excel in the future?
- Quality performance.
- Quality.
- Motivated workforce.

 Learn

Innovation and learning perspective

- Can we continue to improve and create value?
- In which areas must the organisation improve?
- Product diversification.

311

- % sales from new products.
- Amount of training.
- Number of employee suggestions.
- Extent of employee empowerment.

 Learn

Financial perspective
- This is concerned with the shareholders view of performance.
- Shareholders are concerned with many aspects of financial performance.
- Amongst the measures of success are:
    - Market share.
    - Profit ratio.
    - Return on investment.
    - Economic value added.
    - Return on capital employed.
    - Cash flow.
    - Share price.

 Learn

Service industry issues

In general services differ from manufacturing since they are:

1. Intangible.
2. Simultaneous.
3. Perishable.
4. Heterogeneous.

Remember the mnemonic SHIP or PISH.

These issues makes the measurement of services more difficult that measurement in a production environment.

Intangible
Services by their very nature are intangible, has no physical substance and difficult to measure. Unlike the production of a unit of product which can easily be quantified the provision of a service is far more difficult to measure.

Simultaneous
The services both offered and received at the same time. This means that it is normally impossible to measure and correct the provision of the service prior to it being received by the customer. The spontaneous nature of such a service means that it is likely that the service will be provided differently each and every time it is performed.

Perishable
A service is often related to time for example a tuition course would relate to a course of so many hours. If the service is not taken up by a student then that service is lost because the time spent by the tutor has been lost forever.

Heterogeneous

Every service is different, the specific needs of a customer will differ from one to another. Additionally, the same service provided may be accepted in a very different manner depending on the position of the recipient to receive it.

Again if we consider a university course, the service provided will be received differently by students based on their background, level of academic achievement and degree of consciousness.

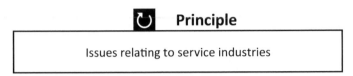

Principle

Issues relating to service industries

The building block model

This model is particularly suited to service industries.

Fitzgerald and Moon divide performance measurement into three areas:

1. **Standards**

This refers to the targets that are set within the organisation. These should be:

* High enough to motivate.
* Be owned by the employees (through participation in target-setting).
* Be seen to be equitable.

Learn

2. **Rewards**

This refers to what the organisation (and the employee) is trying to achieve. The employee will only work hard towards the achievement of a goal if there is a perceived link between working hard and receiving a bonus or benefit from that work.

* The organisation's objectives should be clearly understood.
* Employees should be motivated to work towards these objectives.
* Employees should be able to control areas over which they will be held responsible.

Learn

3. **Dimensions**

This refers to how performance will be measured. The areas are:

* Results measures:
  - Financial;
  - Competitive performance.

- Determinant measures:
  - **Quality** of service;
  - **Flexibility**;
  - (Resource) **Utilisation**;
  - **Innovation**.

You can remember the dimensions by using the mnemonic QUIF FC.

 # Learn

Results measures

The results measures relate to the need for a company to achieve results both in terms of profit (financial) but also relative to the market as a whole (competitive).

Determinant measures

To achieve the level of result there are fundamental aspects of the business that need to be measured. Those will determine the underlying performance of the business.

EG Learning example 14.2

Scotty provides services in the form of consultations to customers, the business being related to health and fitness.

The budgeted information for the year is as follows.

Non-financial data	Budget
Total client enquiries	
– new business	50,000
– repeat business	30,000
Number of client consultations	
– new business	15,000
– repeat business	12,000
Mix of client consultations	
– medical	6,000
– dietary	12,000
– fitness	9,000
Number of consultants employed	
– medical	6
– dietary	12
– fitness	9
Number of client complaints	270

Financial data

Clients are charged a fee per consultation at the rate of: medical £30; dietary £35 and fitness £25.

Each customer enquiry incurs a variable cost of £3, whether or not it is converted into a consultation.

Consultants are each paid a fixed annual salary as follows: medical £30,000; dietary £25,000; fitness £20,000.

Suggest ways in which each of these performance measures could be measured.

1. Competitiveness.
2. Flexibility.
3. Resource utilisation.
4. Quality.
5. Innovation.

14.2 Not-for-profit organisations and the public sector

In a not-for-profit environment there are specific problems:

1. Low emphasis on financial aims
2. Multiple stakeholder
3. Potential lack of financial understanding and control

Low emphasis on financial aims
In simple terms the basic objective of a not-for-profit is to provide a service without making a loss, a profit or surplus simply being either a timing issue or a means to an end where funds are being raised for future investment in the service.

Multiple stakeholders
Rather than having an overriding key stakeholder in the form of shareholders or owners many not-for-profit organisations have many competing stakeholder groups with their own unique interests all with substantial influence in the decision making process.

Potential lack of financial control
It is common for the senior management of these organisation to have little interest or ability to control the finances of the organisation. This leads to a higher likelihood of fraud and mismanagement as a result.

The wider issue is that the organisation is providing a service of social or moral worth. We can attempt to measure this service.

14.2.1 Objectives of a not-for-profit entity

The objective for such an organisation will differ widely from one organisation to another. They may include one or more of the following:

1. Client satisfaction
2. Employee satisfaction (particularly when volunteers are a substantial part of the workforce)
3. Maximisation of surplus (perhaps to assist in growth or protect against loss of future funding)
4. Growth
5. Usage of facilities (for example library services)
6. Maintenance of capability (for example a fire service or army)

The key to remember in the exam is that for every not-for-profit organisation there will be multiple objectives that have to be addressed as opposed to a profit-making organisation where profit is the key aim for satisfying the owners or shareholders.

14.2.2 Problems of performance measurement of a not-for-profit entity

1. **Multiple objectives** – As seen above most organisations will have competing objectives. The difficulty arises when attempting to identify the relative importance of the objectives.
2. **Measurement of services provided** – the nature of many services is that they are more qualitative than quantitative. When measuring such outputs it is often very difficult to get meaningful aggregate measures of performance.
3. **No profit motive** – measures such as ROI and RI cannot be used to gain an overall measure of performance
4. **Identification of cost unit** – the cost unit is likely to be relatively complex and there is likely to be more than one cost unit. For example what is a cost unit for a hospital/ there are likely to be multiple such cost units being used by a single patient.
5. **Key constraint** – For most organisations the key constraint is the level of finance available. A charity is limited to its donations and a government department is limited to its allocation from the finance department. This constraint is separate in most organisations to their end objective.
6. **Political intervention** – unlike commercial entities, not-for-profit entities are far more likely to be affected by political influence, either directly in the form of elected officials or indirectly by public sentiment.
7. **Legal considerations** – it is likely that adherence to restrictive legal rules are going to impact on a not-for-profit entity because of the nature of the organisation or the links to government at a local or national level.

 **Principle**

Difficulties associated with performance measurement in not-for-profit organisations

14.2.3 Effective performance measures

In order to establish meaningful measures within such an environment we can employ the following solutions

1. **Input measurement** – in the absence of easily measured output then more consideration can be put into the costs and resourcing of an organisation.
2. **Independent scrutiny and target setting** – There is need for fine judgement when setting qualitative targets. By use of independent experts measures can be set that reflect performance levels appropriate without introducing bias.
3. **External comparison** – A powerful assessment of the performance of an organisation is to benchmark that performance in relation to similar organisations. This allows for both historical results to be used but also best practice measures to be developed.

 Principle

> Approaches to measuring performance in not-for-profit organisations

14.2.4 Value for money (VFM)

Value for money is a framework by which not for profit organisations can be measured. It separates the performance of the business into three areas, the three E's:

1. Effectiveness
2. Efficiency
3. Economy

Effectiveness (an output measure)
This may be described as how well the organisation meets its objectives. Perhaps an easier way of understanding it would be to see how well the output of services match the client need.

Efficiency (the relationship between input and output)
This describes how well resources are utilised, it measures the output of services for a given level of resource or input.

Economy (an input measure)
This considers the cost of sourcing the input resources. The aim being to minimise the costs of the input for a given standard and level of resource.

The key to VFM is to understand that performing in a single area is not sufficient, instead the organisation must achieve in relation to all three aspects in order to provide value for money.

 Learn

14.3 Problems with performance measures

All performance measurement systems have problems associated with them. To gain an exhaustive list of the types of problems we could use the following list:

1. Tunnel vision
2. Ossification
3. Gaming
4. Sub-optimisation
5. Myopia
6. Measure fixation
7. Misrepresentation
8. Misinterpretation

You may use the mnemonic TOGS 4M to remember these better.

Tunnel vision

Undue focus on a performance measure to the detriment of other aspects. For example, the emphasis on efficiency of output to the detriment of quality of output

Ossification

A word that means 'to harden' where a measure is never changed it is 'set in stone'. It is the unwillingness to change a performance measure once it has been set up. This may mean measuring something that is unimportant or measuring it in an inappropriate way because things have changed since the measure was first established.

Gaming

The deliberate distortion of a measure in order to secure a strategic advantage. An example could be where sales are held back in one year in order that the next year's target is not set so high. This is a form of management fraud.

Sub-optimisation

The achievement of some objective at the expense of others. This is particularly likely to occur where performance measures of one area of responsibility impact on another. For example, if a purchasing manager buys lower quality material they achieve a favourable variance that may adversely affect the ability of the production manager to do their job.

Myopia

The medical term for short- or near-sightedness. This simply means short-termism at the expense of poorer long-term performance.

Measure fixation

Behaviour and activity towards achieving a particular value or performance measure even if that measure is impossible to achieve This may lead to other parts of the business suffering due to excessive energy being expended on achieving the goal. This may be particularly apparent when the measure will lead to substantial bonuses.

Misrepresentation

The reporting of acceptable performance that has not been achieved. This is a form of management fraud.

Misinterpretation

Failure of the measure to accommodate the complexity of the environment it is intended to cover.

 **Principle**

Behavioural issues related to performance measurement

14.4 Accounting information systems

Accounting information systems are more than just software. Accounting information systems typically process financial and other data into reports for management. The basis is transactions data (for example sales, purchases) but also adjustments such as deprecation, and judgment issues such as asset valuations. Frequently, these can be purchases on a modular basis (packages such as Sage). This information is used in different ways

It is quite commonly the case that an organisation will have no single 'accounting information system' as such. A firm may use package software to process sales orders, and go to an outsource partner for payroll. Data from both systems may be transferred by journal into a nominal ledger system. Budgeting and financial modelling may be outside the accounting information system, and maybe a manual process involving spreadsheet models of various degrees of sophistication. For example, the accountant preparing the management accounts may access transaction data.

Typically, also, the management accountant may be able to interrogate and drill down into the data, with specialised reports.

So it is probably better to see the 'accounting information system' as more than just a software package, but the organisation and reporting structure as well,

14.4.1   Uses and requirements of accounting information

Management activity	Implications for accounting information system
Strategic planning This is the setting of long term goals, in the light of the environment of the organisation, and its internal capabilities, and the development of plans to achieve the goals	Strategic planning is forward looking, and must incorporate environmental information. A lot of financial modelling will be needed. Furthermore, frequently this is a one-off exercise, with financial models of alternative business plans, and investment cases up for comparison. The plans are incorporated in a strategic budget, which determines resource usage. The accounting system can contribute historic data, but this needs to be aligned with information about market trends and competitors.
Management control	Management control typically relates to performance against budget or prior year, with key performance indicators, both financial and non-financial, as the measurement tool. It is possible that Enterprise Resource Planning systems will aggregate much information to get an overall financial view, but some KPIs are non-financial: for example, the success of digital marketing campaigns are measurable ('click through' rates, and so on). Variance analysis and standard costing apply.
Operational control	This covers short timescales and is likely to be focused on transactions. Bank reconciliations are an example of operational control, for example just to check the accuracy of the processed information. Remedial action over breach of credit limits is an example. As transaction processing systems- see below -
Decision making	Decision making is forward-looking. Typical needs are the identification of fixed and variable costs, opportunity costs, committed and discretionary costs and, importantly, cash flows.

You should not consider that 'strategic planning' is somehow more important than operational control. If operational matters go badly wrong – eg if they show the company is losing cash – then operational controls are very important.

14.4.2   Management information systems (MIS)

MIS converts data from internal sources into information to aid managers to make decisions. Information from these systems tends to be used by tactical managers. It may be manual or automated, but mostly it is automated for timely process of the data to be used in decision making.

The management accounting information system generally has three aims:

1. To gather and process information for costing – products, services
2. To gather and process information needed for planning, control and evaluation
3. To provide information for decision making

 Learn

Management information systems are generally divided into a number of sub-systems.

14.4.3   Transaction processing system (TPS)

TPS captures, stores, batch processes and summarises routine transactions and other accounting data. It is mainly used at the operational level of management. Inventory and ledger records are good examples of routine TPS.

 Learn

A TPS has mainly four functions.

Collection	Storage	Modification	Retrieval
Using source documents	input the data and keep it	processing, real-time or batch	future use of further processing

The transactions may be batch processed or real-time processed

14.4.4   Executive information system (EIS)

Executive information systems aid strategic decision making by providing internal and external information which is relevant to the critical success factors of the organisation.

 Learn

14.4.5   Enterprise resource planning system (ERPS)

An ERP system is a computer system that pulls together information from all parts of the organisation and provides more integration between different parts of the company.

Involves the planning of:

*   Manufacturing
    -   planning for production
    -   planned purchasing of materials
    -   quality management and control

- Sales and distribution
  - management of sales orders and customers
  - transportation and shipping

- Accounting
  - accounts receivables and payables
  - budgeting
  - standard costing

- Human resources
  - training
  - recruitment
  - employee development

 Learn

14.5 Open and closed systems

A system is a set of interacting or interdependent components forming an integrated whole. For example, a car engine is type of system. A business organisation is also a type of system.

An open system continuously interacts with its environment or surroundings, and its components are subject to environmental influences. The interaction can take the form of taking inputs or raw materials and outputting products; or taking transaction data and converting it into information.

In practice, as far as business organisations are controlled, no system is entirely open or entirely closed. Business organisations contain many subsystems, manufacturing, human resource management, financial processes, approval processes and planning processes. Many of these systems are influenced by external factors. For example, the design of many organisation systems might be influenced by legal requirements (eg. to collect data), financial or regulatory requirements and so on. There is, for example, the requirement to retain information for audit trail purposes.

Implications for performance management of open and closed system

	Example	Merits	Problems
Open systems	For performance management this would mean that environmental data could impact all parts of the system. The performance measures of an organisation with high energy use could take average market prices into account, and recalibrate results based on these market conditions. (Airlines often quote fuel costs as a reason for underperformance.)	The organisation's performance will reflect the environment, After all, energy prices will affect the cost base and it seems only fair to reflect this.	This might introduce too much complexity into the system , so that the purpose of the system would be hard to achieve There is no incentive to take measures to deal with the environmental issues. For example, if energy prices go up, can energy usage be reduced? Or can more efficient buying be introduced?
Closed system	In this case, environmental influences are not taken into account. A company that traded overseas might see a big increase in profits as a result of changes in the exchange rate.	There is a focus on what can, in fact, be controlled. Blaming the environment for everything implies an inability to control the system.	Factors relevant to reported performance would be ignored. A closed system would not take this external factor, of the exchange rates, into account, and so the actual operating performance could be worse and artificially flattered by the exchange rate. . A rapid deterioration in the exchange rate could reveal failings elsewhere.

14.6 External considerations in performance management

External considerations arise from two sources:

Comparators' benchmarking

Companies can assess how well they are doing against:

- other companies in the same industry

- companies running similar processes in different industries

(a) Using other companies in the same industry can pose questions as to whether costs are too high or processes inefficient. In the manufacture of aircraft engines, it is said that GE earns a higher return than Pratt and Whitney or Rolls Royce. These broad comparators have to be used with care, given:

- the potential variation of accounting treatments
- different strategic objectives, for example one firm may look to gain market share
- different lifecycle phases, for example comparing a new product in one company with an established product in another company
- different financial objectives
- different age of machinery

(b) Companies running similar processes in different industries

Many industries use call centres (financial services, distribution), and good practice can be transferred from one sector to another. This is not the case for industry-specific processes

Allowing for environmental conditions

Environmental and competitor conditions will affect the performance of an organisation. A sudden reduction in demand could mean lower profits through lower volumes, especially if many costs are fixed. Performance can therefore be measured against the reduced demand in the short term.

However, the management team will be assessed on how well it has prepared for the adverse conditions, what measures it can take etc.

(a) Has it prepared for the downturn, eg by reducing its fixed costs, having a flexible workforce, removed poorly performing products

(b) If facing a new competitor, does it have sales strategies to neutralise the threat

(c) If facing an increase in costs of a key input (eg fuel) what steps has it taken

(d) Has it ensured it will not sacrifice long term for short term

Competitors will be facing the same environmental conditions, and so measuring the performance of an organisation can also be assessed against these benchmarks.

External insight and stakeholder interest

Many organisations exist in a complex stakeholder ecosystem, and have to juggle possibly competing objectives. In a for-profit organisation, it is clear that long term profitability is an overriding benchmark. In a not-for-profit organisation, financial objectives are one of several types of objectives:

A university for example might have the following stakeholders:

- Students
- The local community, if the university is a major employer
- The greater good, eg research outputs
- Academic staff

- The global academic community
- Professional services staff
- Employers looking for a skilled workforce

There are various ranking systems for universities which take variables into account such as:

- Ranking of research departments
- Student experience surveys
- Financial performance
- ...and so on

14.6.1   Performance in the light of external considerations

Method	
External benchmarking of other organisations or processes, and incorporation of benchmarks into KPIs	An organisation can compare performance with other organisations in the sector (eg internet service providers compare download speeds) or other organisations providing similar services. Given there is, frequently, variability in performance, an organisation might seek to improve its performance relative to their peers. British Universities, for example, are listed in various league tables. The sector is highly regulated and there is a National Student Survey on various levels of satisfaction. Performance relevant to the sector is reviewed. If the organisation produces similar outputs, then the indicators can at least alert management to the fact that there may be opportunities elsewhere for improved performance.
Sensitivity analysis and risk analysis	External considerations can be brought into sensitivity analysis of costs and revenues, for identifying breakeven points.
Business scenarios	In strategic planning processes, coherent business scenarios can be developed and organisational forecasts can be reviewed in the light of those scenarios
Continuous budgets	The whole future budget of the business can be reviewed in the light of performance on a rolling basis.

It is also worth noting what is not covered in performance measurement, which are more qualitative factors relevant to the underlying strength or quality of the business. For example, the resilience of a business to a variety of pressures; the quality of the customer base (eg ability to pay) and so on.

14.6.2 Behavioural implications

What gets measured gets managed: over focus on the indicator to the detriment of other important issues	If the performance indicators are linked to reward, there is an incentive to focus on the indicators rather than the underlying mission of the organisation. Other important factors may be lost in the process: for example, output may be maximised at the loss of quality. Sales may be pursued at the expense of credit worthiness.
Gaming the system	At the worst, there may be attempts actively to manipulate the indicators by artificially gaming the data. A large number of corporate scandals (eg Enron) can perhaps be attributed to this. Complex accounting rules can be manipulated.
Risky behaviour	Too narrow focus on some indicators can lead to risky behaviour.
Special pleading	Depending on the organisational target, environmental factors can be used as excuses, as opposed to mere explanations, for underperformance.

14.7 Sources and uses of management accounting information

Internal sources

Source	Use for control purposes
Production department Materials usage reports Breakdown and maintenance Idle time Production schedules Rejects and rework Labour rates	You ought to understand by now how these can be used in variance analysis. Production data can be used to identify peaks and troughs in activity, and when extra resources might be needed, as well as forecasting other costs, and measuring the costs of quality
Despatch and warehouse Total stock holding Obsolete stock holding Accurate stock picking Despatch costs	Despatch costs are variable, and some firms recover this by charging for postage or even seeing despatch as a profit centre. Let us not forget that goods ordered online have to be delivered to someone's doorstep. Also, stock and its depletion and conversion into cash are components of working capital. Just-in-time inventory management would suggest low stock costs are ideal.
Procurement department Prices on key inputs or procurements Major contracts, including service level agreements	Some companies have procurement specialists in-house (or outsource) to manage key overheads, such as travel, facilities. Printing companies have specialist buyers who understand market trends.
Human resource department Total staffing levels Staff turnover and retention Training	High staff turnover can be quite costly. For example recruitment fees, retraining, and overtime for those who have to 'cover', as well as the loss of experienced staff or staff who have close relationships with clients. Training is a way of retaining staff as a result of career development.

Source	Use for control purposes
Customer services Telephone answering speed Dropped calls Types of calls, eg new orders Conversion rates	For example, if there are many dropped calls, this suggests orders are being lost, or given to competitors.
Marketing / business development Website hits Market share and market size	It may be possible to establish a relationship between website visits and sales, and this can therefore be predictive of future revenue. Market share and size data can indicate trends in revenue, provided clients are retained.
Sales department Gross sales revenue Volumes Discount rates Timing of payments (eg on long-term contracts Credit payment terms Sales pipeline (contracts not yet realised) Staffing, commission and business development costs	This enables prediction of revenues and profit margins on products. Combining sales with marketing and despatch information can help identify the costs of serving different customer groups. Credit payment terms also affect cashflow. The sales department has its own overheads, such as personnel and travel. Client contracts might specify service levels, and penalties for non-compliance
Database, loyalty schemes	Some firms 'mine' customer data for behaviour and buying patterns. These enable them to change stock levels or items on sale, to plan for seasonal changes and by constantly reviewing trends they can adjust their plans accordingly, eg by selling some items or withdrawing others

External sources

Source	Use for control purposes
Trade associations, publications, web sites etc	Many industries have trade bodies which provide aggregated data on factors affecting in industry, eg raw material costs
HR and recruitment consultancies	Appropriate salary levels for types of employee Labour market trends These can enable an organisation to identify an appropriate rate
Government departments	Understanding future regulation can help the cost to be modelled The Office of National Statistics publishes industry data, allowing comparability
Commodity exchanges	These give current and future estimated prices of commodities, which are important in some industries (eg manufacturing, food processors, retailers) though less so in others.
Management consultants, accountancy firms etc	These typically have industry practices, which identify trends in the industry
Competitor behaviour	Competitor pricing and behaviour can be a useful reference point
Market research agencies	Some generic data is often produced, but most companies engage them for specific purposes
Customers	Customers have more opportunities to express their feelings, via social media and so on. The level of complaints indicates that customers' service time is taken up in handling complaints as opposed to selling or serving. Corporate clients can give feedback directly to key account managers and so on.

14.7.1 Costs and benefits of external information

Advantages
- Sometimes this data is free

- It is more likely to cover the entire industry or customer segment, and so provide an industry benchmark, against which a firm can compare itself
- It is worth using outside resources for one-off exercises where the cost of data capture and analysis is too high or is impractical
- It is likely to be more objective and not shaped by internal 'political' considerations

Drawbacks

- As it refers to industry benchmarks, it cannot address what an organisation might do uniquely to improve its performance
- It might be too 'general' to be of much value to organisations working in narrowly defined segments of the markets
- Unless specially commissioned, it is available to everyone
- Management consultants and market research exercises can be expensive

14.7.2   Internal information

Internal information is created by the capture, recording and processing of transactions data, and the use of that data to create management reports and answer queries about it.

For example, a customer services executive, who is paid a salary, will pick up a phone, talk to the customer, take the order, code it and input it to the sales order processing system. This sales order purchasing system has been purchased, it is probably being depreciated. This data is used for a number of purposes, to generate invoices. In many cases, standard reports will have been devised. This data may then be transferred to the financial accounting system.

If orders are taken over a website, clearly some of the manual processing goes away. Even so, the firm itself will have invested in the website (a capital cost which will be subject to a depreciation charge), this IT infrastructure will need to be maintained, and integrated to other systems, such as stock and despatch, and so on.

Even though the initial purpose of this is transaction processing, this data is used to create information. The costs of the management information include amongst others, data capture, process and interpretation costs:

- Obtaining the information, which could involve time spent by the staff involved
- The costs of processing the transaction itself, and other outputs (VAT invoices etc), including time, activities, supervision of the customer service team
- The costs of the report writing, transfer to accounting systems, and modelling software to make it into useable management information
- The capital costs of investing in the software, training, IT support and so on
- The costs of management accountants paid to interpret the data
- The costs of any queries or interrogation into the data

Much of this data must be collected anyway: it is translated into management information

The advantages of using internal data are that it is 'real' and reflects genuine transactions. It is also specific to the organisation hence relevant to it.

The disadvantages are that:

- The data collected may not matter particularly to customers, who ultimately pay for goods and services
- It is a truism that 'what gets measured gets managed', and so managers need to ensure that they measure the right things.
- The information systems, especially legacy systems, may not support the management information needs of the organisation
- IT may not incorporate analysis of environmental factors or comparisons that are easily available.

Controls over internal information

Controls over internal information are needed for these reasons

- The information may be commercially sensitive, and may help competitors if stolen
- The information may relate to 3rd party confidential negotiations
- The information may affect the share price of an organisation, and there are rules as to when this should be released
- Organisations are typically bound by data protection legislation
- The information may have a reputational impact
- Social and digital communications media means that leaked information spreads quickly. People 'talk' via email, yet all emails are saved and can be used in litigation; confidential documents are often sent via email. Customers make use of social media, and customers have to respond to this
- A lot more data is collected about customers and users
- Organisations are under threat from organised crime, industrial espionage and other types of hacking.
- Paradoxically, many organisations have to share knowledge internally.

There is no 'one best way' so a number of reinforcing measures are used to protect internal information, no matter how sensitive. These can be deployed with greater degree of rigour depending on the information. It is of course hard to deter the determined hacker or fraudster.

Communications strategy to shape internal messaging	Some organisations have a formal communications strategy with newsletters. As well as letting staff know what is going on, the assumption is that this will be leaked outside, and so the contents are crafted. Even though this is strictly speaking internal information, organisations are porous, and so some internal communications can be drafted with external communications in mind.
Legal and HR measures to create a security culture	(1) Clauses related to commercial confidentiality can be written into all employment contracts; this gives organisations a legal sanction against those who breach it (2) Employment contracts also contain clauses about appropriate email uses (3) HR policies can clearly spell out what is appropriate and not appropriate
Technological and software measures to reinforce the security culture	(1) Data can be stored on different drives, with different sets of permissions. IT administrators are therefore powerful, but permissions and restricted distribution lists (2) Certain documents may only be accessed on shared drives, such as SharePoint sites, for which permission is needed (3) It is possible to restrict forwarding of documents (4) Other measures include regular changing of passwords, virus and malware protection. (5) The IT department can review access attempts
Physical measures	Some information may be stored in one physical location, accessed only by certain people. Typically payroll, the legal department and finance might only be accessed by authorised personnel with passkeys. Simple security such as passkeys, coded locks and so on can protect these floors.

Key Learning Points

Financial performance measures – financial ratios and what they mean. (D4a)
- Non-financial measures:
  - Balanced scorecard model
  - Building blocks model (D4e)

- Performance measurement in not-for-profit organisations (D6b)
- Problems with performance measurement (D6c)

 ## What's the story?

Stop and think through the 'story' of this chapter and how it links with other chapters (use the Overview to help).

Learning example solutions

EG Solution 14.1

Division	North	South	East	West
Profit margin				
Year 1	5%	11.7%	1.5%	3.3%
Year 2	4.4%	7.1%	1.4%	3.5%
Year 3	3.7%	7.3%	1.7%	3.7%

Comments

Profitability differs substantially between divisions considering that they are in the same Industry. East has only a marginal return but it appears attempts have been made to improve this in the final year. East appears locked in a continuous price war in a highly competitive industry.

North is also suffering from a dramatic fall in margins. Maybe this is as a result of fast growth that has led to the need for discounting, this could be an active strategy to grow more quickly than competitors and gain market share.

South enjoys very healthy profitability with a bumper year in year three. This may suggest that South may have a less competitive environment that the other divisions. West is quietly improving the profit margin year-on-year.

EG Solution 14.2

The key to establishing the measures is to try to and prepare a ratio of some sort, one value in relation to another value.

Competitiveness
A measure of competitiveness could be the percentage of consultation to the enquiries. The enquiries reflecting the amount of overall activity and the consultations being the actual units of service being provided. The higher the conversion of enquiries to consultations the more competitive the company could be argued to be.

Flexibility
A difficult measure to quantify, it relates to the ability of the company to satisfy the demands of the customer or alternatively the ability to respond to the changing needs of the market. A measure here could relate to the spread of services and the proportion of resources to each type of consultation. This is probably a more difficult area than most to come up with a measure so focus on other dimensions first in an exam question.

Resource utilisation
A measure that relates input to output, in this situation calculate the consultations per consultant. The higher the number of consultations the better.

Quality

An easy way to measure quality is in terms of quality failure. In this example I would look at the client complaints in relation to the overall level of activity or number of consultations.

Innovation

Innovation relates to change. This again is often problematic to assess. Unless there is an obvious element of change the easy way of measuring change is to focus on the investment of funds to achieve that change.

15

Divisional Performance and Transfer Pricing

Context

This chapter looks at the results of divisions within a company and how to assess how well the division is doing. Some of the measures will be familiar to you at a company level, they have just been applied to a division which allows a comparison to be made.

Secondly we consider the effect of transfer pricing, where goods or services are transferred between divisions within a company. Above all the price should be fair to both divisions so look out to decide if the transfer price is fair.

3Q

1. Can you list the disadvantages of decentralisation of authority and responsibility?

2. Are the overall company performance and individual division performance affected by transfer prices?

3. Do you know what a 'fair' transfer price is?

15.1 Divisional performance appraisal

15.1.1 Responsibility accounting

Decentralisation

Decentralisation is delegating responsibilities to divisional managers or unit heads. In any large organisation it is not possible for the chief executive to manage all parts of the organisation. In this situation there must be some decentralisation of authority and responsibility where the responsibility to achieve results is delegated to junior levels of management.

Decentralisation is normally done by divisionalisation where the organisations are separated into autonomous units based on a process, geographical or product basis.

Advantages

- It increases motivation of the divisional managers as they feel involved in the decision-making of the organisation.
- It is a form of training for the divisional managers and it easy for them to rise through the ranks to strategic positions.
- It should promote goal congruence (see later), as all decisions been taken are all geared towards achieving the objectives of the whole organisation.
- It drastically reduces the time taken to make decisions.

Disadvantages

- Divisional managers may make dysfunctional decisions (decisions that are not in the best interests of the organisation).
- There is a need for a performance appraisal system to assess the performance of individual managers

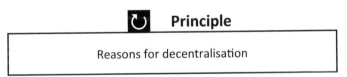

Principle

Reasons for decentralisation

15.1.2 Performance evaluation measures

The basic measure of performance is profit. The measure of profit that is used is normally related to operating profit (or PBIT), this being the measure that is within the control of operational management.

When assessing performance of a manager it is important to only assess the manager on a profit measure that is within the control of the manager. This means that any costs or revenues that are outside the control of the manager should be excluded.

In practice the obvious uncontrollable cost for a division would be apportioned head office costs on the basis that the incurrence of cost is controllable by head office and is charged in an arbitrary manner to the division.

When looking at an investment centre the manager is able to control the amount of investment in the division. It is normal to assess the performance of profit in relation to investment made by head office in the division using either return on investment (ROI) or residual income (RI)

Return on investment (ROI)

$$\text{Return on investment (ROI)} = \frac{\text{Profit before interest and tax} \times 100}{\text{Capital employed}}$$

 Learn

ROI (also called return on capital employed or ROCE) is expressed as a percentage, making it widely understood by managers. It can be used to compare the performance of divisions of different sizes.

Since it is a relative measure it can lead to managers turning down profitable projects (since not profitable enough to maintain the current ROI).

Residual income (RI)

Residual income (RI) = Profit − (Capital employed × the cost of capital)

 Learn

RI ensures that decisions made are in the best interest on the organisation as a whole (if a project has a positive NPV then it also has a positive RI). However, it encourages the use of aged assets. It cannot be used to compare the performance of the divisions on different sizes.

15.1.3   Key issues

The key issues in using ROI and RI are:

1. Goal congruent decision making
2. Short-termism
3. Management fraud
4. Transfer pricing

 Learn

Goal congruent decision making

Performance measures such as ROI and RI should not be used for decision-making. However, because these measures are used to appraise their performance, managers will in turn assess new projects in relation to ROI and RI.

EG Learning example 15.1

There are two divisions with the following performance for the current year:

Division	X	Y
Investment ($m)	10	30
Controllable profit	2	3
Required rate of return	15%	

Required:

Calculate the performance of each division using ROI and RI. Which division has superior performance?

EG Learning example 15.2

Continuing from Learning example 15.1 each division has the opportunity to invest in a new project.

Division	X	Y
Investment ($000s)	500	1,000
Controllable profit	80	120
Required rate of return	15%	

Required:

Using the measures of performance above assess the decisions that would be made by:

    (a) The divisional managers.
    (b) The Head office.

State whether the decisions are congruent with each other.

Short-termism and depreciation of assets

However the performance is appraised, it is normal to appraise divisional managers over one year. When using ROI and RI the investment will fall in value over time as a result of depreciation. This has the impact of increasing the reported performance for each year that investment is not made within the division.

A cynical manager could improve their perceived performance simply as a result of deferring investment and using increasingly outdated assets. This could well have adverse consequences to the business including:

1. Poorer quality output due to worn out machines.
2. Higher risk of machine breakdown.
3. Using outdated technology.

Management fraud

Having a single profit measure or relatively few related measures of performance appraisal allows managers to manipulate the figures underpinning these measures. In simple terms the manager only needs to overstated profits in a period or understate the investment.

Simple ways to overstate of profits:

1. Phasing of apportioned costs to charge fewer costs during the period.
2. Revenue recognition of sales in previous periods or future periods.
3. Ignoring part of the cost base.
4. Incorporate sales from other divisions.
5. Double count sales.

To reduce the opportunity for fraud a range of performance measures should be used that are inter-linked. They will make it more difficult for managers to manipulate the figures for personal gain.

Transfer Pricing

A transfer price is the price which one part of a company charges another part of a company for goods and services its produces. It is 'artificial' but should be set to get all divisions to work in the same way

The setting of the transfer price will have no direct impact on the overall performance of the company but a very real impact on individual divisional performance.

Why transfer pricing is important

1. To control costs, so that divisions demanding services take some responsibility for the costs
2. To incentivise managers to act in the interests of the wider organisation
3. To ensure that, when considering transfer pricing between divisions of the same company in different countries, that the process is lawful. Transfer pricing is used by some corporations a way of shifting profits to low-tax jurisdictions, which mean that these arrangements are scrutinised.

Features of a good transfer price

1. It must be fair, to reflect divisional performance
2. It must not distort business decision making: for example, an artificially high transfer price charged by a supplying division might encourage the buying division to go to an outside supplier, cheaper for the buying division but more expensive for the organisation
3. It must be simple to understand and operate
4. It must be acceptable to tax authorities and not abusive

A price is normally not enough in an intra-business relationship. It may be embedded in a service contract.

Methods of transfer pricing

These will differ if there is an open market value for what is supplied, so we will consider market based approaches and cost based approaches.

1. Transfer price where there is an external market price

The transfer price should equal the external market price, as a clear benchmark. The selling division makes the same profit as it does for external sales; the buying division is indifferent as to whether it buys in-house or outside. At the corporate level, the centre will want as much of the overall profit kept in the business.

A market price (perhaps adjusted for selling costs) fulfils all four criteria above.

Of course, there are some possible adjustments to be made. Like any large client, the buying division may expect a discount for a large order, known well in advance. However, there may need to be some adjustment for capacity.

IE Illustrative example 15.1

If the supplying division of a company has spare capacity that would otherwise be idle, it might charge less to keep the machines running, so the transfer price could simply be set at variable production cost. However, offering discounts to clients to earn some marginal revenue at least could apply equally to outside clients.

2. Transfer price based on full cost

In this model, the supplying division charges full cost (including absorbed overheads). If it only charges its costs, it makes no profit. All the profits are earned in the buying division. If there is an external market for the product, the supplying division has an incentive to sell outside. If not, then the supplying division is effectively just a cost centre.

Full cost plus

To avoid this perverse incentive, the supplying division can charge a mark-up. The total profit is thus spread between the two divisions. This has the benefit of simplicity. Cost plus is also used with external clients.

This does not encourage the supplying division to be efficient or offer a good service if the profit is 'guaranteed'. The threat, at least, of the buying division sourcing from outside will encourage better performance.

The mark-up needs to reflect what would be available on the open market; otherwise the supplying division will make lower profits on sales to other units within its group, and will be incentivised to go outside.

However, if the product made by the buying division is unique, and there is no external market for the product, this issue does not arise but the buying and supplying divisions do need to be incentivised

As far as the buying division is concerned, it is buying units at a defined cost per unit, so the fixed cost element of the component is invisible. The supplying division, however, accounts for its fixed costs separately. It is therefore possible for there to be mismatch, with the supplying division insisting on full recovery of its fixed costs, whereas any sale exceeding variable cost would still make a contribution.

The margin must be set at a level all parties are comfortable with.

3. Transfer price based on variable cost

If fixed overheads are not absorbed, the supplying division may charge variable costs only, with or without a mark-up. Fixed costs are not covered, though a contribution is made. Does this matter? It all depends on how the performance of the divisions are measured and assessed by the corporate centre.

However, variable cost plus a fixed fee might cover this.

4. Other issues

You could consider applying the principles of Activity-Based Costing to a transfer pricing situation; this would show the costs of serving both the internal and external market. Selling to an internal customer may be cheaper, as it will not require an overhead of sales people or marketing; or it may be costlier if the internal customer requires excessive customisation.

The relative tax treatment on transfers between different countries can also affect the transfer pricing decision, as to where profits are booked.

5. Where no intermediate market exists

An intermediate market makes it easier to set a benchmark for a transfer price, but this does not exist for all products, hence the need for other methods.

If there is no intermediate market at all, the following options may be considered.

(a) Do not bother with transfer pricing at all, the supplying department is just a cost centre.
(b) Head office can set a transfer price which maximises the profit for the company overall, rather than let divisions negotiate and bicker with each other: this is particularly relevant where there is a complex international operation.
(c) Set inner and outer parameters for transfer pricing and let the divisions negotiate an agreement.

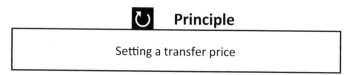

↻ Principle

Setting a transfer price

Key Learning Points

- Divisional performance measurement:
  - ROI = Controllable profit/Divisional capital employed × 100
  - RI = Controllable profit – Cost of capital × Divisional capital employed
  - Goal congruence issues (D5c)

- Transfer pricing is the internal price charged when one division provides goods or services to another division. (D5a)
- The transfer price does not affect the performance of the company as a whole, but will impact divisional performance. (D5b)

 What's the story?

Stop and think through the 'story' of this chapter and how it links with other chapters (use the Overview to help).

Learning example solutions

EG Solution 15.1

	X	Y
ROI	2/10 x 100	3/30 x 100
	= 20%	= 10%
RI	$m	$m
Profit	2	3
Imputed interest	(1.5)	(4.5)
10 x 15%		
30 x 15%		
	0.5	(1.5)

Division X exhibits superior performance both in ROI terms because the percentage is higher and in RI because the RI is positive rather than negative.

EG Solution 15.2

	X	Y
ROI	80/500 x 100	120/1000 x 100
	= 16%	= 12%
Decision		
Division	Reject	Accept
Head office	Accept	Reject

The divisional manager is concerned whether the ROI is greater or less than the existing performance. Head office is concerned whether the ROI is greater or less than the cost of capital. This may lead to a lack of goal congruence where the decision made is different as illustrated above.

RI	$000s	$000s
Profit	80	120
Imputed interest	(75)	(150)
500 x 15%		
1,000 x 15%		

RI	$000s	$000s
RI	5	(30)
Decision		
Division	Accept	Reject
Head office	Accept	Reject

The divisional management are concerned whether the RI positive or negative. This makes sure the decision is consistent with the decision of head office.

Questions

Section A – ALL 15 questions are compulsory and MUST be attempted

Please use the grid provided on page two of the Candidate Answer Booklet to record your answers to each multiple choice question. Do not write out the answers to the MCQs on the lined pages of the answer booklet.
Each question is worth 2 marks.

1. A company manufactures two products, C and D, for which the following information is available:

	Product C	Product D	Total
Budgeted production (units)	1,000	4,000	5,000
Labour hours per unit/in total	8	10	48,000
Number of production runs required	13	15	28
Number of inspections during production	5	3	8
Total production set up costs	$140,000		
Total inspection costs	$80,000		
Other overhead costs	$96,000		

Other overhead costs are absorbed on a labour hour basis.
Using activity-based costing, what is the budgeted overhead cost per unit of Product D?

A. $43·84
B. $46·25
C. $131·00
D. $140·64

2. The selling price of Product X is set at $550 for each unit and sales for the coming year are expected to be 800 units.

A return of 30% on the investment of $500,000 in Product X will be required in the coming year.
What is the target cost for each unit of Product X?

A. $385·00
B. $165·00
C. $187·50
D. $362·50

3. P Co makes two products, P1 and P2. The budgeted details for each product are as follows:

	P1	P2
	$	$
Selling price	10·00	8·00
Cost per unit:		
Direct materials	3·50	4·00
Direct labour	1·50	1·00
Variable overhead	0·60	0·40
Fixed overhead	1·20	1·00
Profit per unit	3·20	1·60

Budgeted production and sales for the year ended 30 November 20X5 are:

Product P1	10,000 units
Product P2	12,500 units

The fixed overhead costs included in P1 relate to apportionment of general overhead costs only. However, P2 also included specific fixed overheads totalling $2,500.

If only product P1 were to be made, how many units (to the nearest whole unit) would need to be sold in order to achieve a profit of $60,000 each year?

A. 25,625 units
B. 19,205 units
C. 18,636 units
D. 26,406 units

4. **Which of the following statements regarding environmental cost accounting are true?**

1. The majority of environmental costs are already captured within a typical organisation's accounting system. The difficulty lies in identifying them
2. Input/output analysis divides material flows within an organisation into three categories: material flows; system flows; and delivery and disposal flows
3. One of the cost categories used in environmental activity-based costing is environment-driven costs which is used for costs which can be directly traced to a cost centre
4. Environmental life-cycle costing enables environmental costs from the design stage of the product right through to decommissioning at the end of its life to be considered

A. (1), (2) and (4)
B. (1) and (4) only
C. (2), (3) and (4)
D. (2) and (3) only

5. To produce 19 litres of Product X, a standard input mix of 8 litres of chemical A and 12 litres of chemical B is required.

Chemical A has a standard cost of $20 per litre and chemical B has a standard cost of $25 per litre.
During September, the actual results showed that 1,850 litres of Product X were produced, using a total input of 900 litres of chemical A and 1,100 litres of chemical B.
The actual costs of chemicals A and B were at the standard cost of $20 and $25 per litre respectively.
Based on the above information, which of the following statements is true?

A. Both variances were adverse
B. Both variances were favourable
C. The total mix variance was adverse and the total yield variance was favourable
D. The total mix variance was favourable and the total yield variance was adverse

6. A budget is a quantified plan of action for a forthcoming period. Budgets can be prepared using a variety of different approaches.

   Which of the following statements regarding approaches to budgeting are correct?

   1. Incremental budgeting builds previous inefficiencies into the budget whereas zero-based budgeting encourages employees to avoid wasteful expenditure
   2. Beyond budgeting uses adaptive management processes and plans on a rolling basis
   3. Activity-based budgeting ensures that the budget is continually updated by adding a new budget period once the most recent budget period has ended
   4. Flexible budgeting recognises different cost behaviour patterns and so takes into account the organisation's overall strategy during the budget process

   A. (1) and (2) only
   B. (1), (2) and (4)
   C. (3) and (4)
   D. (1) and (3)

7. A leisure company owns a number of large health and fitness resorts, but one is suffering from declining sales and is predicted to make a loss in the next year. As a result management have identified a number of possible actions:

5. Shut down the resort and sell off the assets
6. Undertake a major upgrade to facilities costing $4·5m
7. Undertake a minor upgrade to facilities costing $2m

The upgrades are predicted to have variable results and the probability of good results after a major upgrade is 0·8, whereas the probability of good results after a minor upgrade is 0·7.
The company is risk neutral and has prepared the following decision tree.

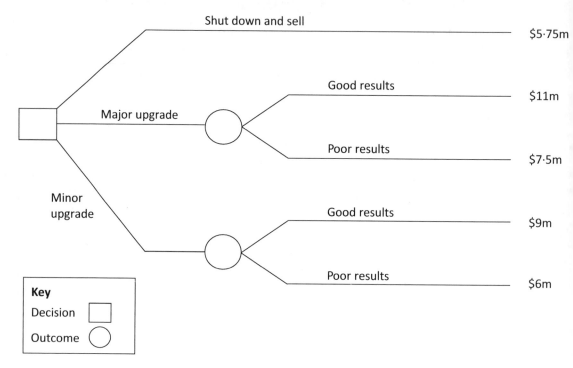

Which decision should the company make?

A. Shutdown and sell
B. Undertake the major upgrade
C. Undertake the minor upgrade
D. Undertake the major upgrade if results are good

8. A company has the following production planned for the next four weeks. The figures reflect the full capacity level of operations. Planned output is equal to the maximum demand per product.

Product	A	B	C	D
	$ per unit	$ per unit	$ per unit	$ per unit
Selling price	160	214	100	140
Raw material cost	24	56	22	40
Direct labour cost	66	88	33	22
Variable overhead cost	24	18	24	18
Fixed overhead cost	16	10	8	12
Profit	30	42	13	48
Planned output	300	125	240	400
Direct labour hours per unit	6	8	3	2

It has now been identified that labour hours available in the next four weeks will be limited to 4,000 hours.

In what order should the products be manufactured, assuming that the company wants to maximise profits in the next four weeks?

A. D, A, C, B
B. D, B, A, C
C. B, A, D, C
D. D, C, A, B

9. Def Co provides accounting services to government departments. On average, each staff member works six chargeable hours per day, with the rest of their working day being spent on non-chargeable administrative work. One of the company's main objectives is to produce a high level of quality and customer satisfaction.

Def Co has set its targets for the next year as follows:

1. Cutting departmental expenditure by 5%
2. Increasing the number of chargeable hours handled by advisers to 6·2 per day
3. Obtaining a score of 4·7 or above on customer satisfaction surveys

Which of the following options allocates the above targets to the correct value for money performance category?

	Economy	Efficiency	Effectiveness
A	(1)	(3)	(2)
B	(2)	(1)	(3)
C	(3)	(2)	(1)
D	(1)	(2)	(3)

10. Different types of information systems provide the information which organisations need for strategic planning, management and operational control.

Which of the following statements are correct?

1. Management information systems (MIS) summarise internal data into periodic reports
2. Transaction processing systems (TPS) facilitate the immediate processing of data
3. Executive information systems (EIS) utilise dashboard facilities and interactive graphics
4. Enterprise resource planning systems (ERPS) can be set up with extranet links to suppliers and customers

A. (1), (2) and (3) only
B. (1) and (3) only
C. (2) and (4) only
D. (1), (2), (3) and (4)

11. The following are all types of costs associated with management information:

1. Use of bar coding and scanners
2. Payroll department's processing of personnel costs
3. Completion of timesheets by employees
4. Input of data into the production system

Which of the above are examples of direct data capture costs?

A. (1) and (3) only
B. (1), (3) and (4)
C. (2) and (3)
D. (1) and (4) only

12. **Which of the following statements regarding life-cycle costing are correct?**

1. It can be applied not only to products but also to an organisation's customers
2. It includes any opportunity costs associated with production
3. The maturity phase is characterised by a rapid build-up in demand
4. Often between 70% to 90% of costs are determined early in the product life cycle

A. (1), (2) and (4)
B. (3) and (4)
C. (1) and (4) only
D. (2) and (3)

13. A company manufactures a product which requires four hours per unit of machine time. Machine time is a bottleneck resource as there are only ten machines which are available for 12 hours per day, five days per week. The product has a selling price of $130 per unit, direct material costs of $50 per unit, labour costs of $40 per unit and factory overhead costs of $20 per unit. These costs are based on weekly production and sales of 150 units.

What is the throughput accounting ratio?

A. 1·33
B. 2·00
C. 0·75
D. 0·31

14. Ox Co has two divisions, A and B. Division A makes a component for air conditioning units which it can only sell to Division B. It has no other outlet for sales.

Current information relating to Division A is as follows:

Marginal cost per unit	$100
Transfer price of the component	$165
Total production and sales of the component each year	2,200 units
Specific fixed costs of Division A per year	$10,000

Cold Co has offered to sell the component to Division B for $140 per unit. If Division B accepts this offer, Division A will be closed.

If Division B accepts Cold Co's offer, what will be the impact on profits per year for the group as a whole?

A. Increase of $65,000
B. Decrease of $78,000
C. Decrease of $88,000
D. Increase of $55,000

15. Which of the following statements regarding Fitzgerald and Moon's Building Blocks model are correct?

1. The determinants of performance are quality, innovation, resource utilisation and competitiveness
2. Standards are targets for performance and should be fair, achievable and controllable
3. Rewards encourage staff to work towards the standards and should be clear, motivating and controllable
4. It is a performance measurement framework particularly suitable for service organisations

A. (1), (2) and (3)
B. (2) and (3) only
C. (3) and (4)
D. (1), (2) and (4)

(30 marks)

Section B – ALL 15 questions are compulsory and MUST be attempted

Please use the grid provided on page two of the Candidate Answer Booklet to record your answers to each multiple choice question. Do not write out the answers to the MCQs on the lined pages of the answer booklet.

Each question is worth 2 marks.

The following scenario relates to questions 16–20.

Glam Co is a hairdressing salon which provides both 'cuts' and 'treatments' to clients. All cuts and treatments at the salon are carried out by one of the salon's three senior stylists. The salon also has two salon assistants and two junior stylists. Every customer attending the salon is first seen by a salon assistant, who washes their hair; next, by a senior stylist, who cuts or treats the hair depending on which service the customer wants; then finally, a junior stylist who dries their hair. The average length of time spent with each member of staff is as follows:

	Cut Hours	Treatment Hours
Assistant	0·1	0·3
Senior stylist	1·0	1·5
Junior stylist	0·6	0·5

The salon is open for eight hours each day for six days per week. It is only closed for two weeks each year. Staff salaries are $40,000 each year for each senior stylist, $28,000 each year for each junior stylist and $12,000 each year for each of the assistants. The cost of cleaning products applied when washing the hair is $1·50 per client. The cost of all additional products applied during a 'treatment' is $7·40 per client. Other salon costs (excluding labour and raw materials) amount to $106,400 each year.

Glam Co charges $60 for each cut and $110 for each treatment.

The senior stylists' time has been correctly identified as the bottleneck activity.

16. **What is the annual capacity of the bottleneck activity?**

	Cuts	Treatments
A	2,400	1,600
B	4,800	4,800
C	7,200	4,800
D	9,600	9,600

17. The salon has calculated the cost per hour to be $42·56.

What is the throughput accounting ratio (TPAR) for both services?

	Cuts	Treatments
A	1·37	1·58
B	1·41	2·38
C	1·37	1·61
D	1·41	2·41

18. Which of the following activities could the salon use to improve the TPAR?

1. Increase the time spent by the bottleneck activity on each service
2. Identify ways to reduce the material costs for the services
3. Increase the level of inventory to prevent stock-outs
4. Increase the productivity of the stage prior to the bottleneck
5. Improve the control of the salon's total operating expenses
6. Apply an increase to the selling price of the services

A. (1), (2) and (4)
B. (2), (3) and (5)
C. (3), (5) and (6)
D. (1), (4) and (6)

19. What would be the effect on the bottleneck if the salon employed another senior stylist?

A. The senior stylists' time will be a bottleneck for cuts only
B. The senior stylists' time will be a bottleneck for treatments only
C. The senior stylists' time will remain the bottleneck for both cuts and treatments
D. There will no longer be a bottleneck

20. Which of the following statements regarding the theory of constraints are correct?

1. It focuses on identifying stages of congestion in a process when production arrives more quickly than the next stage can handle
2. It is based on the concept that organisations manage three key factors – throughput, operating expenses and inventory
3. It uses a sequence of focusing steps to overcome a single bottleneck, at which point the improvement process is complete
4. It can be applied to the management of all limiting factors, both internal and external, which can affect an organisation

A. (1) and (2) only
B. (1), (2) and (3)
C. (2), (3) and (4)
D. (1), (3) and (4)

The following scenario relates to questions 21-25.

Chair Co has in development several new products. One of them is a new type of luxury car seat. The estimated labour time for the first unit is 12 hours but a learning curve of 75% is expected to apply for the first eight units produced. The cost of labour is $15 per hour.

The cost of materials and other variable overheads is expected to total $230 per unit. Chair Co plans on pricing the seat by adding a 50% mark-up to the total variable cost per seat, with the labour cost being based on the incremental time taken to produce the 8th unit.

21. What is the labour cost of the 8th unit?

A. $45·65
B. $75·94
C. $4·32
D. $3·04

22. The first phase of production has now been completed for the new car seat. The first unit actually took 12·5 hours to make and the total time for the first eight units was 34·3 hours, at which point the learning effect came to an end. Chair Co are planning on adjusting the price to reflect the actual time it took to complete the 8th unit.

What was the actual rate of learning which occurred?

A. 65·7%
B. 58·6%
C. 70·0%
D. 76·5%

23. Another product which Chair Co has in development is a new design of high chair for feeding young children. Based on previous experience of producing similar products, Chair Co had assumed that a learning rate of 85% would apply to the manufacture of this new design but after the first phase of production had been completed, management realised that a learning rate of 80% had been achieved.

Which of the following statements could explain why the actual rate of learning differed from the rate which was expected?

1. Staffing levels were stable during the first manufacturing phase
2. There were machine breakdowns during production
3. Assembly of the chairs was manual and very repetitive
4. There was high staff turnover during this period
5. There were minimal stoppages in the production process
6. The design of the chair was changed several times at this early phase

A. (2), (3) and (4)
B. (1), (3) and (5)
C. (1), (5) and (6)
D. (2), (4) and (6)

24. Chair Co uses cost-plus pricing.

Which of the following statements regarding cost-plus pricing strategies are correct?

1. Marginal cost-plus pricing is easier where there is a readily identifiable variable cost
2. Full cost-plus pricing requires the budgeted level of output to be determined at the outset
3. Cost-plus pricing is a strategically focused approach as it accounts for external factors
4. Cost-plus pricing requires that the profit mark-up applied by an organisation is fixed

A. (1), (2) and (4)
B. (1) and (2) only
C. (3) and (4)
D. (1) and (3)

25. Chair Co has also developed a new type of office chair and management is trying to formulate a budget for this product. They have decided to match the production level to demand, however, demand for this chair is uncertain.

Management have collected the following information:

	Demand (units)	Probability
Worst possible outcome	10,000	0·3
Most likely outcome	22,000	0·5
Best possible outcome	35,000	0·2

The selling price per unit is $25. The variable cost per unit is $8 for any production level up to 25,000 units. If the production level is higher than 25,000 units, then the variable cost per unit will decrease by 10% and this reduction will apply to all the units produced at that level.
Total fixed costs are estimated to be $75,000.
Using probabilistic budgeting, what is the expected budgeted contribution of the product?

A. $282,000
B. $357,000
C. $287,600
D. $362,600

The following scenario relates to questions 26-30.
The Hi Life Co (HL Co) makes sofas. It has recently received a request from a customer to provide a one-off order of sofas, in excess of normal budgeted production. The order would need to be completed within two weeks. The following cost estimate has already been prepared:

		$
Direct materials:		
Fabric	200 m² at $17 per m²	3,400
Wood	50 m² at $8·20 per m²	410
Direct labour:		
Skilled	200 hours at $16 per hour	3,200
Semi-skilled	300 hours at $12 per hour	3,600
Factory overheads	500 hours at $3 per hour	1,500
Total production cost		12,110
General fixed overheads as 10% of total production cost		1,211
Total cost		13,321

A quotation now needs to be prepared on a relevant cost basis so that HL Co can offer as competitive a price as possible for the order.

26. The fabric is regularly used by HL Co. There are currently 300 m² in inventory, which cost $17 per m². The current purchase price of the fabric is $17·50 per m².

    The wood is regularly used by HL Co and usually costs $8·20 per m². However, the company's current supplier's earliest delivery time for the wood is in three weeks' time. An alternative supplier could deliver immediately but they would charge $8·50 per m². HL Co already has 500 m² in inventory but 480 m² of this is needed to complete other existing orders in the next two weeks. The remaining 20 m² is not going to be needed until four weeks' time.
    What is the cost of the fabric and the wood which should be included in the quotation?

	Fabric	**Wood**
A	$3,500	$419
B	$3,400	$419
C	$3,500	$255
D	$0	$255

27. The skilled labour force is employed under permanent contracts of employment under which they must be paid for 40 hours per week's labour, even if their time is idle due to absence of orders. Their rate of pay is $16 per hour, although any overtime is paid at time and a half. In the next two weeks, there is spare capacity of 150 labour hours.

There is no spare capacity for semi-skilled workers. They are currently paid $12 per hour or time and a half for overtime. However, a local agency can provide additional semi-skilled workers for $14 per hour.

What cost should be included in the quotation for skilled labour and semi-skilled labour?

	Skilled	Semi-skilled
A	$3,600	$4,200
B	$1,200	$4,200
C	$3,600	$5,400
D	$1,200	$5,400

28. Of the $3 per hour factory overheads costs, $1·50 per hour reflects the electricity costs of running the cutting machine which will be used to cut the fabric and wood for the sofas. The other $1·50 per hour reflects the cost of the factory supervisor's salary. The supervisor is paid an annual salary and is also paid $15 per hour for any overtime he works. He will need to work 20 hours overtime if this order is accepted.

What is the cost which should be included in the quotation for factory overheads?

A. $1,050
B. $1,800
C. $750
D. $300

29. **Which statement correctly describes the treatment of the general fixed overheads when preparing the quotation?**

A. The overheads should be excluded because they are a sunk cost
B. The overheads should be excluded because they are not incremental costs
C. The overheads should be included because they relate to production costs
D. The overheads should be included because all expenses should be recovered

30. Which of the following statements about relevant costing are true?

1. An opportunity cost will always be a relevant cost even if it is a past cost
2. Fixed costs are always general in nature and are therefore never relevant
3. Committed costs are never considered to be relevant costs
4. An opportunity cost represents the cost of the best alternative forgone
5. Notional costs are always relevant as they make the estimate more realistic
6. Avoidable costs would be saved if an activity did not happen and so are relevant
7. Common costs are only relevant if the viability of the whole process is being assessed
8. Differential costs in a make or buy decision are not considered to be relevant

A. (2), (3), (4) and (6)
B. (1), (2), (5) and (7)
C. (3), (4), (6) and (7)
D. (1), (5), (6) and (8)

(30 marks)

Section C – Both questions are compulsory and MUST be attempted

Please write your answers to all parts of these questions on the lined pages within the Candidate Answer Booklet.

31. Carad Co is an electronics company which makes two types of television – plasma screen TVs and LCD TVs. It operates within a highly competitive market and is constantly under pressure to reduce prices. Carad Co operates a standard costing system and performs a detailed variance analysis of both products on a monthly basis. Extracts from the management information for the month of November are shown below:

		Note
Total number of units made and sold	1,400	1
Material price variance	$28,000 A	2
Total labour variance	$6,050 A	3

Notes

1. The budgeted total sales volume for TVs was 1,180 units, consisting of an equal mix of plasma screen TVs and LCD screen TVs. Actual sales volume was 750 plasma TVs and 650 LCD TVs. Standard sales prices are $350 per unit for the plasma TVs and $300 per unit for the LCD TVs. The actual sales prices achieved during November were $330 per unit for plasma TVs and $290 per unit for LCD TVs. The standard contributions for plasma TVs and LCD TVs are $190 and $180 per unit respectively.

2. The sole reason for this variance was an increase in the purchase price of one of its key components, X. Each plasma TV made and each LCD TV made requires one unit of component X, for which Carad Co's standard cost is $60 per unit. Due to a shortage of components in the market place, the market price for November went up to $85 per unit for X. Carad Co actually paid $80 per unit for it.

3. Each plasma TV uses 2 standard hours of labour and each LCD TV uses 1·5 standard hours of labour. The standard cost for labour is $14 per hour and this also reflects the actual cost per labour hour for the company's permanent staff in November. However, because of the increase in sales and production volumes in November, the company also had to use additional temporary labour at the higher cost of $18 per hour. The total capacity of Carad's permanent workforce is 2,200 hours production per month, assuming full efficiency. In the month of November, the permanent workforce were wholly efficient, taking exactly 2 hours to complete each plasma TV and exactly 1·5 hours to produce each LCD TV. The total labour variance therefore relates solely to the temporary workers, who took twice as long as the permanent workers to complete their production.

Required:

(a) **Calculate the following for the month of November, showing all workings clearly:**
  (i) **The sales price variance and sales volume contribution variance;** (4 marks)
  (ii) **The material price planning variance and material price operational variance;** (2 marks)
  (iii) **The labour rate variance and the labour efficiency variance.** (5 marks)

(b) **Explain the reasons why Carad Co would be interested in the material price planning variance and the material price operational variance.** (9 marks)

(20 marks)

32. Thatcher International Park (TIP) is a theme park and has for many years been a successful business, which has traded profitably. About three years ago the directors decided to capitalise on their success and reduced the expenditure made on new thrill rides, reduced routine maintenance where possible (deciding instead to repair equipment when it broke down) and made a commitment to regularly increase admission prices. Once an admission price is paid customers can use any of the facilities and rides for free.

These steps increased profits considerably, enabling good dividends to be paid to the owners and bonuses to the directors. The last two years of financial results are shown below.

	20X4	20X5
	$	$
Sales	5,250,000	5,320,000
Less expenses:		
Wages	2,500,000	2,200,000
Maintenance – routine	80,000	70,000
Repairs	260,000	320,000
Directors' salaries	150,000	160,000
Directors' bonuses	15,000	18,000
Other costs (including depreciation)	1,200,000	1,180,000
Net profit	1,045,000	1,372,000
Book value of assets at start of year	13,000,000	12,000,000
Dividend paid	500,000	650,000
Number of visitors	150,000	140,000

TIP operates in a country where the average rate of inflation is around 1% per annum.

Required:

(c) **Assess the financial performance of TIP using the information given above.** (14 marks)

During the early part of 20X4 TIP employed a newly qualified management accountant. He quickly became concerned about the potential performance of TIP and to investigate his concerns, he started to gather data to measure some non-financial measures of success. The data he has gathered is shown below:

Table 1

	20X4	20X5
Hours lost due to breakdown of rides (see note 1)	9,000 hours	32,000 hours
Average waiting time per ride	20 minutes	30 minutes

Note 1: TIP has 50 rides of different types. It is open 360 days of the year for 10 hours each day

Required:

(d) **Assess the QUALITY of the service which TIP provides to its customers using Table 1 and any other relevant data and indicate the RISKS it is likely to face if it continues with its current policies.** (6 marks)

(20 marks)

Formulae Sheet

Learning curve

$$Y = ax^b$$

Where Y = cumulative average time per unit to produce x units

a = the time taken for the first unit of output

x = the cumulative number of units produced

b = the index of learning (log LR/log2)

LR = the learning rate as a decimal

Demand curve

$$P = a - bQ$$

$$b = \frac{\text{change in price}}{\text{change in quantity}}$$

$$a = \text{price when Q} = 0$$

$$MR = a - 2bQ$$

End of Question Paper

Answers

Section A

1.   B

Set-up costs per production run = $140,000/28 = $5,000

Cost per inspection = $80,000/8 = $10,000

Other overhead costs per labour hour = $96,000/48,000 = $2

Overhead costs of product D:

		$
Set-up costs (15 x $5,000)		75,000
Inspection costs (3 x $10,000)		30,000
Other overheads (40,000 x $2)		80,000
		185,000

Overhead cost per unit = $185,000/4,000 units = $46·25

2.   D

Return: $500,000 x 30% = $150,000

Total sales revenue = $550 x 800 = $440,000

Therefore total cost = $440,000 – $150,000 = $290,000

Unit cost = $290,000/800 = $362·50

3.   C

The number of units required to make a target profit = (fixed costs + target profit)/ contribution per unit of P1.

Fixed costs = ($1·20 x 10,000) + ($1·00 x 12,500) – $2,500 = $22,000

Contribution per unit of P = $3·20 + $1·20 = $4·40

($22,000 + $60,000)/$4·40 = 18,636 units

4.   B

Most organisations do collect data about environmental costs but find it difficult to split them out and categorise them effectively.

Life-cycle costing does allow the organisation to collect information about a product's environmental costs throughout its life cycle.

The technique which divides material flows into three categories is material flow cost accounting, not input/output analysis.

ABC does categorise some costs as environment-driven costs, however, these are costs which are normally hidden within total overheads in a conventional costing system. It is environment-related costs which can be allocated directly to a cost centre.

5.   D

Mix variance:

Material	AQSM	AQAM	Difference (litres)	Standard cost ($/litre)	Variance ($)
A	800	900	100 A	20	2,000 A
B	1,200	1,100	100 F	25	2,500F
	2,000	2,000			500 F

Yield variance:

Material	SQSM	AQSM	Difference (litres)	Standard cost ($/litre)	Variance ($)
A	779	800	21 A	20	420 A
B	1,168	1,200	32 A	25	800A
	(W1) 1,947	2,000			1,220 A

(W1) 1,850 litres of output should use 1,947 litres of input (1,850/0·95)

6.   A

An incremental budget builds from the previous year's figures and so any inefficiencies will be carried forward and zero-based budgeting starts from scratch with each item justified for its inclusion in the budget and so should encourage the identification of waste and non-value adding activities, so Statement 1 is correct.

Beyond budgeting attempts to move away from conforming to a rigid annual budget and uses adaptive processes to encourage management to be responsive to current situations which facilitates the use of rolling forecasts, so Statement 2 is correct.

Rolling budgeting are budgets which are continuously updated throughout the year and so forces managers to reassess plans more regularly, whereas activity-based budgeting involves defining the activities which underpin the financial figures and using the activity to allocate resources for the budget, so Statement 3 is incorrect.

Flexible budgets are designed to show the changes in financial figures based on different activity levels and so will recognise different cost behaviour patterns, however, it is activity-based budgeting which ensures that the overall strategy is taken into account because it attempts to manage the business as interrelated parts, not separate activities, so Statement 4 is incorrect.

7.　C

EV for major upgrade = (0·80 x $11m) + (0·2 x $7·5m) = $10·3m

EV for minor upgrade = (0·70 x $9m) + (0·3 x $6m) = $8·1m

Decision

Shutdown and sell	$5·75m
Major upgrade (10·3m − 4·5m)	$5·8m
Minor upgrade ($8·1m − $2m)	$6·1m

As the minor upgrade has the highest expected return that should be the option chosen.

8.　A

In a single limiting factor situation products should be ranked based on their contribution per unit of limiting factor, which in this case is labour hours.

Product	A	B	C	D
Contribution per unit ($)	46	52	21	60
Number of labour hours required per unit	6	8	3	2
Contribution per labour hour ($)	7·67	6·50	7·00	30·00
Ranking	2nd	4th	3rd	1st

9.　D

Target 1 is a financial target and so assesses economy factors. Target 2 is measuring the rate of work handled by staff which is an efficiency measure. Target 3 is assessing output, so is a measure of effectiveness.

10.　D

Management information systems do summarise data from TPS into periodic reports for management to use for decision-making.

Transaction processing systems do facilitate the immediate processing of data.

Executive information systems draw data from the MIS and support senior managers to make strategic decisions. They usually have dashboard and interactive graphics so that the big picture can be seen.

Enterprise resource planning systems can have extranet links set up with customers and suppliers.

11.　A

Direct data capture costs is a type of data input in which there is no data entry but instead it is captured for a specific purpose. Therefore the use of bar coding and scanners and the completion of timesheets are examples of direct data capture costs.

Time spent by the payroll department processing personnel costs and the input of data into the production system are examples of process costs.

12.   C

Customer life-cycle costing can be used by organisations.

It has been reported that the majority of a product's costs are determined early on, i.e. at the design phase.

Life-cycle costing does not include any opportunity costs associated with production.

The growth phase is characterised by a rapid increase in demand.

13.   A

Return per factory hour = ($130 – $50)/4 hours = $20

Factory costs per hour = $20 + ($40/4) = $15

TPAR = $20/$15 = 1·33

14.   B

Increase in variable costs per unit from buying in ($140 – $100) =$40

Therefore total increase in variable costs (2,200 units x $40) = $88,000

Less the specific fixed costs saved if A is shut down = ($10,000)

Decrease in profit = $78,000

15.   C

The determinants of performance are quality, innovation, resource utilisation and flexibility. Competitiveness is a result of the determinants.

Standards should be fair, achievable and staff should have ownership of them. Controllability is a feature of the rewards block.

Rewards should be clear, motivating and controllable, so this is correct.

It is a framework designed to attempt to overcome the problems associated with performance management in service companies.

Section B

16. C

Total salon hours = 8 x 6 x 50 = 2,400 each year.

There are three senior stylists, therefore total hours available = 7,200.

Based on the time taken for each activity, they can perform 7,200 cuts (7,200 hours/1 hour per cut) or 4,800 treatments (7,200 hours/1·5 hours per treatment).

17. A

Cuts

Return per hour = (Selling price – materials)/time taken on the bottleneck = (60 – 1·50)/1 = 58·50

TPAR = Return per hour/cost per hour = 58·50/42·56 = 1·37 (to two decimal places)

Treatments

Return per hour = (Selling price – materials)/time taken on the bottleneck = (110 – 8·90)/1·5 = 67·40

TPAR = Return per hour/cost per hour = 67·40/42·56 = 1·58 (to two decimal places)

18. C

The factors which are included in the TPAR are selling price, material costs, operating expenses and bottleneck time. Increasing the selling price and reducing costs will improve the TPAR.

Increasing the time which each service takes on the bottleneck (the senior stylists' time) will only reduce the number of services they can provide, so this will not improve throughput.

Throughput accounting does not advocate the building of inventory as it is often used in a just-in-time environment and there is no point increasing the activity prior to the bottleneck as it will just create a build-up of work-in-progress. Neither of these will improve the rate of throughput through the process.

19. B

The existing capacity for each activity is:

	Cut	Treatment
Assistants	48,000	16,000
Senior stylists	7,200	4,800
Junior stylists	8,000	9,600

If another senior stylist is employed, this will mean that their available hours will be (4 x 2,400) = 9,600.

This will give them capacity to now do 9,600 cuts (9,600 hours/1 hour per cut) and 6,400 treatments (9,600 hours/1·5 hours per treatment).

As a result, the senior stylists will still be the bottleneck activity for treatments but for cuts the bottleneck will now be the junior stylists as they can only do 8,000 cuts compared to the senior stylists of 9,600.

20.   A

The theory of constraints is focused on identifying restrictions in a process and how to manage that restriction (commonly termed a bottleneck).

It is based on the concept of managing throughput, operating expenses and inventory.

It does use a series of focusing steps but it is not complete once the bottleneck has been overcome. In fact it is an ongoing process of improvement, as once the bottleneck has been elevated it is probable that another bottleneck will appear and the process will continue.

It cannot be applied to all limiting factors as some, particularly those external to the organisation, may be out of the organisation's control.

21.   A

Learning curve formula = $y = ax^b$

Cumulative average time per unit for 8 units: $Y = 12 \times 8^{-415} = 5 \cdot 0628948$ hours.

Therefore cumulative total time for 8 units = 40·503158 hours.

Cumulative average time per unit for 7 units: $Y = 12 \times 7^{-415} = 5 \cdot 3513771$ hours.

Therefore cumulative total time for 7 units = 37·45964 hours.

Therefore incremental time for 8th unit = 40·503158 hours − 37·45964 hours = 3·043518 hours.

Total labour cost for 8th unit = 3·043518 x $15 = $45·65277

22.   C

Actual learning rate

Cumulative number of seats produced	Cumulative total hours	Cumulative average hours per unit
1	12·5	12·5
2	?	12·5 x r
4	?	12·5 x r²
8	34·3	12·5 x r³

Using algebra: $34 \cdot 3 = 8 \times (12 \cdot 5 \times r^3)$

$4 \cdot 2875 = (12 \cdot 5 \times r^3)$

$0 \cdot 343 = r^3$

$r = 0 \cdot 70$

Therefore the learning rate was 70%.

23.   B

An 80% learning rate means that the learning was faster than expected.

Factors which are present for a learning curve to take effect are a highly manual and repetitive process (so staff can become quicker the more they perform the same series of tasks), no stoppages to production (so the learning rate will not be lost whilst staff are idle) and a stable workforce (so the learning process does not have to keep restarting).

If there is high staff turnover, stoppages in production and continual design changes, then the learning rate will not be effective and should be slower.

24.   B

As marginal costing is based on variable costs, it is easier when a readily identifiable variable cost has been established.

The budgeted volume of output does need to be determined for full cost-plus pricing as it would be used to calculate the overhead absorption rate for the calculation of the full cost per unit.

Cost-plus pricing is internally focused and a drawback of the technique is that it fails to consider external influences, like competitor pricing strategies.

The mark-up percentage does not have to be fixed; it can vary and be adjusted to reflect market conditions.

25.   D

As the variable cost per unit is changing depending on the production level, contribution for each level needs to be calculated and then the probabilities applied to the outcomes.

Demand (units)	Contribution (per unit)	Total contribution	Probability	Expected budgeted contribution
10,000	17·00	170,000	0·3	51,000
22,000	17·00	374,000	0·5	187,000
35,000	17·80	623,000	0·2	124,600
				362,600

26.   A

Fabric is in regular use, so the replacement cost is the relevant cost (200 m² x $17·50) = $3,500.

30 m² of wood will have to be ordered in from the alternative supplier but the remaining 20 m² which is in inventory and not needed for other work can be used and then replaced by an order from the usual supplier (30 m² x $8·50) + (20 m² x $8·20) = $419.

27.   B

Skilled labour:

There is no cost for the first 150 hours as there is spare capacity. The remaining 50 hours required will be paid at time and a half, which is $16 x 1·5 = $24.

50 hours x $24 = $1,200

Semi-skilled labour:

There is no spare capacity, so the company will either need to pay overtime or hire in additional staff. The cost of paying overtime would be $18 per hour, so it would be cheaper to hire in the additional staff for $14 per hour. 300 hours x $14 = $4,200

28.   A

The electricity costs are incremental as the machine will be used more to produce the new order (500 hours x $1·50) = $750.

The supervisor's salary is not relevant as it is paid anyway; however, the overtime is relevant (20 hours x $15) = $300.

29.   B

The general fixed overheads should be excluded as they are not incremental, i.e. they are not arising specifically as a result of this order. They are not sunk as they are not past costs. This is a common misconception.

30.   C

An opportunity cost does represent the cost of the best alternative forgone, however, if it is an historic (past) cost, it would not be relevant.

Fixed costs can be incremental to a decision and in those circumstances would be relevant.

Committed costs are costs the organisation has already agreed to and can no longer influence and so are not relevant.

Notional costs are used to make cost estimates more realistic; however, they are not real cash flows and are not considered to be relevant.

Avoidable costs are saved if an activity is not undertaken and if this occurs as a result of the decision, then they are relevant.

Common costs are relevant if the whole process is being evaluated; however, they are not relevant to a further processing decision.

Differential costs are relevant in a make or buy decision as the organisation is trying to choose between two options.

Section C

31.

(a)

(i) **Sales price variance and sales volume variance**

Sales price variance = (actual price – standard price) x actual volume

	Actual price	Standard price	Difference	Actual volume	Sales price variance
	$	$	$		$
Plasma TVs	330	350	−20	750	15,000 A
LCD TVs	290	300	−10	650	6,500 A
					21,500 A

Sales volume contribution variance = (actual sales volume – budgeted sales volume) x standard margin

	Actual sales volume	Budgeted Sales volume	Difference	Standard margin	Sales volume variance
				$	$
Plasma TVs	750	590	160	190	30,400 F
LCD TVs	650	590	60	180	10,800 F
	1,400	1,180			41,200 F

(ii) **Material price planning and purchasing operational variances**

Material planning variance = (original target price – general market price at time of purchase) x quantity purchased ($60 – $85) x 1,400 = $35,000 A

Material price operational variance = (general market price at time of purchase – actual price paid) x quantity purchased ($85 – $80) x 1,400 = $7,000 F

(iii) **Labour rate and labour efficiency variances**

Labour rate variance = (standard labour rate per hour – actual labour rate per hour) x actual hours worked

Actual hours worked by temporary workers:

Total hours needed if staff were fully efficient = (750 x 2) + (650 x 1·5) = 2,475.

Permanent staff provide 2,200 hours, therefore excess = 2,475 – 2,200 = 275.

However, temporary workers take twice as long, therefore hours worked = 275 x 2 = 550.

Labour rate variance relates solely to temporary workers, therefore ignore permanent staff in the calculation.

Labour rate variance = ($14 – $18) x 550 = $2,200 A

Labour efficiency variance = (standard labour hours for actual production – actual labour hours worked) x standard rate (275 – 550) x $14 = $3,850 A

(b) **Explanation of planning and operational variances**

Before the material price planning and operational variances were calculated, the only information available as regards material purchasing was that there was an adverse material price variance of $28,000. The purchasing department will be assessed on the basis of this variance, yet, on its own, it is not a reliable indicator of the purchasing department's efficiency. The reason it is not a reliable indicator is because market conditions can change, leading to an increase in price, and this change in market conditions is not within the control of the purchasing department.

By analysing the materials price variance further and breaking it down into its two components – planning and operational - the variance actually becomes a more useful assessment tool. The planning variance represents the uncontrollable element and the operational variance represents the controllable element.

The planning variance is really useful for providing feedback on just how skilled management is in estimating future prices. This can be very easy in some businesses and very difficult in others. Giving this detail could help to improve planning and standard setting in the future, as management will be increasingly aware of factors which could create volatility in their forecasts.

The operational variance is more meaningful in that it measures the purchasing department's efficiency given the market conditions which prevailed at the time. As can be seen in Carad, the material price operational variance is favourable which demonstrates that the purchasing department managed to acquire the component which was in short supply at a better price than expected. Without this breakdown in the variance, the purchasing department could have been held accountable for the overall adverse variance which was not indicative of their actual performance. This is then a fairer method of assessing performance and will, in turn, stop staff from becoming demotivated.

32.

(a) TIP's financial performance can be assessed in a number of ways:

Sales growth

Sales are up about 1·3% (W1) which is a little above the rate of inflation and therefore a move in the right direction. However, with average admission prices jumping about 8·6% (W2) and numbers of visitors falling, there are clearly problems. Large increases in admission prices reduce the value proposition for the customer, it is unlikely that the rate of increase is sustainable or even justifiable. Indeed with volumes falling (down by 6·7% (W6)), it appears that some customers are being put off and price could be one of the reasons.

Maintenance and repairs

There appears to be a continuing drift away from routine maintenance with management preferring to repair equipment as required. This does not appear to be saving any money as the combined cost of maintenance and repair is higher in 20X5 than in 20X4 (possible risks are dealt with in part (b)).

Directors' pay

Absolute salary levels are up 6·7% (W3), well above the modest inflation rate. It appears that the shareholders are happy with the financial performance of the business and are prepared to reward the directors accordingly. Bonus levels are also well up. It may be that the directors have some form of profit related pay scheme and are being rewarded for the improved profit performance. The directors are likely to be very pleased with the increases to pay.

Wages

Wages are down by 12% (W5). This may partly reflect the loss of customers (down by 6·7% (W6)) if it is assumed that at least part of the wages cost is variable. It could also be that the directors are reducing staff levels beyond the fall in the level of customers to enhance short-term profit and personal bonus. Customer service and indeed safety could be compromised here.

Net profit

Net profit is up a huge 31·3% (W7) and most shareholders would be pleased with that. Net profit is a very traditional measure of performance and most would say this was a sign of good performance.

Return on assets

The profitability can be measured relative to the asset base which is being used to generate it. This is sometimes referred to as ROI or return on investment. The return on assets is up considerably to 11·4% from 8% (W8). This is partly due to the significant rise in profit and partly due to the fall in asset value. We are told that TIP has cut back on new development, so the fall in asset value is probably due to depreciation being charged with little being spent during the year on assets. In this regard it is inevitable that return on assets is up but it is more questionable whether this is a good performance. A theme park (and thrill rides in particular) must be updated to keep customers coming back. The directors of TIP are risking the future of the park.

(b) **Quality provision**

Reliability of the rides

The hours lost has increased significantly. Equally the percentage of capacity lost due to breakdowns is now approaching 17·8% (W9). This would appear to be a very high number of hours lost. This would surely increase the risk that customers are disappointed being unable to ride. Given the fixed admission price system, this is bound to irritate some customers as they have effectively already paid to ride.

Average queuing time

Queuing will be seen by customers as dead time. They may see some waiting as inevitable and hence acceptable. However, TIP should be careful to maintain waiting times at a minimum. An increase of 10 minutes (or 50%) is likely to be noticeable by customers and is unlikely to enhance the quality of the TIP experience for them. The increase in waiting times is probably due to the high number of hours lost due to breakdown with customers being forced to queue for a fewer number of ride options.

Safety

The clear reduction in maintenance could easily damage the safety record of the park and is an obvious quality issue.

Risks

If TIP continues with current policies, then they will expose themselves to the following risks:

o   The lack of routine maintenance could easily lead to an accident or injury to a customer. This could lead to compensation being paid or reputational damage.

o   Increased competition. The continuous raising of admission prices increases the likelihood of a new competitor entering the market (although there are significant barriers to entry in this market, e.g. capital cost, land and so on).

     o   Loss of customers. The value for money which customers see when coming to TIP is clearly reducing (higher prices, less reliability of rides and longer queues). Regardless of the existence of competition, customers could simply choose not to come, substituting another leisure activity instead.

     o   Profit fall. In the end if customers' numbers fall, then so will profit. The shareholders, although well rewarded at the moment, could suffer a loss of dividend. Directors' job security could then be threatened.

Workings:

(W1)   Sales growth is $5,320,000/$5,250,000 = 1·01333 or 1·3%.

(W2)   Average admission prices were:

        20X4: $5,250,000/150,000 = $35 per person

        20X5: $5,320,000/140,000 = $38 per person

        An increase of $38/$35 = 1·0857 or 8·57%.

(W3)   Directors' pay up by $160,000/$150,000 = 1·0667 or 6·7%.

(W4)   Directors' bonuses levels up from $15,000/$150,000 or 10% to $18,000/$160,000 or 12·5% of turnover. This is an increase of 3/15 or 20%.

(W5)   Wages are down by (1 – $2,200,000/$2,500,000) or 12%.

(W6)   Loss of customers is (1 – 140,000/150,000) or 6·7%.

(W7)   Profits up by $1,372,000/$1,045,000 = 1·3129 or 31·3%.

(W8)   Return on assets:

        20X4: $1,045,000/$13,000,000 = 1·0803 or 8·03%

        20X5: $1,372,000/$12,000,000 = 1·114 or 11·4%

(W9)   Capacity of rides in hours is 360 days x 50 rides x 10 hours per day = 180,000.

        20X4 lost capacity is 9,000/180,000 = 0·05 or 5%.

        20X5 lost capacity is 32,000/180,000 = 0·177 or 17·8%.

Specimen Exam Marking Scheme

					Marks
Section A					
Each question is worth 2 marks					<u>30</u>
Section B					
Each question is worth 2 marks					<u>30</u>

				Maximum marks	Marks awarded
Section C					
31	**(a)**	**(i)**	Sales price variance – Plasma TVs	1	
			Sales price variance – LCD TVs	1	
			Sales volume contribution variance – Plasma TVs	1	
			Sales volume contribution variance – LCD TVs	1	
				<u>4</u>	
		(ii)	Material price planning variance	1	
			Material price operational variance	1	
				<u>2</u>	
		(iii)	Actual hours worked	3	
			Labour rate variance	1	
			Labour efficiency variance	1	
				<u>5</u>	

	(b)	Controllability	2
		Material price planning	3
		Material price operating	3
		Other valid point – planning or operating	1
			———
			9
			20
32	**(a)**	Sales growth	3
		Maintenance	3
		Directors' pay	2
		Wages	2
		Net profit	2
		Return on assets	2
			———
			14
	(b)	Reliability of rides	2
		Average queuing time	2
		Risks	2
			———
			6
			20

Index

Index